AF539384

Public Relations and Media

Public Relations and Media

Ruchika Gupta

RANDOM PUBLICATIONS
NEW DELHI (INDIA)

Public Relations and Media

ISBN 978-93-5111-490-1

Published in 2015 in India by

RANDOM PUBLICATIONS

4376-A/4B, Gali Murari Lal, Ansari Road
New Delhi-110 002
Phone : +9111-43580356, 011-23289044, 011-43142548
e-mail: sales@randompublications.com,
info@randompublications.com, randomexports@gmail.com

Reprinted 2024

Type Setting by : Friends Media, Delhi-110089
Digitally Printed at : Replika Press Pvt. Ltd.

Preface

The relationship between the media and the Public Relation (PR) industry is a complex and increasingly symbiotic one. The media is the central vehicle for much of the PR industry's messages. PR practitioners want to place their stories in the news or other publications and programmes. Without being able to do this, PR would lose one of its main avenues for communication with the public.

The media in turn has become more dependent on PR to supply content to fill air time or column inches. Whilst newspapers have been steadily shedding staff over the last couple of decades they have simultaneously managed to produce ever thicker publications, and the ever growing ranks of PR are happy to help fill the pages.

Public relations can't function without the media. PR professionals spend most of their day maintaining existing relationships and cultivating new ones with journalists and other members of the mass media. Many journalists have a distrustful attitude to PR. They need to have a wariness of professional story-pitchers. In order to overcome this barrier, the PR agencies aim to build ongoing relationships with journalists and media sources. The more and better relationships they can build, the more influence they can exert on the media.

The present book is a comprehensive and detailed introduction to the theories and practices of the public relations industry. Tracing the development of public relations, it explores the issues which affect the industry, examines its relationship with media, lobbying organisations and journalism, assess its professionalism and regulation and advises on training and entry into the profession. It will be an all-inclusive manual for a student, or for a teacher who needs to prepare his or her lessons.

Author

Contents

1

Introduction

Public relations (PR) is the practice of managing the flow of information between an individual or an organization and the public. It may include an organization or individual gaining exposure to their audiences using topics of public interest and news items that do not require direct payment. The aim of public relations by a company often is to persuade the public, investors, partners, employees, and other stakeholders to maintain a certain point of view about it, its leadership, products, or of political decisions. Common activities include speaking at conferences, winning industry awards, working with the press, and employee communication.

PR is distinct from advertising as it is generally not aimed at selling a particular product from a particular business, and, for further comparison, propaganda, sometimes carried out for political purposes by governments. Many of the same PR techniques may be employed in all these areas. Within the industry, those involved in marketing may consider public relations a subfield of marketing; those involved in PR may disagree.Precursors to public relations can be found in publicists who specialised in promoting circuses, theatrical performances, and other public spectacles. Later, most PR practitioners were and are still recruited from the ranks of journalism. Journalists concerned with ethics question former colleagues for using their inside understanding of news media, helping clients receive favorable media coverage. Highly paid PR positions remain a popular career change choice for many journalists.

Historical Background

Public Relations is as old as human civilisation. It has existed in one form or the other. There are umpteen examples of its varied form, content and end use. An ancient clay tablet, found in Iraq, told the Sumerian farmers how to grow better crops. That was over 4000 years ago. The Arabian tales relate how the celebrated Sultan Haroon-Al-Rashid used to wander about every night in disguise to see for himself as to what the people really felt about his administration.

Anceint Greeks used word *sematikos* (to signify, to mean) for public relations. The Semantikos means semantics, which can be defined as how to get people to believe things and do things. That is not a bad definition of public relations. In 50 B.C. Julius Caesar wrote the first campaign biography, *Caesar's Gallic Wars*. He publicised his military exploits to convince the Roman people that he would make the best head of state. Candidates for political office continue to publicise themselves with campaign biographies and accounts of military exploits to this day.

In 394 A.D., St. Augustine was a professor of rhetoric in Milan, the capitol of the Western Roman Empire. He delivered the regular eulogies to the emperor and was the closest thing to a minister of propaganda for the imperial court. Thus, St. Augustine was one of the first people in charge of public relations. The modern equivalent would be the President's press secretary or communication director.

In 1776, Thomas Paine wrote "The Crisis," a pamphlet which convinced the soldiers of Washington's army to stay and fight at a time when so many were prepared to desert so they could escape the cold and the hardships of a winter campaign. Paine was a master of political propaganda whose writing could get people to do things and believe things.

Benjamin Franklin made it a rule to forbear all contradiction to others, and all positive assertions of his own. He would say, "I conceive" or "'I apprehend" or "I imagine" a thing to be so, or it appears to be so. Franklin pioneered the rules for "personal relations" in an era before mass media had made possible a profession called "public relations."

In the middle of the 19th century appeared a man who was to become one of the leading publicists of all time, P. T. Barnum. His accomplishments include the founding of the American Museum and the establishment of the Barnum and Bailey Circus. Barnum was a master of promotion who could fill his enterprises with customers by using what we today would call sleazy methods of publicity. For example, he announced that his museum would exhibit a 161-year-old woman who had been Washington's nurse. He produced an elderly woman and a forged birth certificate to make his case.

William Seward, Lincoln's secretary of state in 1861, gained a large American audience through his understanding of how to use the press. He told his friend Jefferson Davis: "I speak to the newspapers—they have a large audience and can repeat a thousand times what I want to impress on the public."

A number of American precursors to public relations are found in the form of publicists who specialised in promoting circuses, theatrical performances, and other public spectacles. In the United States, where public relations has its origins, many early public relations practices were developed in support of railroads. In fact, many scholars believe that the first appearance of the term "public relations" appeared in the 1897 *Year Book of Railway Literature*. Later, practitioners were recruited from the ranks of journalism. Some reporters concerned with ethics criticise former colleagues for using their inside understanding of news media to help clients receive favourable media coverage.

Some historians regard Ivy Lee as the first real practitioner of public relations, but Edward Bernays, a nephew and student of Sigmund Freud, is generally regarded today as the profession's founder. In the United Kingdom Sir Basil Clarke (1879-1947) was a pioneer of public relations.

The First World War helped stimulate the development of public relations as a profession. Many of the first PR professionals, including Ivy Lee, Edward Bernays, John W. Hill, and Carl Byoir, got their start with the Committee on Public Information, which organised publicity on behalf of U.S. objectives during World War I.

In describing the origin of the term Public Relations, Bernays commented, "When I came back to the United States [from the war], I decided that if you could use propaganda for war, you could certainly use it for peace. And propaganda got to be a bad word because of the Germans... using it. So what I did was to try to find some other words, so we found the words Counsel on Public Relations".

Ivy Lee, who has been credited with developing the modern news release, espoused a philosophy consistent with what has sometimes been called the "two-way street" approach to public relations in which PR consists of helping clients listen as well as communicate messages to their publics. In the words of the Public Relations Society of America (PRSA), "Public relations helps an organisation and its publics adapt mutually to each other." In practice, however, Lee often engaged in one-way propagandising on behalf of clients despised by the public, including Standard Oil founder John D. Rockefeller. Shortly before his death, the US Congress had been investigating Rockefeller's work on behalf of the controversial Nazi German company IG Farben.

Bernays was the profession's first theorist. Bernays drew many of his ideas from Sigmund Freud's theories about the irrational, unconscious motives that shape human behaviour. Bernays authored several books, including *Crystallising Public Opinion* (1923), *Propaganda* (1928), and *The Engineering of Consent* (1947). He saw public relations as an "applied social science" that uses insights from psychology, sociology, and other disciplines to scientifically manage and manipulate the thinking and behaviour of an irrational and "herdlike" public. "The conscious and intelligent manipulation of the organised habits and opinions of the masses is an important element in democratic society," he wrote in *Propaganda*, "Those who manipulate this unseen mechanism of society constitute an invisible government which is the true ruling power of our country."

In the 1890s when gender role reversals could be caricaturised, the idea of an aggressive woman who also smoked was considered laughable. In 1929, Edward Bernays proved otherwise when he convinced women to smoke in public during an Easter parade in Manhattan as a show of defiance against male domination. The demonstrators were not aware that a tobacco company was behind the publicity stunt.

One of Bernays' early clients was the tobacco industry. In 1929, he orchestrated a now-legendary publicity stunt aimed at persuading women to take up cigarette smoking, an act that at the time was exclusively equated with men. It was considered unfeminine and inappropriate for women to smoke; besides the occasional prostitute, virtually no women participated in the act publicly.

Bernays initially consulted psychoanalyst A. A. Brill for advice, Brill told him: "Some women regard cigarettes as symbols of freedom... Smoking is a sublimation of oral eroticism; holding a cigarette in the mouth excites the oral zone. It is perfectly normal for women to want to smoke cigarettes.

Further the first women who smoked probably had an excess of male components and adopted the habit as a masculine act. But today the emancipation of women has suppressed many feminine desires. More women now do the same work as men do.... Cigarettes, which are equated with men, become torches of freedom." Upon hearing this analysis, Bernays dubbed his PR campaign the: "Torches of Liberty Contingent".

It was in this spirit that Bernays arranged for New York City débutantes to march in that year's Easter Day Parade, defiantly smoking cigarettes as a statement of rebellion against the norms of a male-dominated society. Publicity photos of these beautiful fashion models smoking "Torches of Liberty" were sent to various media outlets and appeared worldwide. As a result, the taboo was dissolved and many women were led to associate the act of smoking with female liberation. Some women went so far as to demand membership in all-male smoking clubs, a highly controversial act at the time. For his work, Bernays was paid a tidy sum by George Washington Hill, president of the American Tobacco Company.

Another early practitioner was Harry Reichenbach (1882-1931) a New York-based American press agent and publicist who promoted movies. He claims to have made famous the Paul Chabas painting, September Morn. Supposedly, he saw a print in a Chicago art store window. He made a deal with the store owner who had not sold any of his 2,000 prints. Reichenbach had hired some boys to "ogle" the picture when he showed it to the moralist crusader Anthony Comstock. Comstock was suitably outraged when he saw it. Comstock's Anti-Vice Society took the case to the court and lost. However, the case aroused interest to the painting, which ultimately sold millions of copies.

In 1950 PRSA enacts the first "Professional Standards for the Practice of Public Relations," a forerunner to the current Code of Ethics, last revised in 2000 to include six core values and six code provisions. The six core values are "Advocacy, Honesty, Expertise, Independence, Loyalty, and Fairness." The six code provisions consulted with are "Free Flow of Information, Competition, Disclosure of Information, Safeguarding Confidences, Conflicts of Interest, and Enhancing the Profession."

Emergence of Modern Public Relations

Viewed as a professional endeavour, public relations is most often defined as the management function that seeks to establish and maintain mutually beneficial relationships between an organisation, commercial or non-commercial, and the audiences or "publics" on which the success of these entities depends. These publics may include any of several possible constituencies: customers, investors, employees, suppliers, legislators, competitors, government officials and other "influentials."

Working within the context of the prevailing public opinion, laws, politics and societal norms of the country or countries in which they work, public relations practitioners develop programs and craft messages aimed at creating favourable support for the goals of the organisations they represent. Obtaining significant, positive news and feature coverage in the print and broadcast media is a key objective. Unlike advertising or marketing, with which it is often confused, professional public relations is more "soft sell" than "hard sell." It emphasises information and persuasion as opposed to packaging and paid media, diplomacy as opposed to force. Owing to its subtleties, it is occasionally viewed as "propaganda" or, in more current jargon, "spin," the intentional manipulation of public opinion without regard for what is accurate or true.

Although professional public relations has certainly been misused from time to time, its record of historical achievement suggests a much deeper and abiding respect for and adherence to openness and honesty in its dealings and communications. Public relations blossomed as a professional endeavour in the 20th Century, most conspicuously in the United States, but its roots, both philosophical and pragmatic, can be traced throughout civilisation.

Edward Bernays, whom many have considered the founder of modern public relations, wrote, "The three main elements of public relations are practically as old as society: informing people, persuading people, or integrating people with people. Of course, the means and methods of accomplishing these ends have changed as society has changed."

For Bernays and other historians of the practice, professional public relations has always gone hand in hand with civilisation. In their eyes, much of recorded history can be interpreted as the practice of public relations. Whereas primitive societies ruled mainly through fear and intimidation, more advanced cultures depended on discussion and debate. As rulers sought to build consensus, persuasion became less and less grounded in force and more and more grounded in words, although force or the threat of force—witness the 9/11 tragedy—too often still drives the deliberations. With the invention of writing, public relations in the formal sense took shape.

Whether they were promoting their image as warriors or kings, leaders of ancient civilisations such as Sumeria, Babylonia, Assyria, and Persia used poems and other writings to promote their prowess in battle and politics. In Egypt much of the art and architecture (statues, temples, tombs) was used to impress on the public the greatness of priests, nobles, and scribes. In ancient Israel, the Bible and other religious texts became a powerful means for moulding the public mind. With the growth of the Hellenic world, the word, both written and spoken, exploded as a force for social integration. And the Athens marketplace became a centre of public discussion concerning the conduct of business and public life. Oratory flourished, and the public interest became a central concern of philosophical speculation.

Public relations continued to develop even during medieval times, using the "new media" of that day, such as the Bayeaux Tapestry, a woven wall hanging that extolled the Norman Conquest of England in 1066. It was not until the Renaissance and Reformation that the foundation of the modern world arose—and with it the underpinnings of the kind of public relations that has become vital to the management of public and private institutions. Great documents of liberty crystallised the power of public opinion.

When the French Revolution arrived, the stage was set. In their *Declaration of the Rights of Man and Citizens* (1789), the leaders of the French Revolution proclaimed the right of citizens to express and communicate thought freely. In 1792 the National Assembly of France created the first propaganda ministry. It was part of the Ministry of the Interior and it was called the Bureau d'Esprit, or "Bureau of the Spirit." It subsidised editors and sent agents to various parts of the country to win public support for the French Revolution.

England's rebellious American colonies produced a host of public relations experts who used oratory, newspapers, meetings, committees, pamphlets, and correspondence to win people to their cause. Included among them were Paul Revere, Benjamin Franklin, John Peter Zenger, Samuel Adams, Alexander Hamilton, James Madison, and John Jay. Adams has been called the great press agent of the American Revolution for fashioning the machinery of political change. Hamilton, Madison, and Jay are credited with winning ratification of the Constitution by publishing letters they had written to the press in 1787–1788. These letters became known as the Federalist Papers.

The other great documents produced by the founders of the United States—the *Declaration of Independence*, the *Constitution*, and the *Bill of*

Rights—may all be seen as master-works of public relations. These documents, essential to the notion of tying one's destiny to the public interest, also helped establish the United States as the breeding ground for pursuing public relations as a profession that represented the diverse interests of democracy and free enterprise.

Many American legends are the result of public relations campaigns. For example, the story of Daniel Boone was created by a landowner to promote settlement in Kentucky. And Davy Crockett's exploits were largely created by his press agent, Matthew St. Clair, to woo votes away from President Andrew Jackson. The master of all nineteenth-century press agents was Phineas T. Barnum. Showman par excellence, Barnum created a wave of publicity stunts and coverage that made his circus, "The Greatest Show on Earth," an irresistible draw in every city and town it visited after its inception in 1871. Press agentry was so successful that it became an essential undertaking for companies that depended on the public's attention. Indeed, the success of Barnum and his colleagues in manipulating the press was so great that, to this day, the media still harbor skepticism toward anything that suggests commercial promotion.

It was in the last two decades of the nineteenth century and the early years of the twentieth century that professional public relations bloomed. This was the era of America's wild and woolly development as the centre of capitalist enterprise, when industry, the railroads, and utilities exploded across the face of the nation. The hard-bitten attitudes of businessmen toward the public were epitomised in 1892 by the cold-blooded methods of Henry Clay Frick in his attempt to crush a labour union in the Carnegie-Frick Steel Companies plant in Homestead, Pennsylvania. The employees' strike was ultimately broken and the union destroyed by the use of the Pennsylvania State militia. Brute force won the battle for immediate control, but public opinion, framed in the struggle of the workers, won the war. Much of public relations history is woven into this unending struggle between employer and employee, though today, fortunately, the war is waged by discussion and negotiation, not private police or armed guards.

Corporations quickly learned the value of combating hostility and courting public favour through professional public relations. Corporations also learned the value of publicity in attracting customers and investors. Companies across America established press bureaus to manage the dissemination of news favourable to themselves and unfavourable to their competitors. The “battle of the currents” between Westinghouse (advocate of alternating-current, or AC, power transmission) and Thomas A. Edison’s General Electric (advocate of direct current, or DC, transmission) is one of the earliest examples of how public relations was first conducted in the United States by powerful economic interests. Using former newspapermen as their publicists, the companies fought each other tooth and nail for media attention, political influence, and marketing advantage. Trade associations also caught the public relations fever in the late 1800s. The Association of American Railroads claims it was the first organisation to use the term *public relations* in its 1897 *Year Book of Railway Literature*.

In the 1900s, public relations evolved from individual press agents and publicists to counselling firms that offered their services as experts in the field. The nation’s first publicity firm, The Publicity Bureau, was founded in Boston in 1900 by George V. S. Michaelis, Herbert Small, and Thomas O. Marvin. In 1906 the bureau came into prominence when it was hired by the nation’s railroads to oppose adverse regulatory legislation that was then in Congress. The firm failed in its efforts, but soon after, the majority of railroads established their own public relations departments.

The Bell System

One of the most famous corporations in history was the American Telephone and Telegraph Company (AT&T), founded in the 1870s, with its 23 Bell Telephone companies, a manufacturing and supply unit (Western Electric), and several other technical and research entities, including Bell Laboratories. Collectively, it was known as “The Bell System” or more affectionately, Ma Bell. Until the U.S. government split it into several different companies in January 1, 1984, it was the most formidable telecommunications giant in the world. Although it made great products, had an almost monopolistic control over telephony, and thrived on high-end technical research and development, a central aspect of the company’s success over the years was its use of professional public relations. The practice was integrated as the critical tool for communicating and managing its relations with employees, suppliers, legislators and, most important, consumers.

Post–World War Development

With the post–World War II economic boom, which turned the United States into the wealthiest country on earth, public relations prospered as never before. New and old institutions of business, government, and not-for-profit enterprise had seen what public relations had done for the war effort, and they wanted to tap its evolving power for purposes of publicising their products and services for the burgeoning consumer markets, both at home and abroad.

In the 1930s and 1940s, several organisations were founded to represent the interests of public relations practitioners, culminating in 1948 in the formation of the Public Relations Society of America (PRSA). Today, the PRSA remains the world's largest public relations membership association with more than 20,000 members, primarily in the United States.

By the late 1960s, public relations had matured into a full-blown professional enterprise, comprising, in the United States, several hundred public relations agencies, large and small, and more than 100,000 individual practitioners whose ranks mushroomed to double that number by the year 2000. Public relations specialists became an integral part of top management, often reporting directly to the president or CEO of the institutions they served.

Part of the driving force for this growth in the 1960s and into the 1970s was the great burst of political turbulence that engulfed the world. Part was also the burgeoning consumer movement that sought to protect the average person against unsafe products, unsanitary working conditions, unfair pricing and other breaches, real and alleged, of the expanding social contract that said, in effect, the "Customer is King." Corporations, in particular, found themselves crafting "Bills of Rights" for their customers, recasting their credit agreements in "plain English," and instituting numerous other reforms to guarantee consumer satisfaction. Colleges and universities were particularly affected, as their campuses became hot-beds of social action. Like business and government, they, too, had to pay attention to their "publics" or suffer the consequences.

In the 1980s and 1990s, the struggle for equality among the races and sexes continued, even as massive change in these areas became the norm, but new issues arose to spark other manifestations of activist militancy—much of it focused on environmental and quality-of-life issues. Business and government became the primary targets for initiatives aimed at curbing air pollution, water pollution, deforestation, and the general threat of ecological disaster caused by global warming and the destruction of the world's natural habitats.

Over time, public relations professionals are called upon to handle a multiplicity of assignments. At the most rudimentary level, they disseminate news and other non-controversial information about their employer's operations and accomplishments. At a more sophisticated level, especially at the highest reaches of government or in the world's largest corporations, they manage communications related to more substantive issues such as industrial accidents, environmental disasters, product recalls, and unfair labor practices. The list of challenges is endless. Corporations are particularly vulnerable to public antipathy toward irresponsible social behaviour or breaches of accepted standards of institutional conduct. Some headline situations since the 1980's underscore the social and political impact that various kinds of crises can have for corporations:

i) Union Carbide's Bhopal (India) chemical plant explosion
ii) Perrier's benzene-tainted bottled water
iii) Dow Corning's faulty silicone breast implants
iv) Nike's unfair labor practices in Asian plants
v) Coca-Cola's tainted beverage scare in France and elsewhere in Europe
vi) Shell Oil environmental pollution in Ogoniland, Nigeria
vii) Microsoft's fight against U.S. Government charges of monopolistic abuse
viii) Bridgestone/Firestone's faulty manufactured tires and their link to hundreds of deaths and injuries in Ford cars and trucks
ix) Enron's managerial deception and financial malfeasance

Each of these companies faced reverberations around the globe as the press and government authorities took them to task for failing to prevent or minimise the resulting damage, or for misrepresenting the facts and implications once the situations arose. Crises of this magnitude are infrequent, fortunately, but owing to the level of damage, actual or potential, and the degree of controversy they engender, they are usually in the headlines for weeks or months and the effects on the companies involved may linger for years. In some instances, the companies go bankrupt.

Professional public relations has more than fulfilled its role in society despite the many setbacks that seem to go hand in hand with the practice from time to time. What began as mainly a U.S. enterprise in the early 1900s, with a few agencies and a few hundred practitioners, has grown, almost inexorably, to become a global enterprise, far surpassing what even the most visionary of its early proponents imagined. PR practitioners have prospered as the issues with which they concern themselves have grown in magnitude and impact. Along the way, the "legends" and "stars" of yesteryear were replaced by a new breed of highly skilled executives whose names and front-page exploits became far less important as a measure of success than their day-to-day accomplishments as professional communicators. Most of them became well-paid professionals on a par with other major professions, although many practitioners who owned and ran their own consultancies became multi-millionaires for their labours.

PR: Nature and Scope

PR historians say the first PR firm, the Publicity Bureau, was established in 1900 by former newspapermen, with Harvard University as its first client. The First World War also helped stimulate the development of public relations as a profession.

Many of the first PR professionals, including Ivy Lee, Edward Bernays, and Carl Byoir, got their start with the Committee for Public Information, which organised publicity on behalf of U.S. objectives during World War I. Some historians regard Ivy Lee as the first real practitioner of public relations, but Edward Bernays is generally regarded today as the profession's founder. Ivy Lee, who has been credited with developing the modern news release (also called a "press release"), espoused a philosophy consistent with what has sometimes been called the "two-way street" approach to public relations, in which PR consists of helping clients listen as well as communicate messages to their publics.

In the words of the Public Relations Society of America (PRSA), "Public relations helps an organisation and its publics adapt mutually to each other." In practice, however, Lee often engaged in one-way propagandising on behalf of clients despised by the public, including robber baron John D. Rockefeller. Bernays was the profession's first theorist. A nephew of Sigmund Freud, Bernays drew many of his ideas from Freud's theories about the irrational, unconscious motives that shape human behavior. Bernays authored several books, including Crystallising Public Opinion, Propaganda, and The Engineering of Consent. Bernays saw public relations as an "applied social science" that uses insights from psychology, sociology, and other disciplines to scientifically manage and manipulate the thinking and behavior of an irrational and "herdlike" public.

"The conscious and intelligent manipulation of the organised habits and opinions of the masses is an important element in democratic society," he wrote in Propaganda. "Those who manipulate this unseen mechanism of society constitute an invisible government which is the true ruling power of our country." One of Bernays' early clients was the tobacco industry. In 1929, he orchestrated a legendary publicity stunt aimed at persuading women to take up cigarette smoking, which was then considered unfeminine and inappropriate for women with any social standing. To counter this image, Bernays arranged for New York City débutantes to march in that year's Easter Day Parade, defiantly smoking cigarettes as a statement of rebellion against the norms of a male-dominated society.

Photographs of what Bernays dubbed the "Torches of Liberty Brigade" were sent to newspapers, convincing many women to equate smoking with women's rights. Some women went so far as to demand membership in all-male smoking clubs, a highly controversial act at the time.

PR may target different audiences with different messages to achieve an overall goal. Public Relations sets out to effect widespread opinion and behavior changes. Modern public relations uses a variety of techniques including opinion polling and focus groups to evaluate public opinion, combined with a variety of high-tech techniques for distributing information on behalf of their clients, including satellite feeds, the Internet, broadcast faxes, and database-driven phone banks to recruit supporters for a client's cause. According to the PRSA,

"Examples of the knowledge that may be required in the professional practice of public relations include communication arts, psychology, social psychology, sociology, political science, economics, and the principles of management and ethics. Technical knowledge and skills are required for opinion research, public issues analysis, media relations, direct mail, institutional advertising, publications, film/video productions, special events, speeches, and presentations."

Although public relations professionals are stereotypically seen as corporate servants, the reality is that almost any organisation that has a stake in how it is portrayed in the media employs at least one PR manager. Large organisations may even have dedicated communications departments. Government agencies, trade associations, and other nonprofit organisations commonly carry out PR activities. Public relations should be seen as a management function in any organisation. An effective communication, or public relations, plan for an organisation is developed to communicate to an audience (whether internal or external publics) in such a way the message coincides with organisational goals and seeks to benefit mutual interests whenever possible.

As industry consolidation becomes more prevalent, many organisations and individuals are choosing to retain "boutique" firms as opposed to so-called "global" communications firms. These smaller firms typically specialise in only a couple of practice areas and thus, often have a greater understanding of their client's business. And because they deal with certain journalists with greater frequency, specialty firms often have stronger media contacts in the areas that matter most to their clients. Added benefits of smaller, specialty firms include more personal attention and accountability and as well, cost savings. This is not to say that smaller is always better, but there is a growing consensus that specialty firms offer more than once considered.

A number of specialties exist within the field of public relations, including:

— crisis management
— reputation management
— issue management
— investor relations and labor relations
— grassroots PR (sometimes referred to as astroturf PR).

Public relations involves the management and distribution of information to enable an organisation's target audiences to understand its policies and programmes.

The role of public relations is to:

a) place a subject on the public agenda;
b) garner public support and endorsement of a person, product, organisation or idea;
c) extend advertising campaigns; and
d) deliver complex information and messages (which can not be delivered by an advertisement).

Public relations practice is broader than media relations and/or publicity generation. In reality, the activities of public relations practice include:

is "FOR IMMEDIATE RELEASE" across the top (some may instead be embargoed until a certain date), and lists the issuing organisation's media contacts directly below. The media contacts are the people that the release's issuer wants to make available to the media; for example, a press release about new scientific study will typically list the study's lead scientist as its media contact. The bottom of each release is usually marked with ### or -30- to signify the end of the text.

A press release is simply a written statement distributed to the media. It is a fundamental tool of PR work. Press releases are usually sent via a newswire service (such as PR Newswire or Business Wire) to media outlets, where journalists may pick them up and use them as they see fit. Very often the information in a press release finds its way verbatim, or minimally altered, to print and broadcast reports. If a media outlet reports that "John Doe said in a statement today that...", the "statement" was almost always a press release.

The text of the press release is usually (but not always) written as a news story, with an eye-catching headline and an article written in standard journalistic inverted pyramid style. This style is effective for reaching harried, and often skeptical journalists who rarely read entire releases. It also makes it easy for journalists to lift entire passages from a release and insert them into their own article. While this practice is frowned upon in newsrooms, journalism is a deadline-driven industry, and it is not uncommon for reporters to occasionally copy or modify a line or two from a press release. PR practitioners, on the other hand, design releases to encourage as much "lifting" as possible, so in essence, the less professional a journalist is, the more successful the release is judged to be.

The only time that journalists may copy from a press release in good conscience is if the release provides a direct quote, as in: Senator Smith said, "This is the most fiscally irresponsible bill that the Congress has passed since the Buy Everyone A Mercedes Act." In this case, a journalist may copy the quote verbatim into his or her story, although most reporters prefer to try soliciting an individual quote from the speaker before filing their story. However, because press releases reflect their issuer's preferred interpretation or packaging of a story, journalists are often skeptical of their contents. Of course, the level of skepticism, if any, depends on what the story is and who's telling it. Newsrooms receive so many press releases that, unless it is a story that the media are already paying attention to, a press release alone isn't always enough to catch a journalist's attention. With the advent of modern media and new technology, press releases now have equivalents in these media - video news releases and audio news releases.

Other methods are the following

— Publicity events or publicity stunts
— The talk show circuit. A PR spokesperson (or his/her client) "does the circuit" by being interviewed on television and radio talk shows with audiences that the client wishes to reach.
— Books and other writings
— After a PR practitioner has been working in the field for a while, he or she accumulates a list of contacts in the media and elsewhere in the public affairs sphere. This "Rolodex" becomes a prized asset, and job announcements sometimes even ask for candidates with an existing Rolodex, especially those in the media relations area of PR.

Media and the PR Industry

The relationship between the news media and the PR industry is a complex and increasingly symbiotic one. The media is the central vehicle for much of the PR industry's messages. PR practitioners want to place their stories in the news or other publications and programmes. Without being able to do this, PR would lose one of its main avenues for communication with the public.

The media in turn has become more dependent on PR to supply content to fill air time or column inches. Whilst newspapers have been steadily shedding staff over the last couple of decades they have simultaneously managed to produce ever thicker publications, and the ever growing ranks of PR are happy to help fill the pages.

The power of the big agencies and spin doctor goes beyond this however. As the primary point of contact between businesses and the media, PR people can control access to information which journalists want. This gives them tremendous leverage in negotiating with journalists, as they are in a position to refuse information.

One of the primary tools for supplying content to the media is the press release. This was invented as a PR tool by Ivy Lee. Ideally the press release will provide a publishable article that a over-worked (or lazy) journalist can publish with minimal effort. Anyone with much experience of press searching will have noticed how the same article can appear in several different publications under different names, with only minute changes. Newspapers acquire such content from press agencies such as Reuters or the Press Association which employ their own journalists, as well as from PR agencies and some intermediate services such as PR Newswire.

The largest supplier of content to the UK press is the Press Association. The Press Association, formed in 1868 by a group of newspaper publishers, supplies content to every national and regional daily newspaper, to major broadcasters, online publishers and to a wide range of commercial organisations. Customers subscribe to its news and features lists from which they can take stories to print or broadcast.

Much of the Press Associations content is produced by its network of journalists and photographers, and the PA is proud of its reputation for impartiality. However the Press Association's independence is compromised by its relationship with the PR industry.

One of the PA's 27 shareholders is United Business Media, owners of PR Newswire, and other corporate communications companies. In addition the Press Association now offers services to PR agencies, "PA's unique position at the centre of the media industry in the UK enables us to provide support for many PR and marketing campaigns". Space on PA's newswire service is sold in bulk, to other more commmercial newswires and PR agencies. PR agencies gain an extra level of anonymity by having their content supplied by the prestigious Press Association.

More recent developments include the video news release (VNR) and the audio news release (ANR) for TV and radio news respectively. These are pre-edited video or audio news stories sent to broadcast news stations in just the same way that press releases are sent to the print media. VNRs have become quite ubiquitous on US television news particularly on the smaller TV stations which lack the resources to fill airtime with quality news.

In the UK, VNRs have not reached the same penetration into newsrooms but they are gaining ground. The main national news channels are far more assiduous in applying editorial control than their American counterparts. According to VNR producer, Grapevine Communications, " VNRs so far have been most successful with local ITV newsrooms and with satellite and cable broadcasters; BBC is not in favour, and both BBC and ITN take a fully-independent editorial line."

VNRs still wield influence however. Medialink, the market leader in VNR and ANR production, claims to have placed stories on BBC News programs. The BBC was unable to comment on how often VNRs and ANRs are used

In response to inquiries, ITN denied using any VNRs. When presented with evidence suggesting that they had used VNRs, ITN declined to comment.

Building Relationships

Many journalists have a distrustful attitude to PR. They need to have a wariness of professional story-pitchers. In order to overcome this barrier, the PR agencies aim to build ongoing relationships with journalists and media sources. The more and better relationships they can build, the more influence they can exert on the media.

The nature of the relationship is worth probing if we are to understand the modern media/PR system. Neil Macdonald, editor of 'Business Monthly', the newsletter of the American Chamber of Commerce in Egypt, provides some rare insight into the relationship. He tells of how, in the summer of 2002, he was approached by a number of PR practitioners asking him to provide some advance coverage of the IPRA conference, which was to take place in Cairo that year. Despite feeling "uneasy" with accepting a story from PR people, he ultimately concluded that he "couldn't afford to create a bad relationship with PR agencies" and assigned a freelancer "who I figured could take the fall if the individuals being written about didn't like what they read".

"Most journalists will have taken the PR shilling at some point in their career... Most of the time it is a straightforward love-hate relationship," observes Nic Paton, writing in the Media Guardian, "To the journalist, the PR is a necessary evil. And the PR is willing to suffer all that talk about integrity and independence as long as it gets the client those valuable column inches."

A recent report by the International Public Relations Society into 'unethical media practices' concluded that 'cash for editorial' practices are widespread around the world, especially in central and southern Europe and Latin America, in both print and broadcast media.

Although the bribing of journalists and or editors to run certain stories is held to be quite rare in Western Europe and North America (the PR industry's own PR continually stresses its strict adherence to honesty and integrity) some questionable traditions have developed. One relationship-building practice is known as 'selling in'. Journalists are employed as freelancers by a PR agency to write up stories on behalf of a client and to then sell them on to the press. The newspaper then never knows that it is carrying PR and the practice saves a lot of effort for the PR agency. Admitting to 'selling in' is not good for a journalist's reputation and is rarely discussed, so it is virtually impossible to determine how widespread this tactic has become. In spite of qualms of conscience, many journalists end up taking fees from both the PR agency and the publisher.

Like many journalists, Wall Street Journal reporter, Dean Rotbart went on to work for the PR industry. He set up a company TJFR Group to provide intelligence and background information on journalists for PR agencies. "The exclusive subscriber site contains stories, bios, columns, photos and streaming video that are useful to those dealing with and who have an interest in the business media." Such information is doubtless invaluable for media manipulation, enabling them to match the stories they want to place with the journalists most likely to be sympathetic. Rotbart's client list includes the biggest PR companies in the world and some of the largest corporations from every industry sector.

In addition to planting stories in the press, PR agencies may also need to prevent stories from getting published.

Naturally the PR industry has developed a number of ways of doing this. There is always the threat of legal action as a last resort but this may endanger a carefully cultivated relationship with a journalist or media source, so PR pros prefer more subtle methods first. However, "arm-twisting is used all the time," writes New York Post columnist, John Crudele in O'Dwyer's. A PR department may threaten not to cooperate with an unfriendly journalist, but that is a tactic which may backfire by further arousing the journalist's suspicions. One tactic is for the PR practitioner to contend that a story is old news, at the very least this should plant a seed of doubt in a journalist's mind. Convincing the journalist's editor may be more useful in stopping the story. Another more effective option is to feed the journalist a more interesting story. By the time he has finished with that, the first story may well be old news.

Mark Hollingsworth writes of Sir Tim Bell (of Bell Pottinger), "Bell… is a dealer in information. He establishes close relationships with journalists and editors as a way of ensuring that his client's message is conveyed to his liking. He is Mephistopheles to the reporter's Faust. Favours are offered and received: if the story about the client is spiked, the journalist is handed an even better exclusive about someone else. If the article is published, future cooperation is withdrawn."

PR people may go to far greater extremes than this to censor public debate, however. When David Steinman's book, "Diet for a Poisoned Planet" threatened to bring revelations of pesticide and chemical contamination on raisins (amongst other poisons and foodstuffs) to the public's attention, the California Raisin Advisory Board hired PR company, Ketchum, to conduct damage control. Ketchum obtained details of the book tour and TV and radio appearances that Steinman had planned. They called each media outlet and hassled them to drop the interview or to allow an industry spokesman on the show to present a balanced case. Through the American Council on Science and Health, an industry front group and client of Ketchum, they lobbied the US government to work against the book. Dr William Marcus, a senior science advisor for the Environmental Protection Agency, who had written the book's foreword was pressured to withdraw it. He refused and was later fired from the EPA.

One of the most alarming effects of the burgeoning PR industry's relationship with the media, is that it leads to a steady dumbing down of most news outlets.

Today the media is dominated by big corporations. Few newspapers in Britain or America are not owned by a media corporation. And as the press has become more corporate so its emphasis has shifted from traditional news values - investigation and reporting - to market driven values - profitability, and maximising readership. Noam Chomsky suggests that the most important value for the modern press is to deliver audiences for their advertisers, who supply the bulk of revenue. Fewer journalists are employed and less and less time is available for investigation. Instead content is supplied ever more directly from the press release. Investigative journalism becomes rarer and is supplanted by source journalism.

In this environment the PR companies have become a necessary crutch for the media, but not one that the media is keen to investigate and expose to the public, "like an alcoholic who can't believe he has a drinking problem, members of the press are too close to their own addiction to PR to realise there is anything wrong."

PR on the Internet

The PR has not been quick in recognising the importance of the internet, but it is beginnning to develop strategies for dealing with the new medium. Some of the key practices with which PR agencies aim to tackle the internet include, monitoring and intelligence of relevant internet sites and communications, and through 'viral marketing'.

The Bivings Group is a PR company that specialises in internet PR. Working out of offices in Washington D.C., Brussels and Tokyo, Bivings conducts its PR services for clients including Monsanto, Phillip Morris, and BP.

In 2001, when Californian scientists published a report in Nature, showing that Mexican maize had been contaminated by GM pollen that must have travelled over huge distances, it was a potential disaster for the biotech industry. However the two scientists were roundly and falsely condemned in their methods and political sympathies by correspondents to a biotech listserver, and in the resulting scandal Nature published a retraction of the article. Research revealed however that emails sent in by the two scientists' detractors originated on Bivings Group's servers. Bivings denied all knowledge.

References

Aronson, M., Spenter, D., & Ames, C. *The Public Relations Writer's Handbook: The Digital Age*. San Francisco: Jossey-Bass. 2007.

Botan, C., & Hazleton, V. *Public Relations Theory II*. New Jersey: Lawrence Erlbaum Associates. 2006.

Hansen-Horn, T., & Neff, B. *Public Relations: From Theory to Practice*. Boston: Pearson Education. 2008.

Hendrix, J., & Hayes, D. *Public Relations Cases*. Belmont, CA: Thomson Arts and Sciences. 2007.

2

Public Relations: Theory and Practice

Thomas Jefferson (1807) used the phrase "Public relations" in the place of "State of thought" while writing his seventh address to the US Congress. In India, Great Indian Peninsular Railway Company Limited (GIP Railways) carried on publicity in Public Relations campaign in England for promote tourism to India through mass media and pamphlets. During the time of First World War a central publicity board was set up at Bombay (now Mumbai) for disseminating war news to the public and press. After Second World War the Public Relations activity gained importance both privates as well as Government started Public Relations campaigns.

Investing on Public relations will help the organisation to achieve its objective effectively and smoothly. Public Relations is not creating good image for a bad team.Since false image cannot be sustained for a long time. Though the organisation product or services are good it need an effective Public Relations campaign for attracting, motivating the public to the product or service or towards the purpose of the programme. It is not only encourage the involvement from the public and also resulting in better image.

An effective Public Relations can create and build up the image of an individual or an organisation or a nation. At the time of adverse publicity or when the organisation is under crisis an effective Public Relations can remove the "misunderstanding" and can create mutual understanding between the organisation and the public.

PR is a set of methods which can gain publicity and attention for an individual or an organization to limited or widespread audiences. These methods usually make use of topics that are generally do not require direct payment. These are usually topics that are of public interest and news items. The exposure that public relations provides is channeled through third party sources which have acceptable and solid credibility so that the information disseminated will acquire legitimacy associated with the credibility of the third party source. This credibility which is deficient withadvertising and is what adds to the functions of public relations.

The benefit that an organization acquires from exposure to their audiences is essential to any business that needs a positive image. Public relations can be used to establish and develop relationships with various demographics. Politicians use public relations to present their platforms to their constituency. Customers and potential customers are also objects of PR campaigns.

Although there is still no unified theory of public relations there are several models which can come close to a description of a real world scenario. One of these is the model proposed by Carl H. Botan and Vincent Hazleton in their book called *Public Relations Theory 2.*

Botan proposes that there are two main branches of public relations. These are the theoretical branch and the applied branch. Each of these branches approaches public relations from a different angle of perspective. The theoretical branch first approaches public relations according to its significance to society as a whole only after which does it then address its role of supporting business.

Questions regarding how and what the contributions of public relations to society are significant and relevant to the theoretical branch. The applied branch represents public relations from the traditional perspective. This business oriented view addresses its role in an organization-publics function.

The central difficulty in public relations is the evaluation of the effectiveness of the program and which model or theory to use in the evaluation. In the most common model which is the process paradigm the assessment is made by examining the method as a set of routine steps or procedures which is in a continuous cycle.

These steps are generally recognized to be problem identification, planning, implementation, and evaluation. If these steps are undertaken correctly then the public relations campaign is deemed to be successful.

At present public relations is a fundamentally a management function that addresses the symmetrical or two way communication and the encouragement of mutually advantageous relationship between an organization and its publics.

This also means that that management must promote an organization's ability to listen and respond to those individuals whose symbiotic relationship with the organization is essential to the fulfillment if the organization's goals.

Contemporary theorists are opening new ways to think about public relations. Public relations scholar have hitherto borrowed theories from the adjacent disciplines of communication, psychology, sociology, and organisation studies. At the end of the twentieth century, J. Grunig's four-model concept of public relations was the only modern theoretical approach that could be said to have originated from within public relations scholarship. Even J. Grunig's perspective is rooted in political theory. But the 21st century's burgeoning critical and professional interest in ethical public relations has produced a flurry of discipline-specific, theoretical initiatives.

Grunig's Four-model Concept of Public Relations

Grunig's ongoing defence and development of his 'symmetrical' approach to public relations theory has been the touchstone of much public relations theoretical work over the last two decades. His insistence on 'symmetry' has its roots in:

> ...a theory of politics called interest group liberalism...Interest group liberalism views the political system as a mechanism for open competition among interest or issue groups. Interest group liberalism looks to citizen groups to champion interests of ordinary people against unresponsive government and corporate structures.

In 1984, Grunig and Hunt advocated the 'symmetrical model' of public relations over the 'asymmetrical', 'information', and 'press agent/publicity' models. Grunig held to this claim despite the admission that most people believe professional public relations is best described as operating to an 'asymmetrical' rather than a 'symmetrical model'. The 'asymmetrical model' represents public relations programs aimed at advancing the standing and the projects of the organisation that pays for public relations work. 'Asymmetrical' programs are not aimed at advancing the interests of the publics involved with the sponsoring organisation to the same extent:

> Some critics of the symmetrical worldview—both practitioners and theorists—claim that the approach is unrealistic or idealistic. They argue that organisations hire public relations people as advocates to advance their interests and not as "do-gooders" who "give in" to outsiders with an agenda different from that of the organisation. In short, these critics believe that organisations would not hire a public relations person who does not practice asymmetrically.

J. Grunig and L. Grunig nonetheless claim that there are findings that symmetrical public relations programs are the most effective. Symmetrical public relations programs are those that try to make sure the targeted publics benefit as much as the programs' sponsors or originators:

> Although research supports the idea that the two-way symmetrical model makes public relations more ethical, senior managers of organisations who are oriented to the bottom line also want to know whether it pays for their organisations to be ethical. Research to date suggests that it does. Several studies have shown the ineffectiveness of the press agentry, public information, and two-way asymmetrical models.

Critics of the symmetrical model raise objections such as:

> It is simply absurd to suggest that an interaction between, for example the Shell Oil company and a public consisting of unskilled workers in a developing country can be symmetrical just because the interaction is symmetrical in form. It is even more absurd to suggest the reverse, that the interaction between this worker public and Shell Oil can be symmetrical if the workers adopt the correct attitude and are willing to compromise.

J. Grunig's more recent response to such critics is:

> Both the disciples of the symmetrical theory and critical scholars who debunk it seem to have reconstructed the theory inaccurately in their minds-to the extent that the theory appears to be ridiculous. In my conceptualisation by contrast, symmetrical public relations does not take place in an ideal situation where competing interests come together with goodwill to resolve their differences because they share a goal of social equilibrium and harmony. Rather it takes place in situations where groups come together to protect and enhance their self-interests. Argumentation, debate and persuasion take place. But dialogue, listening, understanding and relationship building also occur because they are more effective in resolving conflict than are one-way attempts at compliance gaining.

Heath' Rhetorical Approach to Public Relations

Heath has taken a major initiative to try to make rhetorical theory the primary perspective through which public relations should be understood. Heath explains his view of the rhetorical process in his *Handbook of Public Relations*.

> This book champions humans' commitment to rhetorical dialogue as the process for forging conclusions and influencing actions. The process is a two-way one. Through statement and counter-statement, people test each other's views of reality, value, and choices relevant to products, services and public policies.

Rhetoric, like PR, has negative connotations. However, the term originated as the surely very welcome mode of persuasive discourse that accompanied the advent of putative democracy. It was an important aspect of the way complex, ancient Greek society governed itself through public debate and persuasion, rather like our present court and parliamentary processes, reducing the need for oppression and violence. For Heath, the public relations practitioner and the client whom they represent are engaged, rather like ancient rhetors, in a "wrangle in the marketplace".... "Professional communicators have a major voice in the marketplace of ideas—the dialogue on behalf of various self interests". Heath echoes J. Grunig's 'symmetry' when he says that this wrangle must be conducted on the basis of a level playing field in order for it to constitute ethical public relations practice:

> A rhetorical view presumes that, in terms of their right to speak, all parties are symmetrical... In a utopia people have what they need and have no reason for dispute-rhetoric or public relations. Thus public relations as a discipline seeks to advance marketplace and public policy discourse by pursuing relational excellence in actions (organisational responsibility) and discourse that lead to the co-creation, co-management, or co-definition of meaning (zones of meaning) that reconcile strains and alienation and foster mutually beneficial relationships.

Heath suggests that rhetoric "is symmetrical because each idea placed in the marketplace or public policy arena stands on its own merits". For critics, however, it is not clear how what Heath calls "rhetorical enactment rationale" makes public relations more ethical or acceptable, except if those engaged in contesting their views are equally resourced. This of course, as in the Leitch and Nielson critique of J. Grunig above, is often an impossible situation. We are led to the conclusion that, like "symmetrical public relations", "rhetorical enactment rationale" is another 'ideal type' of public relations—a theoretical construct against which the ethicality and efficacy of public relations initiatives in a democratic society can be compared.

For Skerlep, there is an advantage in the rhetorical theoretical approach towards public relations in that it allows public relations people to gain other perspectives on situations in a way that problematises the notion of 'Truth'. 'Truth' is often a very contested terrain when interest groups are in public confrontation. Skerlep suggests:

> The naive belief in truth, objectivity and impartiality as the normative criteria of validity of public relations discourse that is professed by public relations textbooks does not elucidate on the discursive dimension of polemical confrontations…the positivistic concept of truth [has] become controversial with the ascent of postmodern relativism…".

Skerlep underlines Aristotle's realisation that rhetorical argumentation—the open public contest of ideas as advocated by Heath—does not lead to 'absolute truths'. But this does not mean that the rhetor is allowed to speak untruths or to manipulate the public either. Instead: "In the situation of public contention on a controversial issue the speaker can only marshal the best arguments for his or her case…The 'truth' can only be reached through argumentative dialogue that reveals which of the participating parties has better arguments". This is probably an approach that many environmental and human welfare lobby groups would reject. Such groups would point to empirical studies to argue that there IS a 'truth' to do with environmental protection or public health.

Relationship Management Approach

An important public relations theory initiative in 2000 was the publication of the book *Public Relations as Relationship Management: A relational approach to the study and practice of public relations,* edited by Ledingham and Bruning. The editors claim in their introduction that:

> The emergence of relationship management as a paradigm for public relations scholarship and practice calls into question the essence of public relations—what it is and what it does or should do, its function and value within the organisational structure and the greater society, and the benefits generated not only for the sponsoring organisations but also for the publics those organisations serve and the communities and societies in which they exist.

The 'relational management' approach to public relations is centred on the 'dimensions' or 'parameters' of "relationship management". These Efficiency [synergy] dimensions or parameters are aspects in the relationship between the organisation sponsoring the public relations work and the target of that project. They are factors in the relationship such as:

— Adaptation
— Assuring legitimacy
— Asymmetry (unequal power)
— Being constructive
— Being open
— Commitment
— Cooperation
— Creating win-win situations
— Credibility
— Efficiency (synergy)
— Interdependence/power imbalance
— Intimacy
— Investment
— Legitimacy (justification)
— Mutual goals
— Necessity (legal requirements)
— Networking—common friends
— Openness
— Passion
— Performance satisfaction
— Reciprocity (cooperation)
— Satisfaction
— Shared technology
— Sharing tasks
— Social bonds
— Stability
— Structural bonds

— Trust
— Understanding
— Openness
— Involvement
— Investment

Advocates of the relationship management approach say that various inclusions and absences of these 'dimensions' are often unproblematically conflated within the term 'relationship'. That is, often authors do not say which of the above aspects of 'relationship' they are referring to, nor which they do not mean, when they use the term 'relationship'. They imply that better analysis of such components would enable people to understand public relations better. In the 'relational' paradigm the aspects or 'dimensions' of a relationship may not be symmetrical.

There may not be equivalent access or ownership of such things as: shared technology; sharing tasks; social bonds; stability: structural bonds (employment, contracts). Even such concepts as "trust", "openness", or "satisfaction" do not imply a necessary symmetrical reciprocity. For these reasons it is hard to compare the relationship management approach to public relations directly with the J. Grunig or Heath approaches above. It could be argued that 'relationship management' may in fact be more of an instrumental procedure. It may be an approach to mapping a multitude of ways public relations may be 'done' rather than a way to get to the essence of any normative notion of what public relations 'is' or should be. This is despite Ledingham and Bruning's claim to "a paradigm for public relations scholarship and practice" in their introduction. Another possibility is that 'relationship management' is to do with a rediscovery, elaboration, and analysis of the 'goodwill' aspect of public relations, an aspect which is still prominent in some definitions that descend from the UK definition of public relations:

> Public relations is the discipline which looks after reputation, with the aim of earning understanding and support and influencing opinion and behaviour. It is the planned and sustained effort to establish and maintain goodwill and mutual understanding between an organisation and its publics.

Public Relations as Engendered Practice

Organisations make choices about the careers of the increasing numbers of women entering public relations based not on merit but rather on gender. L. Grunig, Toth, and Hon, compare the posited "feminist values" of "cooperation, respect, caring, nurturance (sic), interconnection, justice, equity, honesty, sensitivity, perceptiveness, intuition, altruism, fairness, morality and commitment" with the "norms of public relations practice." They find the latter wanting. The above authors imply that there are feminine attributes that make women particularly suited to carry out public relations work. They further suggest that, despite this suitability, a 'masculine ideology' dominates senior public relations management levels. This ideology discriminates against the appointment of women to senior levels and opposes the promotion of feminine values when public relations strategy is decided:

> Over the past 10 years, gender discrepancies in hiring, salaries, and promotion have been found in quantitative and qualitative studies in public relations. Although there have been a few critics of these studies, surveys and focus groups continue to offer valid and reliable statistics and experiences attesting to the fact that, although the public relations profession is almost 70 per cent women today, men are often favoured for hiring, higher salaries, and promotions to management positions.

Aldoory and Toth contribute to what they call "burgeoning theory in this area". They suggest that the "scholarly body of knowledge in public relations requires its own theory of gender discrimination in a gendered profession". Their review of studies compares career discrimination against women in public relations with career discrimination against women in other areas such as marketing. They find that women are discriminated against for the usual reasons: being looked upon as home makers and child bearers; for socially held notions of the role and psychology of women; that 'career women' are the exception, and so on. However, Aldoory and Toth theorise that, in public relations, there is an additional concern because:

> (A)s the number of men decreases throughout the profession, attempts to recruit and retain them become stronger. These stronger attempts lead to favouritism towards males in terms of salaries, promotions and benefits...[This] leads to a lack of attention towards young women's needs for skills and knowledge, such as negotiation tactics and assertiveness.

This downgrading of women's employment is despite suggestions that women tend to have better social and psychological 'values' than men to carry out 'symmetrical' public relations. In the view of many leading public relations theorists, symmetrical public relations is the best form of public relations. Discussion about attitudes towards engendered values and roles is hard to summarise without making stereotypical generalisations. Leading female scholars of public relations L. Grunig, et al. make the point that:

> (M)uch confusion surrounds any discussion of women and public relations. When we think about women, are we really thinking about gender, which we consider biological, or a constellation of socially determined sex roles, which encompass stereotypical qualities associated with either femininity or masculinity? We all know that not all people biologically classified as "women" act alike. People of either gender may have feminine characteristics. We value the qualities associated with femininity, but of course not all women exhibit female characteristics or are feminine. Not all men act "masculine" and not all traits considered masculine are antithetical to feminism.

Having pointed out the problems, L. Grunig, et al., say:

> Some scholars have suggested that the most effective public relations grows out of an entire world view that is feminine. That is, public relations that is practised as balanced, two-way communication between an organisation and its stakeholder groups stands to make the greatest contribution to organisational effectiveness.

L. Grunig, et al. then associate the "feminist values" which are listed at the start of this section: "cooperation, respect, caring..." etc., as those values that best orient a public relations strategist towards the two-way symmetrical attitude.

Postmodern Perspective on Public Relations

Some recent theories verge on an alternative politics of public relations. Holtzhausen, for example, advocates a postmodern perspective on public relations. She implies that management thinking within major organisations needs to be critiqued by public relations people to challenge dominant ideas that overlook the diversity of views and perspectives current in the postmodern condition of society. By 'postmodern society' she means a society where political, cultural, social, and economic views and mores are very diverse. In postmodernism there is no one guiding principle as there is in a theocracy, or a society guided by 'scientific progress', or as is implied by the expression 'The American Dream'. As the public relations person is often the conscience and the spokesperson/advisor of organisations, the responsibility for this postmodern critique importantly resides in the public relations department:

> Postmodern theories urge public relations practitioners to acknowledge the political nature of their activities and to be aware of the power relations inherent in everyday practice. Public relations is about change or resistance to change, these political acts are manifest in the everyday use of organisational language and symbolism and are influenced by the organisation's cultural and social environment. This redefines the boundary spanning role. Instead of claiming objectivity, practitioners are forced to choose which side they are on.

Holzhausen gives examples from South Africa of an internal corporate communications department persuading a tourism board to align with animal rights activists to campaign against a government policy to cull elephants. The same department assisted in a trade union linked campaign to oppose discrimination against black people and women within the tourist board. Holzhausen says:

> It should be the responsibility of the public relations function to create opportunities for dissent, for opening up opportunities for debates without forcing consensus, to create possibilities for change...Scholars and practitioners can create a postmodern condition by being critical and by exposing the irony and contradictions of public relations practice.

Holzhausen is clearly the most radical of the public relations theorists discussed so far and it is not obvious how the necessarily changing political conditions of South Africa can be projected generally. Her ideas are to some extent in line with Heath's notion of rhetorical dialogue, although it is not clear that Heath has in mind internal dialogue rather than dialogue between cohesive organisations and other groups who have other perspectives. Interestingly, J. Grunig sees Holzhausen's 'internal revolutionary' ideas as in line with his own strictures for organisations to be symmetrical with their publics: "I concur with Derina Holzhausen that public relations is a postmodern force in organisations that gives voice to public in management decision making—an in-house activist" J. Grunig.

Another element challenging established public relations thinking is the omnipresent internet. The internet has made protest against corporations and other dominant organisations easier. But they go on to explain that the internet has also created a new class of protesters. The micro-activists are individualists opposed to capitalism, but also opposed to big organisations such as political parties of the left and organisations such as Greenpeace. Micro-activists believe such campaigning organisations compromise and 'sellout'. They are all part of the "oppressionism" of a violent and environmentally malfunctioning world. While rejecting macro organisation, the internet enables micro-activists to cooperate very effectively as they did at Seattle.

Similar 'lateral connection' changes can be observed among corporations' stakeholders facilitated by the increasing adoption and development in sophistication of the internet. What writings on internet activists and writings on stakeholders' use of the internet both indicate for the public relations theorist is that simple models of communication between 'an organisation and its publics' are either redundant, or at least should be viewed with the utmost suspicion. This puts into question simple communication models such as the 'sender-receiver' model and such concepts as 'opinion leaders', 'third party endorsement' via journalism, 'gate-keeping' by editors, and 'agenda setting' through sponsorship, event management, and other tactics. Though these concepts may still have some relevance, theories of communication are needed that help map the apparently teeming and far harder to see and understand lateral communication between targeted publics and others. Simplistic concepts of symmetrical communication would seem to be made redundant by this realisation. However, J. Grunig's alignment with public relations as postmodern activism would seem to keep his approach abreast of the fragmented and multi-directional nature of contemporary public relations influences. It is not clear how Heath's rhetorical approach is implicated in internet developments other than to say that Heath welcomes dialogue.

PR and Change Theory

Of all the theories important to the effective performance of public relations, change theory may be the most vital. Virtually every thing we do in the professional field of public relations is related to the accomplishment of change whether changes of attitudes, opinions, or behaviours. Even when our public relations mission is to maintain existing relationships that contribute to customer, legislator or public support, as would be the case in maintaining loyalty to a product or service, knowledge of the factors relating to the way social change takes place gives the practitioner an edge in management counselling and in public relations planning.

In some cases, change theory knowledge allows public relations managers to counsel management on the cost an organisation will confront in resisting change or in changing public opinions, attitudes or behaviours. It may also help us to know when the best management counsel may be defining the reasons why the timing for a public opinion change campaign is simply wrong. In the 1980s, utility companies faced an up-hill challenge in gaining public acceptance for the construction of nuclear power plants. Executives, at that point in time, would have been better served through counsel based on change theory research as to why the battle to win favourable public opinion simply could not be won. Unfortunately, some members of top management may have interpreted failure as the ineffectiveness of public relations counsel in achieving the successful persuasive communication needed.

Employee Change

You probably think of the use of change theory and strategy as it may relate to employee change. Certainly knowledge of effective change strategy is essential when faced with needs related to mergers, downsizing, or a change in corporate culture. The public relations executive's knowledge needs may relate to the direction of the activity or as a contributing member of the change management team. In all change planning, however, the role need of public relations counsel should be that of an executive with expertise in his or her knowledge of facilitating change with the least disruption to the relationships needed to achieve and advance organisational goals.

Target Audience Change

There is also a need for implementation of change theory knowledge in the strategic planning process in any change activity such as a change of public behaviour for health, safety, environmental, or conservation benefits. Even the trial and use of a new product or service on the part of a target audience involves a change in attitude, opinion, and behaviour. Knowledge of change factors provides another set of guidelines for increasing the effectiveness public relations problem solving strategies.

Organisational Change

Probably the most critical role of the senior public relations executive, however, is that of keeping his or her own CEO and executive management team open to change. It is a role that is not always recognised because of all of the other public relations responsibilities placed on a public relations manager. Yet, if organisations are to achieve two-way symmetrical public relations performance, then the role is critical. It may also be critical to the public relations manager's status as a member of an organisational management team. The ability of the public relations executive to contribute to this task will depend on the demonstration of knowledge of change theory in his or her day to day management counsel, a public relations program that includes the monitoring of changes and trends in the organisation's social environment, and the ability of a public relations executive to convey to management what public relations can contribute to a management team's ability in responding to social change.

Value of Change Theory

Knowledge of change theory provides the ability to identify strategic communication needs and allows identification of the obstacles to the accomplishment of change. Most importantly it empowers the public relations executive in influencing executive management in understanding the importance of environmental, stakeholder, and target audience research and communication of the results to the management team on a continual basis.

Change theory also teaches patience in the achievement of change as well as the importance of flexibility on the part of management in achieving change objectives. It also teaches us that in relation to change, there is nearly always an action by a change agent followed by a reaction on the part of the targeted audience or population. The end result is some type of integration. An understanding of this end result teaches us, as practitioners, patience and recognition of the importance of management flexibility in the achievement of the change. It is a critical change theory understanding that must be shared with a management team.

Cultural Theory of PR

Public relations is a multicultural field that entails an ongoing competition and cooperation among a finite number of cultural voices. Public relations not only contributes to cultural discourse; it also is a site of an ongoing cultural contest. Cultural theory in anthropology on the elementary relational structures proposes that "plural rationalities" organise social discourse. Cultural theory scholars labeled these different rationalities as "cultural biases." A cultural bias is a worldview that cognitively supports a particular way of organising social relations. Each cultural bias has an accompanying set of preferred argument structures or cultural topoi. These CT organise discussions of value conflicts in society. These cultural biases also organise discourse about public relations. This competition of cultural voices appears in histories of public relations, accounts of professional practice, estimates of public relations's future trajectory, and normative prescriptions for public relations practice.

Think of culture as essentially a dialogue that allocates praise and blame. Then focus particularly on the blame. Cultural theory proposes that "culture" is an ecosystem inhabited by a finite number of ways of life. Culture emerges in the contentious conversation among the ways of life. A way of life consists of a preferred pattern of social relations and a cultural bias or set of shared values and beliefs about people and the natural world. These configurations of belief and social relations are "reciprocal, interacting and reinforcing. Adherence to a certain pattern of social relationships facilitates a distinctive way of looking at the world; adherence to a certain worldview legitimises a corresponding type of social relations".

A way of life is viable only as long as its cultural bias and its pattern of social relationships are compatible with each other. "A cultural voice" will refer to instances when the premises of a "cultural bias" are articulated in argument. In addition, a "cultural tribe" will refer to an "interpretive community" that shares a particular cultural bias. Cultural theory posits that the social construction of reality operates within set limits. There are only five enduring voices in the cultural competition; only fatalism, egalitarianism, hierarchy, autonomous individualism (AI), and competitive individualism are coherent enough to attain long term viability. A cultural bias is an internally consistent template that structures human relationships.

The core propositions of each cultural bias are also argument structures. A topos or topic structure is a general theme that can be used to develop persuasive arguments on a wide set of topics. A cultural topos is a systematic argument that reinforces a preferred pattern of social relationships. Each cultural voice has a core set of CT. The most fundamental arguments of each cultural voice are its assertions about "nature" and "human nature."

"That's the way the world is" or "That's the way people are" are final arguments put forward to quell further disputation. These beliefs about reality are associated with a supporting value imperative, a decision making principle, a justice principle, and an activity principle. The cultural voices fundamentally disagree with one another in their assertions about reality and the preferred structure of social relations.Thetopoi of the culturalvoices are ordered from left to right, from the simplest to the most complex, and in terms of the degree of strategic calculation required to sustain each type of social relations.

According to cultural theory, the five ways of life constitute a cultural ecosystem. Each way of life defines itself relative to its competitors, and each way of life competes for adherents. Each way of life waxes or wanes relative to the success that its topoi have in predicting, interpreting, and managing events. CT have great durability in cultural debates, even extending over several centuries. However, societal events can increase the allure of a cultural voice and diminish the potency of competing cultural voices. The terrorist attacks of September 11th strengthened the appeal of hierarchy (i.e., national security). Likewise, the collapse of Enron gave some new impetus to egalitarian initiatives like campaign finance reform. These gains have been at the expense of competitive individualist (CI) topoi that dominated discourse during the 1990s stock market boom.

Each cultural bias provides lenses for interpreting the world. Each way of life clearly sees what the other ways of life do not see. As with optical illusions, one can only see one thing at a time. To see differently, one must change lenses. Even when they agree on nouns and verbs, theways of life disagree on adjectives and adverbs. CIs celebrate the elegant efficiency in markets, but egalitarians bemoan wasteful and vindictive conspicuous consumption that markets enable.

Cultural theory proposes that each way of life is incomplete. "Eachway of life needs each of its rivals, either to make up for its deficiencies, or to exploit, or to define itselfagainst. To destroy the other (wayof life) is to murder the self". Away of life contains contradictions and pathologies. The ways of life compete and give form to culture. Each group develops its own set of compromises and social institutions. One voice may dominate discourse or two voices may form a dominant coalition. The remaining voices tend to be ignored or marginalised. Representative democracy is a coalition of cultures in which each voice is articulated somewhere in the differentiated institutions of representative democracy.

The cultural voices also collaborate. Two ways of life may share values and preferred means. They may support the same means for different reasons.

Hierarchical advocates endorse school uniforms because they symbolise order, but egalitarian advocates embrace uniforms because they mute displays of social inequality. Cultural alliances and oppositions shift as historical circumstances change. For culture, there "is no final equilibrium point. Change is inherent in the different competencies and biases of different cultures". The hierarchical and egalitarian voices privilege the"common good" and disparage the opportunism of CIs and fatalists.

Egalitarians and individualists dislike the regimentation of hierarchical culture. Individualist and hierarchical voices defend the virtues of social inequality. The fatalist voice can be engaged in alliances of evasion and passive resistance. Fatalists may help individualists evade the organising impulses of hierarchy or passively assist hierarchy in preserving the status quo against the attacks of egalitarian reformers. Groups make difficult tradeoffs between the values embedded in the different cultural biases when they decide how to allocate scarce resources.

People experience anxiety, ambivalence, or outrage when they encounter such trade offs. For instance, an explicit discussion about how much an HMO should be required to spend on experimental medical treatments to save one individual's life causes us discomfort. Ordinarily, it is taboo to discuss such topics. To put a dollar value on human life offends our sensibilities.

The CT perspective applies inanycontextwherepeople argue about how they should organise their social relationships. This chapter employs a mix of discourse exemplars from public relations scholarship and professional publications that are available to public relations practitioners, as well as texts that criticise existing public relations institutionsandpractices. This approach emphasises the similarities and continuities between these different discourse genres. It also attempts to demonstrate that the CT framework has heuristic value: It is flexible and is applicable to discourse in each domain. A "rational text" uses a consistent set of topoi in its arguments.

However, some texts are internally inconsistent. A person may also believe that one domain (i.e., family life) fits one model, but that another domain (i.e., professional life) fits another model. The cultural voices also may agree on an ideological point. One sometimes must scrutinise arguments at a microlevel before the differences in underlying topoi become evident. The cultural voices also differ in how frequently they voice their concerns (e.g., fatalism). Mapping the subterranean features of argument also requires persistent attention to what remains unsaid.

Fatalist Voice

Fatalist culture is indifferent to disputes about the nature and obligations of public relations. The other cultural camps often disparage it. The fatalist tribe has low expectations for public relations as a whole. The fatalist voice is underrepresented in the discourse of professional associations. It seldom argues for or justifies the public relations function. Fatalist culture does not debate these issues because it perceives that public relations practitioners lack the power to order their situation. The factors that really affect public relations practice lay beyond practitioners' control (i.e., practitioners have an external locus of control). It offers few visions about the future of practice. Popular culture portrayals of fatalistic public relations depict public relations practitioners as obsequious, cynical, isolated, and unfulfilled.

The fatalist voice does not proselytise, but it is a voice of resistance. It speaks through inattention and excuses for inaction. It resists the exhortations to engage in programmatic action. When asked to support a programme to enhance the influence of public relations, the fatalist voice demurs because the proposed course of action is futile. Collective action will not make a significant difference. Closed ended survey questions seldom find the fatalist voice. However, in depth interviews and ethnographic observation can locate the fatalist voice as they probe practitioners' daily routines. It also becomes audible when outsiders appraise the discipline or when professionals confide about their disillusionment with the profession.

The fatalist voice also murmurs in despotic environments where practitioners perceive that unpredictable and capricious forces determine their fates. Celebrity public relations can be unpredictable and capricious. Publicity becomes an end in itself because it creates a celebrity premium that people are willing to pay for. However, "high visibility public relations" can be a high stakes, zero-sum game. The number of celebrities who can be created and maintained is rather finite and inelastic. "The more popular the sector, the more violently a person's celebrity status will fluctuate".

The fortunes of public relations promoters are driven by the fickle hand that determines who is hot and who is not. Even if celebrity public relations is successful, "the bad news is that publicists are often not included as an important player at the center of the visibility marketing process and are not financially rewarded at the same level as agents and managers". Indeed, the celebrity industry usually maintains a low profile. The ghost writer selectively sorts the facts of a life and creates a celebrity narrative that cannot publicly acknowledge the writer's contribution. The practitioner also must cope with the caprices of temperamental and neurotic celebrities. Hand holding is listed as one of the essential duties of the celebrity promoter because Celebrities often need reassurances and smiles of pseudo-intimacy.

...In a world in which it is very hard to evaluate with any precision what you're doing from day to day, a hand-holder supplies the important services of confidence building and ego maintenance. Moreover, creating a celebrity often creates an uncontrollable ego that "often grows into cockiness and arrogance". These tendencies often are cultivated by the "entourages of obsequious support personnel that surround the celebrity". Press agentry is often characterised as a residue of public relations practice from a different era that has been replaced by more productive and ethical public relations models. However, the chroniclers of "high visibility" declared that "celebrity worship and visibility seeking is in an explosive growth phase" that is spreading to all sectors of society. The fatalist voice emerges when "high visibility public relations" becomes a capricious zero-sum game.

The fatalist voice also appears in organisational public relations. Fatalist culture does not consider public relations to be a self-defining and self regulating system. Public relations is whatever top management says it is: a marginal organisational function that is not seated at the management roundtable. For instance, public relations may be subordinated to another organisational function. "PR has generally been treated as a marketing stepchild, an afterthought to more serious promotional planning". Within public relations research, a great deal of attention has been devoted to the study of the role that practitioners play within the organisation. The prevailing consensus is that most public relations practitioners work as technicians rather than as managers.

Unless a public relations department has at least one practitioner in a management role, the organisational influence of public relations will be minimised. In such environments, one might expect to find a fatalistic worldview. Leichty and Springston found that one of their five public relations role clusters endorsed aspects of the fatalistic voice. This group, which Leichty and Springston labeled as externals, thought the public relations department was peripheral to the communication flows in the organisation. They also thought the public relations department had little influence or power. This type of practitioner was usually the only full time public relations professional in the organisation. These practitioners had few opportunities for professional advancement within their organisations.

Some aspects of the fatalist voice also appear in the Personal Influence model of public relations. The personal influence modelwas defined as "a quid pro quo relationship between the public relations practitioner and strategically placed individuals such as government regulators, media persons and tax officials". The personal influence model is most likely to be employed in those nations in which public opinion is not well articulated in the media and where governmental officials are the most important audience for public relations messages.

Ehnographic account of public relations practice in Southern India found that public relations practitioners spent much of their time ingratiating themselves with powerful people. Practitioners provided small favors to gain personal favor and influence with powerful targets. Personal influence activities included "hospitality, giving gifts and brokering of influence, to build lasting friendships with strategically placed individuals with the aim of seeking favors in return". Most of the practitioners in his sample had public relations titles, but had little power to influence policy decisions in their organisations. Practitioners desired professional autonomy, but "most were reluctant to express this to their superiors because they thought that it would not make any difference".

The personal influence model was most likely in social contexts where there is a high deference to authority by subordinates and an intolerance of subordinates' viewpoints by superiors. Wherever low practitioner power and a capricious environment combine, personal influence will be cultivated as a means of coping. The fatalist view of public relations also appears in the disinterested assessments of outsiders. Peter Drucker, the renowned management consultant, opined:

> There is no public relations. There's publicity, promotion, advertising, but "relations" by definition are a two-way street. And the more important job and the more difficult is not to bring the business and execution to the outside but to bring the outside to terribly insulated people.

Drucker said public relations professionals fail to "tell the truth to management. Public relations people today don't do that because they are scared; because the people they work for don't like to hear what they don't want to hear". Several developmental trajectories lead to a fatalistic view of public relations practice. One trajectory is the route of dashed expectations. A public relations professional may begin with an idealistic vision of how to practice public relations, but become cynical when these expectations are dashed.

A fatalistic viewpoint may develop when a practitioner encounters a chaotic environment that subverts normal public relations practice. Among high-tech companies, the quest to prop up a company's stock price often subverted public relations values. "When the stock price was up, all of us were heroes. When it was down, we were scapegoats". When the stock price starts to drop, "strategy for the most part, goes out the door. Forget setting goals and objectives and creating strategies and tactics. Forget the well thought out public relations plan that was created and approved at the beginning of the year". A practitioner may also embrace fatalist topoi after a precipitous career decline.

Fatalist culture shrugs off the insults of hierarchical culture, the malign neglect of individualist culture, and the proselytising fervor of egalitarian culture. It is better to face some of the unpleasant facts of public relations practice than it is to live in a fantasy world. It is best to persevere through the bad and to enjoy the good when it comes.

Egalitarian Voice

The egalitarian voice is a prophetic voice. It animates activists who seek to reduce social inequality. It has manifested itself in the abolitionists, the muckrakers, and many social movements in the 20th century. Although there is a fledgling in-house egalitarian public relations voice, this voice usually speaks from the periphery of public relations. It prefers to critique the establishment rather than to negotiate with it. Its voice animates conversations about the nature of public relations. Unflattering egalitarian characterisations of public relations are a feature of popular culture's depictions of public relations. Its stark characterisations of public relations practice energise the cultural voices of the dominant coalition to declare, "Public relations isn't at all like that".

Egalitarian critics of public relations accuse it of distorting communication and undermining the processes of participatory democracy. Stauber and Rampton accused public relations of having an antidemocratic bias. "This contemptuous attitude toward democracy is the heritage of Edward Bernays, the father philosopher of public relations who saw corporate 'engineering of consent' as away to eliminate the 'chaos' in democratic society". However, democracy is "chaotic, messy and unpredictable and most bothersome of all to PR practitioners, it often produces decisions that their clients are unable either to predict or control".

Authentic democracy "must be lived daily, its valueswoven into the fabric of society. ...Democracy is not like fast food. It can't be standardised, mass-produced, made predictable and convenient". Public relations threatens democracy because "raw money enables the PR industry to mobilise private detectives, attorneys, broadcast faxes, satellite feeds, sophisticated information systems and other expensive, high-tech resources to out-maneuver, overpower and outlast true citizen reformers". However, corporate public relations has an Achilles heel. "Today's opinion industry is a powerful giant, but like Goliath, it is a giant with a fatal weakness. When the public is educated about its techniques, it often loses its ability to mislead and manipulate".

According to the egalitarian voice, public relations operates by stealth, because it proposes tradeoffs relating to the value of human life that it cannot defend in public. The egalitarian voice searches for a treacherous tradeoff to publicise and thereby mobilise outrage. This provides riveting entertainment for the mass media and gives public relations's dominant coalition indigestion. Stauber and Rampton this tack in pointing to the inherent corruption of corporate public relations. "The need to maximise profit drove antifreeze makers to hire a PR spy so they could fight a lawthatwould save children's lives at a price of only two cents a gallon".

Unmasking public relations's deceits is difficult because public relations practitioners conceal their work. Rampton and Stauber took aim at public relations's cultivated use of third party expert endorsements. The guiding mantra for public relations practitioners was to "put your words in someone else's mouth. The 'someone elses' become Potemkin authorities, faithfully spouting the opinions of their benefactors while making it appear that their views are 'independent'". This approach "offers camouflage, helping to hide the vested interests that lurks behind a message".

Public relations's egalitarian critics are particularly critical of "pseudograssroots" movements. "Astroturf" organising deprives social movements of their natural advantage in public debates: public skepticism about the intentions of corporate interests. "Recognising that industry lacks credibility on environmental issues, industry's public relations modus operandi often is to create front groups to advocate its interests sometimes well-cloaked, other times thinly veiled, and always with Orwellian names". Front groups enable "corporations to take part in public debates and government hearings behind a cover of community concern". "Astroturf public relations" confuses the public as to who the heroes and the villains are. This sows doubt about the authenticity of the egalitarian voice and makes it difficult to mobilise outrage.

In recent years, the egalitarian voice has begun to articulate an affirmative vision of public relations that embraces a communitarian ethic. Public relations scholars have been at the head of this effort. The affirmative egalitarian vision proposes to reform corporate public relations along egalitarian lines and to expand the definition of public relations to include the organising activities of activist groups. The reformers propose to rebuild public relations on the usable parts of public relations practice.

"Community relations is the paradigm case of public relations". Public relations should embrace community building. Interest in community welfare, social order, and progress can be addressed by public relations practitioners. As a social center, through a concern for art and a concern for community play, the organisation can help to enhance community. Practitioners can help the community share aesthetic experience, religious ideas, personal values, and sentiments. Practitioners will not only do advocacy, but also will foster communication that "offers an immediate enhancement of life, which can be enjoyed for its own sake". The feminist critique of public relations is the most developed egalitarian effort to transform corporate public relations.

Feminist research has identified structural changes that are necessary to make public relations a more equitable profession, including making public relations's body of knowledge more inclusive and gender sensitive. These inquiries have sensitised researchers to the inequitable power arrangements in gendered relationships and have increased the discipline's sensitivity to the experiences of public relations practitioners. Although some practitioners have worried that the increasing proportion of female practitioners threatens the organisational status of public relations, feminist theorists believe that "women's emergence in public relations is an opportunity for a more responsible and effective practice".

The discipline will be transformed as students and practitioners come to embrace feminist values (e.g., cooperation, valuing relationships, altruism). The classroom may be the ideal setting in which to consider that the development of personal feminist values that have implications for public relations practice. Such consideration would benefit all students and may be an important step toward realisation of our aspirations for a practice that is truly professional, truly ethical and truly effective. Explicitly embracing feminist values should "help define the field and, in particular, clarify its purposes. Those purposes such as reinstitution of community, the development of relationships, and the resolution of conflict will be grounded in the character of those who work in public relations".

Egalitarian theorists insist that public relations must embrace diversity for both moral and practical reasons. As every domain of public relations practice becomes more diverse, "practitioners and educators must become more sensitive to this environmental change by enacting diversity as a concern relevant to their professional lives and by responding to it interactively". Instead of seeking similarity and harmony, we need to recruit people and pursue ideas that challenge the status quo.We should not just seek out identifiable minorities, but also people who have demonstrated a sensitivity to cultural diversity and a commitment to helping others become responsive to it.

The affirmative egalitarian vision of public relations also seeks to expand the definition of public relations. The activities of activist groups are also within the boundaries of public relations. Smith argued, "The exclusion, or misrepresentation, of activist organisations in the scholarly and pedagogical literature limits our understanding of public relations". The distinction between organisational public relations and social movements is a false dichotomy. Activists must organise to pursue their goals. Once they do, they also "face challenges that require public relations programmes". The activist organisation must compete with other activist organisations for attention and resources to maintain its membership. "One of the realities of activism is that simple survival requires a great deal of time and energy".

Critical theorists criticise public relations research because it subsidises "commercial and state communications at the expense of other segments of the population". Public relations research has "privileged or subsidised certain segments of the population and marginalised others to the periphery of public discourse". Public relations's body of knowledge is inaccessible to most people. Only commercial and state entities have the professional experience and material resources to apply the body of knowledge. Public relations scholars should develop knowledge that equips ordinary citizens to enter into public discourse. "Public communication skills and resources must be extended to all segments of society if communication symmetry is to be recognised". Researchers should focus on the "types of communication practices that are within the reach of resource poor segments of society".

Public relations can contribute to grassroots democracy through activism and radical politics. Pointing to the inevitable contradictions within public relations's ideology, "This perspective opens the door for public relations practitioners to act as community activists, an approach that is not only radical but also ethical and desirable". Enlarging the scope of public relations will require dramatic shifts in public relations education. "The field's case studies, texts and research give preference to public relations as a management function of capitalist organisations, including state organisations". This will involve some conflict among practitioners, as "public relations practitioners line up on opposite sides of the trenches, but so do legal practitioners, marketing experts, and many other professionals in everyday life".

The postmodern environment will be so turbulent that the predictive tools of social science will be of little use. "Hot issue publics and the media skills of activists call into question the ability to deal proactively with activists". Fluid interactions between organisations and publics will replace issues management. For the postmodern version of public relations, it will "be the responsibility of the public relations function to create opportunities for dissent, for opening up debate without forcing consensus, to create possibilities for change".

Tactics are not the product of careful cold reason, they do not follow a table of organisation or plan of attack. Accident, unpredictable reactions to your actions, necessity and improvisation dictate the direction and nature of tactics...the tactic itself comes out of the free flow of action and reaction. The egalitarian voice differentiates between strategic public relations and public relations tactics. It is anxious that the strategic use of public relations by large organisations subverts participatory democracy, but the egalitarian voice embraces public relations tactics as essential tools for promoting social change.

In the parallel egalitarian movement of public journalism, publicity emerged as an essential tool for mobilising action and developing community. Rejecting "strategy" and embracing "tactics" is faithful to the underlying egalitarian tendency to value spontaneity in action. Although it is often excluded from the debates of public relations's dominant coalition, the egalitarian voice has profoundly influenced public relations practice. It makes the cultures of the dominant coalition nervous. As a gadfly culture, the egalitarian voice is always ready to sting. In its affirmative form, it seeks to make public relations work for the common good. It is not yet a part of public relations's dominant coalition, but its influence is increasing.

Hierarchical Voice

The hierarchical voice has long been a member of public relations's dominant coalition, along with the CI voice. It frequently appears in accounts of public relations history and practice. It aims to improve the status of public relations and to institutionalise public relations as a core management function. It has used public relations history to enhance the discipline's status. Its version of public relations history depicts a process of steady evolutionary progress. Despite its origins in the tawdry practice of press agentry, public relations has come of age as a knowledge based discipline.

Edward Bernays consistently articulated the hierarchical voice. Bernays portrayed public relations counselors as societal psychotherapists. "Society has become more complex and its processes have been speeded up over the last few centuries. The rate of progress of the many forces that make up society has been uneven with consequently increased maladjustment and tension". Bernays wanted to solve irrational communication problems. "Maladjustments in many fields, commerce, industry, religion, and government, are based upon the misunderstanding of realities and communications processes....Conflict that is based on misunderstanding, ignorance, and apathy is unnecessary and wasteful".

Bernays saw public relations as "a vital tool of adjustment, interpretation, and integration between individuals, groups and society". Public relations "is vitally important today because modern social science has found that the adjustment of individuals, groups, and institutions to life is necessary for the well-being of all". It is an activity "that makes competition, another factor of our society, more efficient and effective". The public relations counselor must overcome the ignorance of clients and publics. Although the "highest level of adjustment is reached at the point of enlightened self-interest. The public relations counsel must ensure that such enlightenment prevails [italics added]". Bernays recognised that much of public relations practice fell short of the hierarchical ideal. He attributed this imperfection to the lack of controlled barriers to entry into the profession.

"There are too few trained and skilled practitioners. In the early years of the profession, many crowded in who had little specialised knowledge, aptitude or experience". Throughout his life, Bernays championed the cause of licensing public relations practitioners. He thought licensing would help secure public relations's boundaries and exclude unscrupulous and incompetent practitioners. Bernays remained optimistic about public relations's prospects and projected a rising curve of disciplinary growth and maturation. Life in the democratic age was vexing, but with advice of public relations counselors, leaders could navigate these rapids with confidence.

The hierarchical preference for dispassionate expertise also appeared in Hill's account of how Hill and Knowlton operated. Hill was proud that his firm was the first to

a) Offer a broad range of specialised public relations services.

b) Apply cost accounting and budgeting procedures to agency work.

c) Develop an international presence in public relations.

d) Create a professional research division.

He celebrated the breadth and depth of his professional staff by reciting their years of public relations experience, their educational pedigrees, and their international experiences. Displaying a faith in the hierarchical themes of content specialisation and hierarchical integration, he wrote, "Only by such a variegated grouping of education, experience, talent and linguistic capabilities can a large public relations firm meet the requirements of its clients".

Hill portrayed public relations work as a dignified enterprise. He believed that teamwork among experts would "replace the lone-wolf operator-the 'Big I Ams'-as an important factor in the public relations business". He insisted that his firm not solicit business because "we have tried over a period of three and a half decades to build a reputation for high standards of service". Referrals from existing clients provided the needed business. In a tone similar to current manifestos of relationship marketing,

Hill opined, "The relations of public relations firms with their clients ordinarily is intimate and deeply immersed in policies and activities". He wrote, "Fortunately, the public relations counseling business is unlike advertising in that among the top grade firms the shifting of accounts from one firm to another is indeed a rarity".

Philip Lesly represented a more pessimistic strain of the hierarchical viewpoint. Surveying the rise of egalitarian movements in the United States, Lesly counseled executives on how to prevail over the forces of anarchy. Lesly was pessimistic about the possibilities for societal adjustment and integration. He believed that egalitarianism was a rising menace that needed to be neutralised.

Lesly asserted "The first responsibility of an executive is to create and maintain orderly procedures....The effective manager is naturally repelled by disorder and threats to smooth operations". The climate of public opinion was "an attack upon leadership. It presumes that all organisations are suspect and that the leaders of those organisations are probably scoundrels or oppressors". He feared that hierarchy would be "replaced by a tyranny of the crowd, in which the assertiveness of groups of people prevents any orderly functioning". Executives must defend their organisations. "It is evident on all sides that it is those who defy authority disclaim any responsibility for their in-surgence; and it is the established institution that needs to defend itself against siege".

Lesly also lamented the "balkanisation" of public relations. Public relations was increasing in its scope, but itspoweris being dissipatedbycompetition for the spotlightamongitsvaried practitioners. Each function of the field...is seeking to define itself as public relations, rather than recognising that it is onlyoneelementin averybroadfield. In defining the field, one should "stress the gestalt of public relations rather than the segment. Give primacy to the really vital functions and base everything in public relations education to breadth and depth".

Lesly preferred a far-sighted systems-oriented perspective. The hierarchical voice for public relations shares the common desires for (a) distinct boundaries for defining public relations, (b) a definitive body of knowledge that hierarchy can apply, and (c) regulative mechanisms to defend the boundaries of public relations (i.e., keep charlatans and unqualified persons out of the profession). The stock arguments of the hierarchical voice have been quite consistent. If an applied social science approach is taken, public relations can develop a body of theoretic knowledge that meets and distinguishes the practice of public relations from the craft of the communication technician....Such a body of knowledge...is the foundation stone on which public relations can develop more and more professionalism. A standardised body of knowledge would guide public relations practice, help standardise public relations curricula, generate respect for the profession, and repel the epitaphs of "public relations flack."

A body of knowledge would ease hierarchy's fears about the discipline's foundations. Many believe that public relations theory and scholarship are steadily progressing toward this goal. The aim is to integrate relevant knowledge into a systemic and predictive theory. For instance, crisis public relations is moving from crisis communication toward anticipatory models of crisis management. Where media planning once required little planning, the current situation is starkly different. The sheer number of publicity outlets has expanded, increasing the direct costs to provide materials and making it difficult to approach every potential outlet effectively.

In this more complex media landscape, public relations practitioners need to "practice and think about media broadly and strategically. An effective public relations programme must employ techniques ranging from broad-based traditional mass communication to highly individualised interpersonal communication. Moreover, the process of selecting media must be rationalised". However, some fear that the process of "rationalisation" is not proceeding fast enough. Speaking of the "fad" of integrated marketing communication (IMC), "is little more than a confession that nonintegrated or disintegrated communications have been the norm in the past".

The real debate should be about the "relationship between what might be termed integrated marketing and integrated communication". However, this debate was not being engaged because public relations was unilaterally ceding its turf to marketing, as "marketing scholars and practitioners are methodically redefining marketing as public relations". Some of the organisational functions were assimilating high-order public relations functions such as investor relations. This was not due to marketing imperialism, so much as it was due to the failure of public relations scholarship to "define itself and to develop sophisticated and progressive theory".

In the view of some practitiners the legitimacy of the public relations function was precarious. "There remains a need for public relations to define its intellectual and practical domain, especially vis-á-vis marketing, to regain control over its destiny". Within the hierarchical tribe, the optimists and pessimists disagree on the soundness of the discipline's intellectual underpinnings. The ambitious projects of the hierarchical voice are far from completion. The hierarchical voice faces formidable cultural challenges. In particular, the CI voice objects that public relations practice is too situational, fluid, and emergent to be thoroughly rationalised. Despite these challenges, many hierarchical adherents remain optimistic, anticipating that the 21st century will be the golden age of public relations.

AI Voice

AI is the refuge of the free spirit. "This way of life is distinguished from the other four 'engaged' ways of life by its intellectual independence and lofty detachment". For enlightenment to be attained, human nature must be liberated from attachment and dependency. AIs avoid coercive entanglements, especially coercive demands for "right thinking." Human relationships must have exit points; individuals must be able to withdraw from associations that become oppressive. "To the extent that we are capable of detaching ourselves from the fray and rising above it, we are likely to appreciate the partiality of those below".

Cultural theory considers the AI culture to be rare. However, Fiske's equality matching model showed how AI interdependence is structured. An equality matching relationship maintains equality of input and reward (e.g., two couples trade babysitting services). In work settings, equality matching synchronises the contributions of group members so that each works at the same rate. Equality matching ensures that neither party accumulates long term debt. This exchange minimises long term dependence and maintains mutual autonomy. To the extent that the AI culture participates in public relations discussions, it mainly seeks to preserve a public relations niche for cooperative and noncoercive relationships.

In politics, the Natural Law Party articulates the AI voice. Human problems "result from a narrowness of vision that fails to comprehend life's essential unity". However, "with maximally expanded comprehension, individuals naturally behave in their own best long term interests while promoting the interests of society as a whole action fully aligned with natural law". With proper enlightenment, the need for governmental regulation will diminish. People who practice public relations as a part time craft may represent this position. Some public relations partnerships have features similar to the AI model.

In a study of executive conflict, found a work culture that characterised as "silent hives." The social relationships in these partnership firms maximised professional autonomy, discretion, and equality. They also minimised overt expressions of conflict. In agency public relations, partners may share the costs of doing business, while each practitioner maintains his or her own accounts and independent areas of expertise.

If information is a "neutral medium," one can function as a journalist in residence by responding to inquiries about the organisation. In a more proactive form, one might put out information for people to use as they see fit. An AI representative might prefer the job title of "information specialist." The AI perspective provides scholars with an important refuge. The "intellectual domain requires a conscious uncoupling of intellectual agenda from the thoughts, actions and preoccupations of practitioners". For most people, the AI perspective represents a temporary stopping point.

"Adherents to the different engaged ways of life argue with each other with different premises, but often reserve a special contempt for philosophers who merely interpret". The AI framework encourages one to stand aloof from social life. Adams speculated that AI might "induce a resigned fatalism or provide the three activist ways of life with superior insight into the behavior of competing ideologies, an insight that they may seek to exploit in their own management of risk". Practitioners must have a "breadth of perspective" to interpret management to publics and vice versa. However, public relations practitioners had such a comprehensive perspective. A practitioner's organisational position and role limits her vision. "Theoretically, it is questionable that practitioners can develop the perspective they have claimed to offer".

However, the AI perspective does not require superhuman intuition because the relational models are part of our social knowledge. Perspective taking requires a clear memory to avoid cultural myopia.

CI Voice

The CI voice is a powerful voice in the dominant public relations coalition. The CI voice celebrates public relations practice as a virtuoso performance.

CI culture cultivates the biography of the great person. Ivy Lee articulated this voice in the discipline's infancy. Hiebert's historical biography of Lee captured the CI spirit. Hiebert wrote, "Lee was impressed by the important and newsworthy people. He made the most to cultivate his contacts with prominentmenand then in making an impression with his own talents and personality".

According to Hiebert, "Lee's respect for the great men of his time never waned". Lee chastised his associate Daniel Pierce by saying, "Dan, you spend toomuchtime with unimportant people". Leeassiduously cultivated thisnetwork of influential people. Hiebert concluded that Lee "put himself squarely into the circle of his day. From his position hewas able to win wide respect for the new profession of public relations". Lee held his ground with the titans of industry as he promoted his mantra of informing the public. Hiebert noted that Lee was "one of the few men who could make millionaires wait for him". Lee was a 20th century Renaissance Man. He had more than 10,000 books in his library and could quote verbatim from many hundreds of them.

Hiebert wrote that Lee was most interested in "the spread of ideas in which he believed. Indeed his disregard for money bordered on improvidence". Lee had an eclectic interest "in the whole range of human relationships, trade, employee, industrial, government, community and international". In contrast to the specialised tasks of Hill's public relations, Lee sought intuitive solutions. Bernays characterised Lee's work as an "art" and labeled his own work as more "scientific". In an era of knowledge explosion, expertise becomes increasingly narrow and hinders decision making. Brummet argued that disciplines like public relations must use narrative to reduce the complexity of public domain communications to manageable proportions. The CI voice bristles at the hierarchical strictures of corporate public relations.

In another venue, complained that bureaucratic corporate cultures were subverting public relations practice. "Public relations managers themselves are quarantined from the daily combat of opinion making by staff and staff is cushioned from accountability by specialisation". Public relations is "a unique profession. Because it deals with the unpredictable-opinions, attitudes, impressions-it has to be flexible, dynamic, instantaneous and exceptionally skilled". The dynamic environment of public relations meant that public relations "must be entrepreneurial not bureaucratic! In attitudes, approach and activity".

The CI voice emphasises the contextual variations of public relations. Public relations theory cannot encompass all of the unique niches that public relations contains. Moreover, the public relations environment is always changing. Theory lags behind practice and is often outmoded by the time it is developed. Newprofessionals must have apprenticeships and practical experience to learn the ropes.

You simply cannot learn public relations from a book. This belief in flux and change appears in how the CI voice constructs the public relations implications of the Internet. Where the hierarchical voice projects that the Internet will be integrated with existing public relations practices, the CI voice declares that public relations needs to be reinvented to fit the world of the Internet. The Internet offers just another message delivery tool, with limited and impatient audiences. This view is on par with the horse-and-buggy operator criticising the Model-T Ford for being too loud. The Internet is not just a new medium; it's rapidly becoming a platform for all other media, and more. In the end, the CI voice is not anxious about names or labels.

Ivy Lee never selected one label to describe what he did, "confessing at the end of his life that even his own children did not know what to call him". The CI voice is more concerned with making things happen than it is with definitions and labels. CI culture exudes confidence about the future. It will be the best of times for those who are willing to learn and willing to grasp the rings of power.

References

Alan B. Bernstein and Cindy Rakowitz. *Emergency Public Relations: Crisis Management In a 3.0 World.* 2012

Grunig, James E. and Hunt, Todd. *Managing Public Relations.* Orlando, FL: Harcourt Brace Jovanovich, 1984.

Jensen Zhao. *Encyclopedia of Business,* 2nd. Ed. Retrieved fromfindarticles.com

Rubel, Gina F., *Everyday Public Relations for Lawyers*, Doylestown, PA: 1 ed. 2007.

Seitel, Fraser P. *The Practice of Public Relations.* Upper Saddle River, NJ: Pearson Prentice Hall, 2007.

Toth E. & Heath R. (Eds.), *Rhetorical and critical approaches to public relations* (pp. 17-36). New Jersey: Lawrence Erlbaum. 1992.

3

Communication and Public Relation

Public relations refers to the practice of enhancing an organization's reputation in the eyes of public, stakeholders, employees, investors and all others associated with it. Public relations experts are specially hired by organizations who work hard towards maintaining brand image of organization.Communication plays an essential role in effective public relations. Two way communication between both the parties is essential and information must flow in its desired form between the organization and public. The receiver must understand what the sender intends to communicate for an effective public relation. The receivers (public, target audience, stakeholders, employees, investors) must clearly understand the sender's message. (organization in this case).The message/information needs to create an impact in the minds of customers for an effective brand positioning. Communication needs to have a strong influence on the target audience for them to remain loyal towards the organization.

In public relations, the receivers play a crucial role than the sender. The sender (organization) must ensure that the receivers interpret the information correctly and also give necessary feedbacks and reviews. It is really essential for the sender to understand its target audience. Public relations experts must do extensive research and gather as much information as they can before planning any public relation activity. Public relation activities would go unnoticed if receivers to not understand it well. Public relation activities must be designed keeping in mind the benefits of the target audience for a better brand positioning.

For example, in cases of hospitals, public relation activities would ensure a smooth flow of information between the hospital authorities or management and the patients and their immediate family members or relatives. Public relations experts from a hospital in a rural area must plan and design their activities in the local language for receivers to interpret and respond well. If the hospital authorities interact in a language not understood by the patients, no real communication takes place and eventually the effect of public relation activities get nullified.

Further the needs of the target audience must be understood well. Remember public relation activities are designed to position an organization in the best light. This happens only when the target audiences are fully satisfied with its services/products. Understand what your target audiences expect from you to design public relations activities for the maximum and desired impact. Make sure your target audiences understand what you intend to communicate.

Public Information and Public Relations

Public information, public relations, communications: international institutions seem to use these words interchangeably, moving from one to another and back again as successive waves of "reform" come and go. In publicly financed institutions such as UNESCO, public information constitutes an organic function. Keeping the public abreast of developments and debates in the worlds of education, science, culture, social sciences and communication is one of the reasons for which UNESCO exists. Doing it and doing it right is not only clever.

It is an essential part of UNESCO's mandate. Reflecting UNESCO's broad and diverse areas of responsibility, its Bureau of Public Information seeks to draw attention to a wide range of activities. It relies to do so on the research and expertise of colleagues throughout the house to spotlight important social and ethical issues, to nurture the democratic debate—with facts, figures and analysis— and to press for change where change is required.

Public information is, in other words, one of the organisation's principal weapons in the pursuit of its fundamental objectives. A recipe for failure There is enormous, probably limitless interest in the public and media for new data and insights on issues like cloning and bioethics in general, the state of oceans and coastlines, the sharing of fresh water resources, the

realistic about what the strategy can achieve within the timeframe, budget and available resources. Remember, the most successful communication campaigns are underpinned by programme support strategies, which deliver the product or service that your communication strategy is addressing.

Clear, specific and measurable objectives are critical to the success of information activities: not only are they critical to the development of an appropriate public relations strategy, but they also form the basis of campaign evaluation. Therefore it is imperative that specific and measurable objectives are stated clearly in your brief. It is a common error to confuse objectives with tasks. When writing your brief be mindful of the following:

Tasks are what you/or your consultants do to achieve your objectives and commonly start with such words as "To develop…" "To implement..." for example:

— to develop an issues management strategy;

— to undertake a national launch of the campaign;

— to implement a three-month public relations campaign.

An objective is what you hope to achieve from your information activities (ie an outcome) and commonly start with such words as "To increase…" "To inform…" "To reinforce…". Research will assist you to develop realistic objectives. Your research will give you a greater understanding of current awareness and attitudes toward your subject matter and therefore provide a starting point for communication activity. When setting objectives you should:

— be realistic within the timeframe, budget and resources;

— ensure they are measurable;

— state what you aim to achieve in terms of the target audience:

Awareness, understanding and knowledge - most campaigns aim to increase awareness, understanding and knowledge of a government policy or programme. Awareness objectives relate to what you want your target audience to be informed or educated about.

Attitudes—favourable or unfavourable feelings about an issue, which are learned, and relatively enduring. It is assumed that changing attitudes will lead to an increase in the positive behaviours a campaign is promoting. Some campaigns aim to reinforce positive attitudes to ensure that positive behaviours are maintained; while others attempt to change negative attitudes.

Attitude objectives are really a statement of how you want the target audience to feel about the issue.

Behaviours—are what you want the target audience to do as a result of being exposed to your campaign. Behaviours are the specific actions which you are encouraging members of the target audience to undertake. Some examples of objectives are:

— To increase awareness with 18-40 year olds:
— of the immediate and longer term health effects of smoking;
— that every cigarette does physical damage; and
— that support for quitting smoking is available in various forms.
— To generate/strengthen:
— personal relevance to the health messages of the campaign;
— a sense of the 'immediacy' of the health effects depicted in the campaign advertising; and
— the confidence of people aged 18-40 in their own ability to change their behaviour.
— To increase intentions to:
— quit/attempt to quit smoking; and
— access available support services.

The public relations brief should not introduce objectives not outlined in the communication strategy. However, you might not necessarily wish to just replicate all the objectives found in the strategy. It may be that emphasis is placed on achieving some specific objectives in the public relations component of the campaign.

Target Audiences

Exactly who do you want to receive your message? Target audiences should be described in terms of:

— current behaviour
— level of awareness
— level of knowledge
— preferred methods for receiving information
— motivations/barriers to hearing and believing/accepting the information.

You should describe your target audiences in as much detail as possible. Broad descriptions such as the "general public" are less likely to lead to a successful campaign than a tightly defined target. The more thoroughly you understand your target audience/s, the higher the probability of success.

— *Primary Target Audience* —people/groups who will be directly affected by your message or need to be exposed to your message.

— *Secondary Target Audience*—people of less importance who you wish to receive the campaign messages, people who will also benefit from hearing the campaign messages or people who influence your target audience now or in the future: for example, general practitioners.

— *Stakeholders*—Other people/groups who might be directly or indirectly involved in, affected by or with a stake in your campaign.

The key messages should encapsulate the purpose of your communication activity in as few words as possible. Key messages do not need to be catchy. They are not the "slogan" or the "jingle" for your campaign or the actual words to be used as your message. There is time later, during campaign development, to mould your message into a form that is appropriate for your audience/s. Research indicates that the following types of messages are likely to be rejected:

— messages which are global in nature;

— messages which are a series of 'motherhood' statements;

— messages which are self congratulatory; or

— self-promotion without substance.

Effective key messages should include details of the programme or policy being promoted, the benefits of the initiative for the target audience, and a clear "call to action" outlining what the target audience should do as a result of receiving your messages. You should remember that public relations has the ability to deliver the more complex campaign messages and provide a level of detail which the advertising campaign can often not achieve. Careful consideration should be given to which messages are best suited to the public relations versus the advertising strategy.

PR and Communication Mix

It is useful to outline the proposed components of the communication campaign to enable the consultant to understand the context within which the public relations activity will occur. For example, it is useful for the public relations consultant to know that a mass media advertising campaign is planned so that they can ensure synergy between the advertising and public relations strategies. If it is the intention of your department to carry out some of the public relations activities in-house, you must detail in the document exactly what the external public relations consultant will be responsible for and what the department will be managing.

Research: Research is used to guide the development, implementation and evaluation of information activities. It can, and does, prevent resource wastage by ensuring that the campaign is indeed necessary and appropriate for the target audience/s. You should include in your public relations brief details of any research conducted or proposed as part of the campaign, including:

— developmental research which has underpinned the strategy and messages;
— concept testing (to assist in selecting the advertising agency and refining creative concepts for advertising and products);
— benchmark and tracking the campaign (testing strategies, reporting on coverage and readership of your issue, checking recall); and
— evaluating the outcomes (checking for changes in target audience attitudes, knowledge, behaviour).

PR consultants should also be reminded to provide the department with details on how they propose to evaluate the effectiveness of the public relations strategy they are to implement.

Key Issues

Include details of any constraints on your information activities to give consultants the opportunity to consider issues that might impact on the campaign when preparing their proposals. Examples of issues for consideration include:

— subtleties of the communication task, such as "musts" and "must nots" in communicating the message and design;
— sensitive issues;
— the need to work in consultation with other consultants (eg market researcher, advertising agency, or a specialist non-English speaking background or indigenous Australians communications consultant);

— regional or geographical constraints;
— financial constraints;
— the need for materials to be approved by particular positions or by interest groups before release; and
— the approval process for campaign strategies and materials.

Tender Task

The consultant must be provided with specific details on what is expected of them as part of the tender process. This is distinct from the task required of the successful consultant which is defined in the final contract with the department. For example, as part of the tender process the consultant will be expected to:

— Develop a written proposal The proposal must include:
    — an outline of how the public relations strategy will be developed and implemented, if successful;
    — a rationale for the proposed strategic approach;
    — a proposed approach to launching the campaign;
    — strategic advice regarding other suitable publicity events;
    — details of an appropriate publicity programme including an issues management strategy;
    — an outline of a proposed approach to stakeholder management;
    — recommendations on and a rationale for information materials, if applicable;
    — a detailed timeline for implementing the strategy;
    — a detailed costing of services, including daily/weekly/hourly rates;
    — details of personnel who will be working on the strategy, clearly identifying roles and, if applicable, hourly rates;
    — details of similar projects worked on including the contact details of (three) referees;
    — an explanation of how the public relations strategy will be evaluated; and
    — details of reporting and invoicing formats and procedures.
— To assist the selection process, you should also detail in the brief that consultants must:

- restrict the written proposal to 20 or fewer, A4 single-sided, numbered pages using a 12 point font size (excluding curriculum vitaes and company experience which would be less than 30 pages in an attachment to the main document);
- provide an executive summary of no more than two pages;
- provide a specific number of copies; and
- include a table of contents.

Selection Criteria

State the criteria against which you are going to evaluate the consultants' proposals, which should be kept to a minimum to facilitate the selection process. The following selection criteria cover most requirements, although you can add others which you deem appropriate:

- Understanding of the issues.
- Clarity of the rationale for the proposed strategy.
- The quality of the proposed communication strategy
  - Are there clear links with the communication objectives?
  - Will the target audience/s be reached effectively by the proposed strategy?
  - Are the proposed communication vehicles appropriate for the campaign messages?
  - Do the proposed information materials clearly reflect the strategic approach?
  - Innovation and creativity demonstrated within the strategy.
  - Will the proposed strategy have impact/cut through?
  - Are there ideas beyond standard public relations activities?
- Value for money:
  - an assessment of cost against perceived impact/reach of the strategy.
- No conflict of interest.
- References from previous projects will be used to assess the consultant's ability on:
  - provn capacity to deliver projects on time and within budget; and
  - proven ability to work cooperatively with the department.

- relevant/related experience of the team of people who will work on the business.

Experience could be defined in terms of government experience, social marketing experience, subject matter experience or experience in developing and implementing similar communication activities, whichever is deemed to be most relevant to the campaign.

Task for Consultant

Clearly outline the tasks you expect the successful consultant to perform. The following examples cover a wide range of activities and may not always be relevant. For example:

The successful consultant will be required to:

- refine the winning proposal in consultation with the department;
- confirm the programme of activities/events to be developed as part of the strategy;
- develop and implement:

—the final public detailed relations strategy as agreed with the department

  - a launch strategy for the advertising campaign which includes liaising with the media to ensure maximum media coverage and the development of support materials
  - a publicity programme to garner support for the campaign over a six month period
  - a comprehensive issues management strategy
  - a stakeholder management strategy
- develop, produce and distribute supporting information materials;
- organise and manage publicity events;
- liaise with other consultants and key stakeholders as required;
- report regularly to the department on campaign progress;
- at the campaign's completion, submit a report containing:
  - copies of all media releases, fact sheets, invitation, running sheets, etc
  - print and electronic media clippings
  - outline of other outcomes such as alliances, partnership activity, etc

- summary of the strengths and weaknesses of the approach and recommendations for future public relations action
- budget summary
- an assessment of the outcomes and internal efficiencies
- on completion of the campaign provide all the artwork for creative material to the department.

Public Relations and the Press

Public relations arose as a low-tech, person-to-person activity featuring stunts, events, and cozy relations with the press... all designed to attract attention. When it works, it still does. The underlying science mass communications, opinion leadership, cognitive dissonance, etc. does give public relations a patina of legitimacy. Accreditation of practitioners by the Public Relations Society of America is another gesture in that direction. But the business never strayed far from its roots. Get publicity, get attention. Spell the client's name right.

There's lots of room for real strategic planning and opinion sampling in any PR campaign. Online survey services like www.zoomerang.com, www.clicktomarket.com and www.inetsurveys.com are three URLs that belong on every PR person's short list of bookmarks. It's just that MediaMap, PRNewswire, and Business Wire are going to be tapped a whole lot more in the course of a day's work. That doesn't mean the strategic intelligence of a Harold Burson, Pam Edstrom, or Regis McKenna is outdated. But more than ever before, PR today is about publicity and media, and the consultants performing the worthy function of steering corporations into provident waters are just in a different business. In the dot-com, high tech, and B2Anyone worlds, PR might just as well mean Press Relations... if not Press Releases. That could be one reason PR is headed for the couch. Aside from role confusion, the press we're trying to have relations with is fragmenting right along with the markets it serves.

Audiences are splintered into demographic shards, as prosperity and technology bring in their wake an explosion of interests and the time and money to pursue them. The gazillions of new print magazines, e-zines, and newsletters speak to our fragmented and passionate interests. This proliferation goes to the heart of the New PR practice. The very concept of a "public" as an assemblage of people somehow constituting an audience vanished forever circa 1977 when the first Apple fell from the tree. From that time on, with increasing power, each citizen became an independent node in a communications network... and a publisher at will.

Under the velocity of change, the lines are blurring between traditional media and traditional PR. When Yahoo!, to some folks, is a slick magazine and The New York Times is something you read online in the morning, it's easy to see how online and offline media merge. Today, newspaper editors and online e-zine staff can pull their stories off PR wire services or press rooms on commercial web sites. Independent journalists and staff writers can do a good chunk of their research by going to online material produced by PR people. The forward slash separating Online/Offline, PR office/Newsroom is a permeable membrane. Although the basic paradigm continues unchanged, what has changed, forever, for both media and PR, is the traditional way of reaching those targets. And here is where PR comes into its own.

Only publicity has the option to work both these areas, go beyond the mythical segmented markets, beyond the niche pubs, into the never-never land of chat groups, discussion groups, list servs, and bulletin boards that never saw an ad dollar. PR people, by and large, are hired to get their clients publicity, not strategise. In the course of that work, they're clearly part of the expanding news media universe, integral to the gathering and dissemination of news.

Communication Programme

Communication programme consists of message, media and budget. The word communication is derived from the Latin communis, meaning "common."The purpose of communication is to establish a commonness. The basic elements in communication are the source or sender, the message, and the destination or receiver. Effective communication requires efficiency on the part of all three. The communicator must use a channel that will carry the message to the receiver. The message must be within the receiver's capacity to comprehend. The message must motivate the receiver's self-interest and cause him or her to respond. Communicators need to bear in mind that communication is no substitute for policy and action. A sender can encode a message and a receiver decode it only in terms of their own experience and knowledge. When there has been no common experience, then communication becomes virtually impossible. Commonness in communication is essential to link people and purpose together in any cooperative system. The Communication programme includes:

(i) Developing the message

(ii) Selection of media

(iii) Appropriate budget for implementing the programme.

Message Development

For achieving the desired result, the message should be developed properly and clearly. The appropriate message will have the following three attributes:

1) Clear
2) Correct and
3) Concise

Clear

The message is free from ambiguity and it is necessary to ensure that slang phrases / usage are avoided and also the message should be free from perceptional distortion problems. As far as possible, one should use simple language, simple style, appropriate words and right tone.

Correct

The credibility of the message is based on the credibility of the source and also the correctness of the content. It is essential to ensure that the information provided (message) is true, to unbiased and there is a source to verify it. It is essential to avoid content based on rumours, hearsay as well as source of no origin.

Concise

Since message dissemination involves time and effort for transmitting as well as receiving or absorbing. Hence message should be crisp enough to give information and at the same time not occupying more time of the receivers valuable time. The content should revolve around the core element of the message; frills and verbose / ornamental language need to be avoided. The effectiveness of the message is depend upon the above three attributes and if even component is missing or negative, the result will also be negative or not as per the expectations.

Some Specific Guidelines

Practitioners and executives alike can profit close study of these guidelines developed by an experienced counselor, Chester Burger:

1. *Talk from the viewpoint of the public's interest, not the organization's.* The soft drink bottler who launches a campaign to collect and recycle bottles can frankly admit that it does not want to irritate the public by having its product litter the landscape.
2. *Speak in personal terms whenever possible.* When many people have worked on developing a new product or adopting a new policy, it becomes difficult for the executive to say "I."
3. *It you do not want some statement quoted, do not make it.* Spokespersons should avoid talking "off the record," because such statements may well wind up published without the source.
4. *State the most important fact at the beginning.* The executive's format may first list the facts that led to the final conclusion, but such organization will fail when talking with the news media.
5. *Do not argue with the reporter or lose your cool.* Understand that the journalist seeks an interesting story and will use whatever techniques necessary to obtain it.
6. *If a question contains offensive language or simply words you do not like, do not repeat them even to deny them.* Reporters often use the gambit of putting words into the subject's mouth.
7. *If the reporter asks a direct question, give an equally direct answer.* Not giving one is a common error executives are prone to make.
8. *If a spokesperson does not know the answer to a question, one should simply say, " I don't know, but I'll find out for you."* With this, the spokesperson assumes the responsibility of following through.
9. *Tell the truth, even if it hurts.* In this era of skepticism and hostility, the most difficult task is often simply telling the truth.
10. *Do not exaggerate the facts.* Crying wolf makes it harder to be heard next time out.

These guidelines simply add up tot he rule that profitable press relations require adherence to the " Five Fs": dealing with journalists and programme producers in a manner that is fast, factual, frank, fair and friendly.

Essentials of Good Copy

Essentials of good publicity copy are essentials of good news writing. A few reminders can serve as a checklist.

— Will the information or news really interest the intended audience?

— Does the information answer every reasonable question that readers or listeners may ask?

— Is the significance of the information explained in terms of audience?

— Is the copy sufficiently newsworthy to survive stiff competition for public attention?

— Will the information further the objectives of our institution? Is it useful?

— Does the publicity accurately reflect the character and nature of the institution it represents?

— Are the facts, names, and dates accurate? Are the technical terms explained?

— Will the lead catch and hold the busy reader's or inattentive viewer's attention?

— Will it produce a bright, eye-catching headline? Is the lead terse, to the point?

— Do the facts of the story support the lead in fact and spirit?

— Is it readable copy, stripped of superlatives? Good news copy must be curt, clear, concise.

— Is the copy written so as to preclude the charge that it is an effort to get "free advertising"?

— Is the information presented as dramatically as possible with this set of facts?

— Squeeze all the news value you can into your story, but don't exaggerate.

Print Media:

Here are some fundamental principles for print advertising:

1. Use simple Layouts
2. The illustration is usually more important than the Headline

3. Look for story appeal in the illustration
4. Photographs work better than artwork
5. Offer a benefit in the Headline
6. Don't be afraid of long copy
7. Make it easy to read
8. Every advertisement should be a complete sale
9. Break out of the mould
10. Design the advertisement for the medium

References

Bernays, Edward *Public Relations*. Boston, MA: Bellman Publishing Company. 1945.

Blood, R. "Activism and the Internet: From e-mail to new political movement" . *Journal of Communication Management*, 5(2), 160-169. 2000.

Harris, T., & Whalen, P. *The Marketer's Guide to Public Relations in the 21st Century*. Mason, Ohio: Thompson Higher Education. 2006.

Sriramesh, K., & Vercic, D. The *Global Public Relations Handbook: Theory, Research, and Practice.* New Jersey: Lawrence Erlbaum Associates. 2003.

Wilcox, D. & Cameron, G. *Public Relations: Strategies and Tactics*. Boston: Pearson. 2003.

4

Media Relations

Media relations involves working with various media for the purpose of informing the public of an organization's mission, policies and practices in a positive, consistent and credible manner. Typically, this means coordinating directly with the people responsible for producing the news and features in the mass media. The goal of media relations is to maximize positive coverage in the mass media without paying for it directly through advertising.

Many people use the terms public relations and media relations interchangeably; however, doing so is incorrect. Media relations refer to the relationship that a company or organization develops with journalists, while public relations extend that relationship beyond the media to the general public.

Dealing with the media presents unique challenges in that the news media cannot be controlled — they have ultimate control over whether stories pitched to them are of interest to their audiences. Because of this, ongoing relationships between an organization and the news media is vital. One way to ensure a positive working relationship with media personnel is to become deeply familiar with their "beats" and areas of interests. Media relations and public relations practitioners should read as many magazines, journals, newspapers, and blogs as possible, as they relate to one's practice.

Working with the media on the behalf of an organization allows for awareness of the entity to be raised as well as the ability to create an impact with a chosen audience. It allows access to both large and small target audiences and helps build public support and mobilizing public opinion for an organization. This is all done through a wide range of media and can be used to encourage two-way communication.

Importance of Media Relations

The term "media relations" refers to a business or organization's relationship with professional journalists or media outlets. Similar to public relations, this department works on building a rapport with these venues in order to communicate the organization's goals, ideas, intent and newsworthy events. The term "public relations" is often considered a synonym for media relations, but it is not, since public relations is a more general department.

Public relations is different in that information is not just released or available to journalists, but the general public overall. Some companies choose to focus on this broader publicrelations approach rather than try to build a relationship with the media specifically. This is a decision entirely up to the company or organization.

A business or company may have just one person working with the media, or they may hire outside help from one of the many firms in existence. People working in the field may work for a consulting firm, as a part of a company, or as a freelance or independent contractor.Media relations firms employ many highly skilled individuals.

The first step toward building effective media relations is to build a plan. This plan outlines the elements needed to build a relationship with local, regional and national news outlets. It also specifies how this will be done, the image the organization intends to portray, and other noteworthy events that may tie into the company's goals.

Media relations can involve the writing and distribution of press releases. People who work in this field must deal with members of local media organizations and hold press conferences. A department might work closely with an advertising department or agency to maximize the potential outcome of a release, or to find the correct target audience for a company's press releases.

A company's media policy is generally decided by the most senior members of an organization as well as the media relations team. The policy doesn't just affect those at the top of the corporate food chain. It might require employees or members of a group to speak with management before speaking to members of the press about company issues or events.

The practice of media relations involves working with various media outlets to inform the public about a company's news and policies in a positive, consistent and credible manner. This means communicating directly with those responsible for producing news and features in the mass media.

It is common to refer to media relations and public relations in the same breath, but they are different. Media relations refers to the relationship a company builds with journalists, while public relations extends that relationship beyond the media to the general public.

The objective of media relations is to maximise positive coverage in the mass media without paying for it directly through advertising, so essentially, (apart from your time) it is free!

It is also a much more powerful method to communicate your products and services, with so much more kudos attached to a piece of editorial than an advert.

Dealing with the media presents challenges in that the media cannot be controlled. They have power over whether stories presented to them are of interest to their audience.

Therefore, developing a fruitful and ongoing relationship between your company and journalists and keeping them regularly updated is crucial.

Media Relations Tools

Historically the core of public relations, media relations, includes all efforts to publicise products or the company to members of the press—TV and Radio, newspaper, magazine, newsletter and internet. In garnering media coverage, PR professionals work with the media to place stories about products, companies and company spokespeople. This is done by developing interesting and relevant story angles that are pitched to the media. It is important to remember that media placements come with good stories and no payment is made to the media for placements. In fact, in order to maintain the highest level of credibility, many news organisations bar reporters from accepting even the smallest gifts (e.g., free pencils with product logo) from companies. Below are descriptions and tips for using the most common media relations tools. A combination of these tools, spread over time, is the basis of a good media relations campaign. Use every available channel of communication to get your message out to the community. Always look for fresh "hooks" to increase your media exposure. Be sure to include a contact name, phone number (alternate phone number if available) and e-mail address on all media documents so interested reporters can get in contact with you.

Media Advisories / Media Alerts

Media advisories/media alerts are brief, one-page, written notices designed to alert the media of an upcoming news event, such as a news conference. Advisories include the who, what, where, when and why of your activity. Examples of what visuals will be available for photographs and video is also a good idea to include. In providing the media with complete information, an advisory should include background information on the existing severity of a traffic safety threat, and introduce the traffic safety program that addresses this problem.

Press Kits

A press package is the foundation of any media relations program. It consists of a series of stories, usually placed in a two-sided folder with pockets, that organises information in a way that is easy for the news media to use. Typically it will include a description of the organisation, key facts and figures, biographies of the principals, a history, and two or three stories on current trends and issues. It functions as instant background material when a story arises. Press packages also usually include photography.

Press Releases/News Releases

Press releases/news releases offer more information than media advisories and reach more contacts in less time than phone calls. A news release may precede a news event you want covered, be used to make an announcement or provide a response to a current issue or recent story. If possible, limit your news release to one page (no longer than two).

Monitor local daily, weekly and monthly publications to determine which reporters cover your issue. At larger publications, it is important to target specific reporters and section editors. At smaller publications, all media materials may pass directly through the Editor. Be sure to organise the information in your news release in order of importance—with the most pertinent information for the public to know positioned at the top and supporting information toward the bottom. This "pyramid" format ensures that as your news release is edited for available space, key information is more likely to remain part of the story. All key information should be in the first two paragraphs. Include quotes from local authorities or well-known community leaders to support your story. When possible, use digital pictures to complement a news release and provoke interest in the subject. In order to increase your organisation's credibility and the likelihood that your release will be read, only send out a release when you have some real news. News releases can be a valuable communication tool, but only if they are really news.

Brief press releases should be issued on such topics as promotions or hiring of new executives, openings of new buildings and the addition of new products. These typically result in one- to two-paragraph stories in publications, and keep your name in front of the target audience.

Major announcements could be a new research development, a major new product or a major new change in business direction. These typically result in 500- to 800-word stories in print publications and often merit radio and television coverage. Occasionally, a press conference or press briefing may be appropriate in conjunction with major announcements.

"Trend" press releases are usually the most valuable to the news media, and will help you establish a reputation as a source. These are about developing trends in your industry and contain information that would otherwise be difficult for the media to obtain. The following are examples of trend releases: What are the "hottest" spots in the Bay Area real estate market? Are more Americans travelling to Russia now and why? Are physicians gaining more clout in negotiating with insurance companies? Are major medical groups paying more or less attention to holistic/alternative medical therapies?

Although a feature story must be newsworthy, in the broad sense of the word, it is also timeless. It can run in today's paper or tomorrow's or next week's. Feature stories are often called "evergreen" for this reason—it's always fresh and will not fade. Unlike a news story, a feature can have a point of view, an "angle", and is often longer than a hard news story on the same subject.

Background video tapes will help get your story on television. Again, they are most useful when a subject is difficult or inconvenient to film.

Examples would be surgery, the inner workings of a computer or restricted areas of an airport.

You may want to do a complete video news release (VNR) when there is an important announcement, or simply have background footage available for various television stations to put together their own stories. Footage must be in professional Betacam format, rather than VHS.

Fact Sheets

Fact Sheets are similar to a media advisory in that they include the same basic who, what, when, where and why of your campaign or event. Fact sheets contain key facts, statistics, dates and milestones and an overall snapshot for readers.

Press Conferences

A press conference consists of someone speaking to the media at a predetermined time and place. Press conferences usually take place in a public or quasi-public place. Press conferences provide an excellent opportunity for speakers to control information and who gets it; depending on the circumstances, speakers may hand-pick the journalists they invite to the conference instead of making themselves available to any journalist who wishes to attend. It is also assumed that the speaker will answer journalists' questions at a press conference, although they are of course not obligated to. However, someone who holds several press conferences on a topic (especially a scandal) will be asked questions by the press, regardless of whether they indicate they will entertain them, and the more conferences the person holds, the more aggressive the questioning may become. Therefore, it is in a speaker's interest to answer journalists' questions at a press conference to avoid appearing as if they have something to hide.

But questions from reporters—especially hostile reporters—detracts from the control a speaker has over the information they give out. For even more control, but less interactivity, a person may choose to issue a press release.

Press conferences should be used when you have a visual story or need to get information out to all media sources at once.

— News conferences should be held in a location that is easily accessible to the media and is relevant to the message you are presenting. For example, consider planning your media event at a local elementary school when promoting bicycle safety or at a high school when promoting teen seat belt use.

— Make sure the site offers adequate electrical, audio and visual access for reporters.

— Choose a time and date that are convenient for reporters. Usually mornings (not before 9:30 a.m.) or early afternoons on Tuesday, Wednesday or Thursday generally work well for reporters. Avoid scheduled broadcasts like noon and 5 p.m. Be sure your news conference is not at the same time as another newsworthy event, as you don't want to compete for media attention. Take the time to investigate other events that might overlap with yours so you can avoid any conflicts well ahead of time.

— Alert the media of a news conference by sending out a media advisory two to three days prior to the event. Follow-up with a phone call to confirm that your information was received by the correct person and take advantage of the opportunity to sell your story.

— Choose spokespeople carefully. If possible, prepare remarks for speakers to keep them on track and avoid duplication of remarks. Make sure all spokespeople (five at the most) speak for a short time (2-5 minutes) and are available after the news conference to answer one-on-one questions.

— Have media kits on hand which include: event agenda, news release, fact sheet, contact sheet with speakers' names, titles and organisations and a brief backgrounder on your program. Media kits can also be sent to those reporters who were unable to attend your event.

Radio and TV Talk Shows

Radio and TV Talk Shows provide a format for guests to present issues and concerns of interest to the community. Identify the most appropriate programs for reaching your intended audience, including local cable or community-access channels. To place a spokesperson on a talk show, send a pitch letter to the talk show producer indicating why the issue is important to listeners and viewers. Follow-up with a phone call to make your pitch. Plan on submitting your request a few months in advance as talk shows often require significant lead time.

Webcasts

This is rapidly becoming a major publicity tool as people take advantage of the Web's multimedia capabilities. Webcasts can be live events or archived and available on demand. They are a cost-effective, instantaneous method to communicate with media all over the world, in a compelling, interactive manner that meets journalists' needs. Using Webcasts, you can extend the reach of your PR efforts, reduce your budget for spokespeople, ensure your message is communicated consistently across all audiences, better fit into journalists' schedules, and provide more compelling supporting elements.

Public Service Announcements

Public Service Announcements (PSAs) are another good way to reach the public. PSAs are used by print and broadcast media as a means of providing community service messages. TV and radio PSAs are generally 15, 20, 30 or 60 seconds in length and are run on radio and television free of charge by the station. To inquire about placing a PSA, call the station's public affairs director and ask what their PSA policy is. Tell them you are interested in producing a PSA and find out how best to proceed. Stations will have different requirements, so it's important to place that call. Competition is fierce for PSA placement, so be sure your topic is timely. The same holds true for print PSAs.

Calendar Releases

Calendar Releases are modified news releases designed to give community calendar editors the basic information about your event. Whenever possible, send calendar releases four to six weeks in advance to ensure inclusion in the media's community calendar. However, check with your local publications to get a more accurate deadline.

Print and Broadcast Editorials

Print and Broadcast Editorials are used to react to a recent editorial, event or news story, to make a point, state a fact or offer an opinion or also to correct misinformation. These editorials can be submitted to a newspaper, TV or radio station.

— *Letters to the Editor* should be submitted within a few days of the event or activity to which you are responding. Timeliness is key in whether or not your letter will be printed. Letters should be well-written, succinct and to the point. Generally, 75-100 words is the maximum length recommended. Find out what is the preferred format (fax, e-mail, etc.) for submitting letters to the editor for each publication to ensure that your letter will receive the best chance of running. Daily newspapers operate on such a quick time frame that e-mail is often the preferred method for submission. By the time traditional mail arrives, the moment may be lost. Letters should be typed, signed and include a contact name and phone number.

— *Op-Eds* should be written in a news article format, but in an opinionated fashion, outlining your organisation's persuasive points and solutions to issues, and citing necessary statistics and facts as back up to your opinions and/or arguments. Op-Eds should be submitted to the Editorial Page Editor of a newspaper. Similar to a letter to the editor, an op-ed piece provides you with a format to react to an issue, state a fact or express an opinion. Op-eds should also be typed and signed. Maximum length is generally 450 to 600 words. This information can also often be found on the Editorial page of the publication.

— *Broadcast Editorials* serve the same purpose as a letter to the editor or op-ed piece—to react to an issue, state a fact or offer an opinion. Broadcast Editorials should be directed to the station manager of a TV or radio station. It's always a good idea to call in advance and ask about the specific requirements for submission, including length and format.

— *Editorial Board Briefings* are another route to consider. In an editorial briefing, key members from your agency or organisation sit down with the editorial board of your local paper and discuss the matter at hand—seat belt use, pedestrian safety, impaired driving, child restraint, etc.—at length. To arrange for an editorial board briefing, submit a letter of request to the editorial page editor. Follow up with a phone call to make your pitch.

Media Contacts

Media contacts are a crucial component of a successful media relations plan. It doesn't matter how newsworthy the story or how great the news release or op-ed piece is if the information is not received by the correct media contact. Contact information is readily available online and can also be obtained by calling the newspaper, television or radio station directly to find out who the news director (radio) or assignment editor (television) is.

Additionally, media databases are available in both hardcopy and electronic format from a variety of sources. These directories are somewhat costly to obtain. Remember, staff turnover in the media industry is relatively high, so be sure to update your contact list on a regular basis.

Wire Services

Wire services, such as Business Wire, PR NewsWire and Associated Press provide another mechanism for distributing your media materials to a large number of media outlets in a short amount of time. Depending on the wire service, you can select the specific geographic region to receive your materials. You can also select applicable trade publications, such as transportation, government, health, etc. Costs associated with using wire services vary depending upon circulation and number of words. Blast fax services are also available to assist with distribution of your materials.

Long Lead Publications

Long lead publications, such as industry newsletters and regional magazines, are another good venue for promoting your program or campaign. Unlike the quick turnaround associated with daily news services, magazines and newsletters require much more lead-time, often several months in advance, to run a story. A bylined article, similar to an op-ed piece can be modified for a magazine or newsletter. Keep in mind that the focus of the article should connect with the intended readers (audience). If you're interested in having an article included in the July issue of a publication, chances are the article will need to be submitted by late April or early May. Careful planning will avoid missed deadlines.

Follow-up and monitoring efforts

Follow-up and monitoring efforts are an important part of any media relations campaign. Distributing the materials is just the beginning. Keep the issue alive by writing letters to columnists and responding to articles and editorials. Make follow-up calls to ensure that your news release, calendar release or oped lands in the right hands. To track successful media placements, utilise online sources, such as Google, or one of the professional media tracking services in your region.

Press Clipping Services

You'll want to know if syndicates and wire services are picking up your story. That's where a subscription to a clipping service can help. These services scan thousands of newspapers, magazines, and websites and monitor television talk shows and news programs looking for mention of your company or product. You can also provide them with key words thereby keeping upto-date on your industry or competition. There are services that still manually clip articles but there are also Web-based services that scan electronic versions of publications and deliver your "clippings" in electronic form. In either case, having these clippings enables you to judge whether your news is reaching your target audience and if your PR plan is effective.

Media Tours

Some new products can be successfully publicised when launched with a media tour. On a media tour a company spokesperson travels to key cities to introduce a new product by being booked on TV and radio talk shows and conducting interviews with print and internet reporters or influencers (e.g., bloggers). The spokesperson can be a company employee or someone hired by the company, perhaps a celebrity or "expert" who has credibility with the target audience. A media tour may include other kinds of personal appearances in conjunction with special events, such as public appearances, speaking engagements or autograph signing opportunities.

From a tactical perspective, a media tour is about meetings with targeted press and analysts in one or more geographical regions when launching a new company, product, or service. But strategically speaking, communicating one-on-one is the best way to build relationships of mutual respect and interest with the press and analysts whose articles, reports and recommendations influence your company's key external audiences.

You want to put your best foot forward with the media, and first impressions are critical. Think of PR counsel as a coach, and your company is gearing up for the season. To reach the finals, you'll benefit from a coach's wisdom to optimise your performance through preparation, motivation and experience.

Adjust the meeting mode as needed to maximise opportunities for interaction with your key contacts. Often a tour is a combination of in-person meetings with press and analysts in multiple metro areas and teleconferences. Phone briefings are an increasingly common element of tours as more writers and analysts work from remote locations.

The press needs fresh news. For instance, if the purpose of your tour is to unveil a product line, don't be tempted to publish related materials such as white papers or datasheets on your website before releasing the news. Working closely with management will keep information about your company's next big thing from getting out before its time.

Press tours are an exciting prospect since they provide the opportunity to raise your company's profile and communicate the latest messages—with the media, no less! Sometimes that enthusiasm leads to a heavy tour lineup. When you hit the road, the only people entering the conference room for the briefing should be one well-prepared spokesperson and you, the PR expert takes at least two months to plan an effective tour, so it's important to communicate regularly with your internal constituents and set expectations about the process. You'll need the time to engage an industry analyst well in advance of the tour for a consulting session to fine-tune your positioning. Conduct spokesperson training with your star player to master effective message-delivery techniques. Prepare a Q&A for your spokesperson, anticipating a wide range of questions about the news, but also about the company, from competitors to funding to sales channels. Create a concise, news-oriented presentation tailored to the press and analyst audience, but be able to deliver the story without using it as a script for the briefing.

Once you're on the road, most tours are conducted over a period of one to two weeks, with follow-up as needed over the next several months. Complete the tour prior to the wire date of your news, taking into account long- and short-lead publication cycles. When dealing with embargoed news on tour, securing reporters' embargo agreements is essential so that no early stories appear, potentially adversely impacting other media coverage possibilities.

Once the meetings are concluded and the news has been wired, you can expect press coverage, although not necessarily immediately afterward. Articles seeded during the tour, especially with monthly publications, can appear up to six months later. Often, the tour is just the first step in the process, since follow-up is necessary to ensure the reporter has all the elements for the story (customer references, graphics, analyst references). Analysts may use the information in a report or research note, and the publication cycle can be up to nine months. Most importantly, with a tour, your company has invested in a foundation for future dialogue with the key media reaching your prospective customers, partners and investors.

Newsletters

Marketers who have captured names and addresses of customers and potential customers can use a newsletter for regular contact with their targeted audience. Newsletters can be directed at trade customers, final consumers or business buyers and can be distributed either by regular mail or electronic means (i.e., e-newsletters delivered via e-mail or rss feed). Marketers using newsletters strive to provide content of interest to customers as well as information on products and promotions. A bookstore may include reviews of new books, information on online book chats and information on in-store or online promotions. A food manufacturer may include seasonal recipes, information on new products and coupons. Online newsletters offer the opportunity to link to stores carrying the marketer's products. Effective newsletters are sought out by and well received by interested audiences.

Many newsletters are published by clubs, churches, societies, associations, and businesses, especially companies, to provide information of interest to their members, customers or employees. Some newsletters are created as money-making ventures and sold directly to subscribers. Sending newsletters to customers and prospects is a common marketing strategy, which can have benefits and drawbacks. General attributes of newsletters include news and upcoming events of the related organisation, as well as contact information for general inquiries.

Newsletters can be divided into two distinct types. Printed (on paper) and digital (on the internet). The digital formats vary from the simplest format, text to highly designable formats like PDF and HTML. The use of more formatting and web 2.0 attributes like video and sound have become a market standard all over the world.

Special Events

These run the gamut from receptions to elegant dinners to stunts. Special events can be designed to reach a specific narrow target audience, such as individuals interested in college savings plans to major events like a strawberry festival designed to promote tourism and regional agriculture. Stunts, such as building the world's largest ice cream sundae during National Ice Cream month captures the attention of an audience in the immediate area, but also attracts the attention of mass media such as TV news and major newspapers, which provide broad reach. The Oscar Mayer Weiner mobile is a classic example, providing a recognizable icon that travels the country garnering attention wherever it visits. As with all PR programs, special event planners must work hard to ensure the program planned conveys the correct message and image to the target audience.

Speaking Engagements

Speaking before industry conventions, trade association meetings, and other groups provides an opportunity for company experts to demonstrate their expertise to potential clients/customers. Generally these opportunities are not explicitly for company or product promotion; rather they are a chance to talk on a topic of interest to potential customers and serve to highlight the speaker's expertise in a field. Often the only mention of the company or its products is in the speaker biography. Nevertheless, the right speaking engagement puts the company in front of a good target audience and offers networking opportunities for generating customer leads.

Publicity Stunt

Publicity stunt is a planned event designed to attract the public's attention to the event's organisers or their cause. Publicity stunts can be professionally organised or set up by amateurs. Such events are frequently utilised by advertisers, celebrities, athletes, and politicians.

Organisations sometimes seek publicity by staging newsworthy events that attract media coverage. They can be in the form of ground-breakings, dedications, press conferences or organised protests. By staging and managing the event, the organisation attempts to gain some control over what is reported in the media. Successful publicity stunts have news value, offer photo, video and sound bite opportunities, and are arranged primarily for media coverage.

It is sometimes hard for organisations to design successful publicity stunts that highlight the message instead of burying it. The importance of publicity stunts is generating news interest and awareness for the concept, product or service being marketed. Stunts are effective communication tools when used well and useless time wasters when they are not.

Trade Shows

Trade shows can be good opportunities to make company announcements—new products, acquisitions, and alliances—because trade journalists are often present. Setting up one-on-one interviews or background meetings can be tricky since other companies are likely doing the same thing. To maximise your trade show presence, use of the internet and your company website can help. By building a virtual presentation, media (and potential clients visiting your booth) can experience a "press conference," view photos or video, get critical background material, obtain third party quotes or request interviews, and be kept up-to-date as information changes throughout the trade show and beyond. Contacting key media in advance and offering time with your executives can be the incentive they need to seek you out and cover your news.

Community Meetings

Often it is important to hold small neighbourhood meetings to explain various portions of a program that will directly or indirectly impact a group of citizens. In addition to an ongoing public relations campaign it may be necessary to reach out to head off any negative publicity caused by lack of accurate information. Examples of appropriate use of community meetings include change in flight patterns over neighbourhoods adjacent to an airport and major base-reuse project.

Working with Media

Public relations was virtually synonymous with media relations, and getting the media to run favorable stories about an organization and its activities was the cornerstone of that process. Although many journalists pooh-pooh the importance of public relations practitioners' leads and claim that the news media come up with their own story ideas, content analyses of major mass media seem to belie this. Researchers consistently find that a high percentage of news stories originate from public relations input.

Whether they willingly admit it or not, in general public relations people and journalists are mutually dependent on one another.

— Public relations practitioners need journalists as conduits for getting messages to various publics.

— Journalists need public relations people as sources for story ideas, leads to authoritative spokespersons, and specific information about stories in progress.

Thus, both can benefit from a positive working relationship. While having such positive working relationships with the mass media is important to public relations people, they're not important as ends in themselves. They're a means to the broader end of building meaningful relationships with the organization's important publics who also happen to be part of the media's audiences. Those audience members are the ultimate focus of the organization's attention; the media are simply the means of reaching them.

As is the case with so many things they do, public relations practitioners' relationships with the media need to be based on and reflect the needs and the orientation of their organizations, not the practitioners' personal likes and dislikes, nor even their notions of journalistic excellence. The best media by journalistic standards, or even the most popular media, are not necessarily the best media for all public relations purposes or for all organizations' messages. Nonetheless, the unfortunate reality is that an inordinate number of organizations direct their media relations efforts at The Washington Post, The Wall Street Journal, major television networks, and a handful of other prestigious media even though these media have little or no audience among the publics that are most important to these organizations.

A promotional brochure from Ruder-Finn Public Relations echoes this concerned by observing, "Too often, public relations efforts are concentrated exclusively on the major media centers; or a company's attention becomes too focused on the business media that reach executives, to the exclusion of the media that reach the customer." The simple fact is that The New York Times, Smithsonian magazine, and National Public Radio's All Things Considered are not ideal media for all purposes or for all organizations. This should be self-evident, but it's often overlooked, especially by organizations that don't do a lot of media relations or that wait until a problem arises to hire a consultant to help them.

Such organizations need to be more thoughtful and careful in making their decisions says Jon Boroshok, the president of TechMarcom, a Boston marketing communications consulting firm. In a recent issue of pr reporter, Boroshok cautioned organizations looking for media relations help to "watch the name dropping. PR firms love to drop names of media contacts, but these may not be the right reporters, editors and analysts." While some practitioners may get a lot of repeat mileage out of a few high-profile media personalities with whom they've worked, Boroshok concluded, "Experienced pros develop new press relationships as needed."

So, it's important that public relations practitioners keep track of their real goals and not fall victim — as many practitioners have done — to media snobbishness by striving to always get their stories in the elite media. Despite the belief of many traditionalists that "print rules," newspapers are not the best way to reach all audiences.

— A social service agency that tries to use newspaper stories and ads to reach illiterate welfare clients is wasting its time and money.

— Spot ads on carefully selected radio stations or television public service announcements would reach a much higher percentage of the desired audience

At the same time, despite its large audience and high penetration of the population, television is a poor choice of medium for an art museum to use in appealing to high-roller patrons of the arts for large contributions. Carefully targeted direct mail, personal phone calls, or visits would be much more appropriate. The key to media relations is to remember your organization's ultimate target audiences and select the media that provide the most effective ways of reaching them. They should be selected and relationships cultivated on the basis of their usefulness, not their reputation, not their journalistic excellence, not their state of the art technology, not their total circulation, and not even their responsiveness to public relations overtures.

Practically speaking, many organizations do not have — and are unlikely ever to have — enough contact with the media to justify having a full-time employee to do media relations. They may go year after year with no media contact. But, that doesn't mean they should totally ignore media relations. Sooner or later something is going to happen that will require them to work with the media.

— It may be something positive — e.g., introducing a new product, opening a new facility, or hiring a new CEO — for which the organization wants maximum publicity.

— Or, it could be negative circumstances — e.g., a serious accident, layoffs, or being named in a product liability suit — which the organization wants to downplay or minimize.

Unless the organization has somehow established honest and mutually beneficial relationships with the media before these circumstances develop, it will have a much more difficult time accomplishing whatever it wants to accomplish. Small to medium-sized companies which deal in business staples or household goods or which provide routine home or business services will probably have very little contact with the news-side of the mass media.

— Their business is so routine and stable that, short of a major accident, financial calamity, new product introduction, or personnel crisis, they're unlikely to attract the attention of the news media, no matter how hard they try. They simply aren't newsworthy.

— They may, however, extensively use the media as advertising outlets and may even have a staff of media buyers who work in their marketing departments. The linked reading Advertising and publicity briefly discusses the differences between these two distinct processes of using the media to gain attention for an organization or its products.

Organizations like this usually do not make media relations a high priority. They tend to devote few of their resources and very little staff time to it. They may not totally ignore it, but media relations may just be one more, occasional duty that's listed in the public relations person's job description. For other organizations, almost every action is newsworthy and their activities receive a lot of attention from the news media whether the organization wants it or not. Their accomplishments — or shortcomings — are reported as news and their executives are profiled in feature stories. They include high-tech companies, high risk ventures, companies which dominate their industries, and companies that emphasize innovative ideas, special events, or celebrity-oriented endeavors. Examples include Microsoft, IBM, Telecommunications Inc., General Electric, Disney, and the Fox Network.

Such organizations are likely to have large public relations operations and may have several people who are assigned full-time to nothing but media relations. Sometimes they're even more specialized than that. Some companies have one specialist assigned to national media relations and another one to local media relations, or they may have a broadcast media specialist and a print media specialist, or a trade media specialist and a consumer media specialist. Many state and federal government agencies have much more extensive and intensive media contact than businesses of comparable size. One reason is that these agencies have a legal mandate to inform the public of their actions. The other side of the coin is that their decisions and actions — e.g., new taxes, zoning laws, or traffic regulations — directly affect the community in ways that make them inherently newsworthy; that's why the news media want to, and need to, cover them.

Different Ways for Media Relationships

There are countless approaches and techniques that public relations practitioners can use in working with the media. The five broad elements identified here are just one of many equally valid ways of conceptualizing and organizing a wide range of media relations activities.

— respond to the media;

— issue media advisories and alerts;

— visit, network, and schmooze;

— issue news and feature story releases;

— host news conferences and other media opportunities.

When public relations practitioners remember to look at their goals and interests through the eyes of the media and the media's audiences, and when they use these insights to relate to the media people with whom they work, media relations is one of the most effective ways to enhance an organization's public relations. It's a cost-effective way of reaching large and varied audiences and, insofar as those audiences are relevant to the organization, it pays big dividends.

At the most basic level, being able to respond to the media means having someone who is accessible to reporters in case they ever have questions about the organization or its activities. It also means that these accessible spokespersons have to be informed enough to be able to provide prompt, accurate information and explanations that will satisfactorily answer those questions. There are some organizations which, because of the nature of their business or the environment in which they operate, need to have a public relations spokesperson on-call 24 hours per day, seven days a week. They include medical centers where lives are at risk, airports and/or places that deal with hazardous materials where an accident could have major consequences, and correctional institutions and law enforcement agencies.

In contrast, there are other organizations which may be called upon to respond to the media less than once a year and which have a very low probability of ever being called by the media. They include small manufacturers, distributors and retailers of non-dangerous, staple household and business products. For them, being accessible requires minimal preparation and effort, and the extent of their media relations activity may be as little as periodically reminding the media of their public relations person's name and phone number.

Most organizations fall somewhere in between. And, most organizations would prefer to have more extensive and more favorable media coverage — if not full blown media relations — than they now have. The first step should always be having well-prepared, knowledgeable people ready and able to respond when the media call. Even organizations which choose to engage in no other media relations efforts should at least have someone designated to respond promptly to media inquiries to avoid the possibility of being portrayed as non-responsive or secretive by the media.

Media Alerts

In issuing a media alert or an advisory, an organization isn't attempting to tell the story itself or to write the story for the media. — News releases are used for that. — As the terms themselves imply, their purpose is simply to alert editors to something they may want to have their reporters cover. Whether or not it's covered, or how it's covered is left entirely up to the editor. For many organizations, especially for-profit businesses, media alerts are a rarity. Some public relations practitioners never issue them. But, government public information officers and public relations people working for charitable or publicly-funded organizations do them all the time.

In many cases, media alerts are a legal necessity because sunshine laws that guarantee public access to government records and open meetings laws at both the state and federal level require government agencies, commissions, and board to post and/or publish public notices of their meetings and of decisions that affect members of the public. Thus, a state or county welfare agency charged with providing financial assistance to needy citizens or promoting abuse prevention, or a public works department that is repairing or upgrading the city's infrastructure might issue a dozen or more media advisories per month.

— In some instances, the laws requiring government programs to publish/ announce their activities are so stringent that those agencies have to purchase advertising space to get their messages out if the local media don't announce the information as news.

— For such government agencies — and the tax-payers who foot the bills — the number, quality, timeliness, and effectiveness of their media alerts is particularly important.

Non-profit organizations also make frequent use of media alerts as one of their tools for getting reporters to attend and cover the special events and activities they sponsor. In the case of an important event, — a major fund-raising activity, for instance — experienced public relations people won't rely solely on a mailed media alert to attract media coverage, they use follow-up phone calls, personal visits, and other gambits to insure the maximum possible media attention. But, you can bet that they won't forget to issue a media alert as one element in their persuasive campaign.

Visiting the media's editorial and/or production offices and getting to know the people who work there well enough to include them in your professional network is one of the best ways to start building an organization's relationships with the media.

— Public relations practitioners don't build relationships with the media per se, they build them person by person with reporters, photographers, editors, publishers, news directors, assignment directors, programmers, and station managers.

Beyond visiting the media's offices and talking with these folks on their turf, it's also very helpful to invite them to come see your office and tour your organization's facilities. Such informative, yet casual interactions help establish a common ground for future contacts that may deal with more specific and more important issues. Once an initial meeting and familiarization are out of the way, visits to the media's office are usually quite rare. Most reporters and editors, even those who welcome a getting to know you visit, do not encourage nor appreciate public relations people who frequently drop in on them. In fact, they're likely to be very suspicious of such activity.

If you're careful to avoid calling near deadline times, and if you make it a point to ask if the reporter or editor you're calling has time to speak with you when you call, most of them will be happy to have you periodically touch base. But don't call just to pass the time or to talk about the weather, have some relevant information you can pass along to them during these calls.

— Ideally, you'd like to have news about your organization to call to their attention. Even if it's not important enough to warrant a news release, you can mention it as a casual reason for your call. Some reporters will appreciate knowing about it.

— But, if there's no news in your immediate organization to tell them about, perhaps you can alert them to something that's happening within your industry. For instance, you might point out an emerging business trend that would make a good story for them even if it doesn't involve your company.

— Another alternative is to offer feedback on stories they've previously written, especially if you have suggestions for possible follow-ups or can tell them about subsequent developments. Here again, in terms of building a relationship with the reporter, it really doesn't matter if the stories don't involve your organization.

Most reporters will appreciate any story leads or ideas you give them, as long as you don't later try to claim ownership or make them feel you're trying to push the story. Above all, don't call with gratuitous compliments or effusive thank yous for stories that don't warrant them. It's likely to backfire. Remember that many reporters have some degree of innate suspicion of public relations practitioners. They really don't like working with public relations people, and they're uncomfortable about doing it even when they're getting useful information.

So, if they start thinking a public relations person is grateful to them or is trying to butter them up, they start worrying that they have been, or are about to be, conned and they may begin to doubt your sincerity about everything. At the very least, media visits, phone calls and other personal interactions should make future exchanges of information easier for everyone involved. At best, they will also be pleasant breaks in the daily routine, mini social occasions, instead of just another business duty.

News Releases

When an organization issues a news release or a feature story release it's putting its own story in words and delivering it to the media in a format the media can make use of. The most common form of release remains words on a page, although many of these pages are now electronically transmitted — by fax, modem, or wire service — rather than being delivered as hard copy.

— Some practitioners also produce news releases on audio tape for radio stations — audio news releases (ANRs) — or on videotape — video news releases (VNRs) — for television use.

— ANRs and VNRs can be shipped to the media on a tape, or they can be transmitted electronically via telephone line, "wire service," or satellite transmission.

The ideal from a public relations' perspective is for the media to use a release exactly as submitted without changing anything. In that case, the organization is telling its own story in its own words instead of having a third party — e.g., a reporter — tell it from his or her perspective. But, that won't happen unless the public relations person who writes the release is thoroughly knowledgeable about media style and values and reflects that in what and how they write.

What's more likely to happen, is that a news release which is perceived as newsworthy by the media will be edited and/or rewritten in ways that turn it into the media's version of the story rather than the public relations person's view of the story.

— The media may cut some things out that are considered self-serving, old news, or unsupported commentary. Sometimes, releases are simply trimmed to fit the space available or to make them more consistent in terms of style.

— An editor who feels the quotes used in the release are too stilted or self-serving but who doesn't want to simply cut them out may call and talk directly to the executives who were quoted to see if they'll express their ideas in other words.

— The media may add additional information to make the story more complete or more relevant to their audiences.

  a) There may be more than one side to the story you're telling, and the media may want to show the opposing sides.

  b) If the story involves a particular industry, they may want comments from a variety of competitors to provide a more complete scope and balance than they've gotten just from your organization.

Whatever happens to releases once they're issued is beyond the control of the public relations person who releases them. These decisions are strictly the prerogative of the editors, news directors, and other media gatekeepers who very jealously guard them. Large or small, local or national, the media control their own content, and public relations practitioners cannot demand anything be included — or excluded — as editorial content. So, much to the chagrin of public relations practitioners who write news releases, many are simply discarded by the media.

In the past, some public relations practitioners operated like news release factories, churning out as many releases as possible and distributing all of them to all possible media, even to the extent of sending copies to several reporters who worked for the same medium. For many it was just a matter of playing the percentages and thinking that the more the sent out, the more likely they were to have at least some of them used. Others justified blanket distribution as a matter of fairness, saying they didn't want to appear to be playing favorites by sending releases to some media but not to others. But, as increasing numbers of practitioners matured beyond the publicity and explanatory phases of public relations and began thinking in terms of building meaningful relationships, even with the mass media, the use of news releases also matured. Practitioners began thinking in terms of tailoring their releases to fit specific media.

For some, this meant paring down their distribution lists to selectively targeted media and distributing fewer copies of each release. For others it meant preparing and distributing multiple, slightly different copies of each release that could be selectively mailed to different media without reducing the total number of media to whom they sent releases. At its most basic level, the latter approach meant preparing a print media version of the release using AP style guidelines and a separate broadcast version using RTNDA style guidelines that might also include sound bites and/or B-roll video. It also meant preparing several localized versions of a release instead of a single version meant for nation-wide distribution.

Practitioners who conscientiously and effectively applied targeted approaches found that they really worked. They experienced a marked increase in the percentage of releases they issued that were actually used by the media, and they often found that the media's stories were longer and more favorable. For some, personal relationships with reporters and editors were also enhanced. Some of the best and most experienced public relations practitioners had used this tactic for years, but it hadn't gotten a lot of attention.

Contrary to the assertion of some critics, news releases are not a dead or obsolete technique. But, their effective use is very different than it used to be. Instead of treating a news release like a shotgun that fires dozens of information "pellets" in a broad, sweeping pattern that might simultaneously hit several targets at one time, savvy practitioners today use their news releases like a sniper's rifle that is very carefully aimed to solidly impact a precise target.

News Conferences

Hosting news conferences and other media opportunities such as interviews with visiting dignitaries or subject matter experts or tours of facilities can be very helpful and very effective in gaining media attention and coverage. But, activities of this type will only work if the media's needs are kept in mind and if what's being presented has substantive content that will be of interest to the media's audiences.

— Neither a news conference nor an interview opportunity — unless it's with the President, the Pope, a head of state, or someone of comparable importance — is newsworthy in and of itself. It becomes newsworthy and worthwhile for the media only when something new and important is going to be said.

— Tours are of interest only if they're rarely done or there's something new and remarkable to see.

News conferences are the most popular and most standardized media opportunity. Some of their popularity is no doubt due to the popularity and glamour of televised presidential news conferences which have inspired corporate executives and public relations practitioners alike to see themselves glibly responding to every tough question thrown at them. Alas, most news conferences aren't as glamorous as the President's.

The sad truth is that an awful lot of press conferences that are called shouldn't have been. Even the public relations practitioners who called them know there wasn't any real news to announce, but they gave in to the prodding of company managers or mid-level public officials who think calling a press conference is a good way to get some extra attention for what is an otherwise insignificant announcement. In defense of these practitioners, we have to admit that when the boss is pushing for a press conference, it can be tough to resist. It's all too easy to fall into the trap of thinking, "What possible harm could there be in doing it?"

We won't bother to consider the possibility that the boss who's pushing so hard for the press conference, and who may envision him/herself taking center stage to banter with reporters, may slip up and make a mistake. Let's simply focus on the fact that calling unnecessary news conferences about non-newsworthy topics is about as popular with reporters as falsely crying "Wolf!" It may may get attention the first couple of times, but it's counter-productive in the long run.

> "If everything can be made clear in a press release, then a press conference becomes superfluous. Don't call a news conference unless you have something world-shaking to announce. Some of your big shots may be so puffed up with their own importance that they think we'll come every time they call, but friends, that isn't the way it works."

Routine information and simple announcements that aren't likely to provoke a lot of questions are much more easily and effectively handled by issuing news releases.

Role of an Editor

The eventual success of your organization's public and media relations efforts depends mainly on how often your news releases are issued and, more importantly, how often the news they contain is selected to run. The latter decision is in the hands of a person whose title is usually editor. Understanding an editor's job will help you do your job better. Can you name the editor of your local computer magazine or local newspaper? The editor is a very important ally in public relations. The editor has overall responsibility for the publication's content. Below him or her, depending on the periodical's size, are subject editors who are assigned to specific beats (often called "departments"). These editors oversee the content for their departments. Sometimes each editor has additional staff, such as reporters, freelancer writers, photographers, copy writers, copy editors, etc.

The information contained in news releases is the primary source of information for most editors. Newsworthy releases are selected and edited or worked into an article. The selected releases are the lucky ones; most never see the light of day. When you consider that the editor at a daily publication receives upwards of 500 news releases on any given day, gauging the statistical possibility of an individual release being picked up for coverage is easy.

Newspapers don't mean just the regular daily newspapers targeted at the general public. There are special-interest newspapers for business, computers, information technology, telecommunications, and other fields. The specialty papers may run weekly instead of daily, but, like their daily counterparts, they are primarily news-driven rather than feature-driven (which is more the case with magazines). Newspaper editors reject many more releases than they use. The larger the paper's circulation or the more active the area being covered, the more releases the editor has to sort through. Most newspapers have a space budget, which is not to be confused with a financial budget. The space budget consists of the total number of pages printed, divided between advertising and news articles.

Advertisements are the lifeblood of a newspaper; ads consistently provide the largest portion of income. The ads must be accommodated first, after which the issue's remaining space is allocated to specific stories and departments by the key editors. The selection of news releases to cover is based on the editor's personal and professional judgment. The main factor in that judgment can be summed up in a single word: "newsworthiness". Unfortunately, newsworthiness is defined by individual editor's opinions. Newsworthy stories are generally those that offer the most information with the most urgency to the most people.

If a news release issued on particular day is not covered in the following day's paper, this does not mean the news will not appear at all. Releases not considered newsworthy enough to appear in a weekday edition may be suitable for the weekend paper, where there is more room and less emphasis on breaking news. Even if a news item is selected for use, the article may still get pulled at the last minute. Perhaps an advertiser cancelled a large insert just prior to deadline, necessitating a layout change, or a big story emerged late in the day. When this happens, more expendable news is sacrificed. What happens to releases that aren't selected for immediate coverage? Some are kept for future use, but more likely they are sent into the editor's trash can.

Magazines operate very much like newspapers, with departments, editors, space budgets, and advertising, but magazines differ in a few important ways. The potential lifespan of a news release is much longer for a magazine. A monthly publication might not use your news for several months. Depending on the printing and preparation schedule, your release could appear as soon as a week or two after you send the release or as late as six-months later. The nice thing is that whenever your news appears, the information remains in front of the reader for a full month instead of just one day.

The editorial focus and format of a magazine are usually more specialized than those of newspapers. "Focus" refers to the subjects a magazine covers; for instance, Linux Journal focuses on Linux in general while ComputerWorld might focus on Linux in the enterprise. "Format" refers to the way in which a magazine's news and information is presented, usually as a particular mix of regular columns, articles, features (main stories), shorter pieces, and editorials (opinion pieces). Magazine stories don't have to be as "newsy" as newspaper stories. To a greater degree, a magazine researches and creates news rather than relying on current events.

General-interest magazines try to appeal to a large segment of the population. Special-interest magazines target a limited, well-defined community of readers who share a particular interest along with associated activities and concerns. Special-interest magazines are good targets for the Linux community, especially those focusing on Linux, operating systems, storage, security, computers, and information technology. Whether special interest or general interest, the closer your news release relates to the audience of a publication and the greater the impact on that audience, the more likely an editor will choose your news to publish. The key factors are editorial relevance and appeal to the publication's target audience.

In television and radio news shows, news editors, some reporters, and even anchors have input on the news to be aired. In other types of shows, often the producer decides which stories to cover in future broadcasts. Segment producers will produce the individual stories for a broadcast, while assistant producers may perform specialized functions, such as finding interview subjects.

The same considerations of "newsworthiness" discussed for newspapers apply to television broadcast news, with the added element of visuals. There are several types of TV programming you will want to consider. These include educational and informational programs, local and community news programs, and perhaps a business program. Understand the types of shows being produced and aired in your regional area, and then pitch your story for an in-studio interview or a feature.

Radio time for news stories is very limited. Usually there is only enough time for headlines and summaries of the day's top stories, but radio still has great opportunities for your organization. Some radio stations offer expanded news coverage and features (this is sometimes called "foreground programming"). Most Linux news has a better chance of getting coverage or an interview in news programming than in regular programming. The best chance of all lies in targeting an all-news station. Approximately 45 minutes of each hour are devoted to news, sports, weather, special reports, and features. (The remaining 15 minutes are for commercials.)

All-news radio stations operate more like a magazine or newspaper, with specific departments and editors, more producers, more reporters, and therefore, more available resources. Stories that interest a significant portion of their listening community or that appeal to deep-pocketed sponsors will be given the most attention. You could pitch a "Linux for business" type of story. Even if your underlying goal is to promote your organization, the story or interview must avoid advertising or commercial overtones of any kind. Nothing kills the news media's credibility faster or turns off listeners more than inappropriate jingoism.

Talk shows, whether on television or radio, are excellent vehicles for covering a wide variety of topics. Talk shows often invite industry experts to be commentators or participants in a panel discussion. In addition, these shows often have phone-in segments, inviting listeners to ask questions or make comments. These characteristics make the talk show an ideal forum for raising your organization's visibility. For these programs, there is usually an assistant producer responsible for lining up interesting guests, as well as a producer who coordinates the overall process. Both email and telephone contact with the assistant producer can prove rewarding. The host, interviewer, or moderator of the show does not usually choose the guests or have final say in who appears. Unless instructed otherwise, contacting the assistant producer or producer is best.

Clearly, editors and producers have to know the interests of their audiences. Often this knowledge comes from the editors' strong identification with their readers, which can develop into an almost paternal attitude. Editors are constantly making decisions about what their readers will and won't see-any editor would correctly say that is their job. Part of this judgment is based on what the editor feels the readers are currently interested in, and part is based on what the editor feels the readers should or will be interested in. An astute editor keeps their sights as much on the future as on the present. Keep in mind that the role of the news media has never been confined to just reporting the news, but also includes analysis and interpretation.

Analysis and interpretation are considered the domain of "experts," which presents a perfect opportunity for specialists in your organization to share their knowledge and bring visibility to your organization. Editors, being journalists, abide by the five Ws tradition of reporting: who, what, where, when, and why (with an unofficial "how"tagging along). Always include clear, engaging answers to the five Ws in all news releases. Also, you can use the five Ws as a guideline for how to most effectively catch the attention of editors. The way in which you present this information is crucial to being accepted by an editor as newsworthy for their audience. You have to "tell a story," make the news interesting and relevant, and choose an appropriate time and place to present the story.

Who: "Who" usually consists of your organization, spokespersons, and authorities quoted in your news releases. Your organization and those speaking as representatives must be presented as professional, authoritative, influential, and with strong credentials for speaking on matters related to your industry. By positioning your organization in this way, you have a much better chance of generating visibility and prestige. The goal is to make your organization a recognized authority in your field. With this distinction, any time you issue a statement, your news will draw the attention of editors whose readers are interested in the specific work you do. All things being equal, the more influential your spokesperson, the better the chance your news has of being selected.

What: The "what" is the subject of your release-a new application, a new appointment, or any interesting event you choose to announce. Naturally, unusual or exciting announcements have a better chance of being covered. Anything you can do to make your story stand out from the ordinary will be viewed as a refreshing change and will increase the chance of your story being published. If the "what" in your story is a personnel appointment (either paid or volunteer), look for some human interest in either the person or the job at hand. If this person is a well-known Linux expert or a pillar of their local community, all the better. The more noteworthy the individual, the more newsworthy the story. If the "what" is an event such as a Linux trade show, that is a plus. Editors regard events as more urgent and newsworthy than other announcements.

Where: The "where" of your release plays a key role. As you begin to understand public relations, you will appreciate the role of staging events to generate news. Since the media appreciates visuals, try to produce events with images as well as a pertinent story. In planning a pitch or a release, ensure that you clearly indicate the address of every event you hope to have reporters attend. Reporters' time is wasted if they have to call for directions to every event. A special media contact person is a good idea to have at all events. This person can prevent reporters from missing important or visual parts of events. Be aware of upcoming events or activities that you might be able to capitalize on or borrow interest from. Again, the goal is promote the unusual, the unique, the unexpected that will pique the editor's curiosity or sense of humor-and get your story into print.

When: Remember that for most organizations, "when" can be just about any time. There is no need to wait for once-a-year events (like trade shows) to provide news. With creative thinking, you can come up with news stories that capitalize on current events. For example, news about the economy and what proprietary operating systems cost organizations to run can provide a background for Linux news. New computer applications running on Linux also present rich opportunities. "When" is extremely important in terms of releasing the news. For instance, if you are publicizing special events or trade show appearances, you want to allow ample time for an editor to assign a reporter to cover the story (if the news is deemed of interest).

If the editor doesn't have enough time to assign a reporter to cover your event, you can count on no reporters being available. Fortunately, though, while timing is critically important, avoiding bad timing is easy. The first rule is always to provide a reasonable amount of advance notice. For news-breaking media such as radio, television, and some newspapers, two days is an absolute minimum, and a week is more prudent. For magazines and trade journals, one to two weeks is the minimum in most cases, and three to four weeks is even better.

The second rule is to use your common sense and avoid scheduling pitches when you know the editor is on deadline or is involved with other events. Also avoid periods when the editor is working with little or no support staff (such as when reporters are away at an important trade show). Generally, business hours between 9:30 a.m. and 2:00 p.m. is best, since this gives reporters time to write and file their stories. Mondays and Fridays are always more difficult than midweek, but don't be afraid to ask if the editor prefers specific days. If you are requesting reporters attend and cover an event, never ask the editor to confirm their attendance.

The editor will not appreciate the pressure, and besides they cannot guarantee they will have the resources (reporters and camera operators) at the appointed time. News changes by the second. A reporter may be ready to go to your event and, at the last minute, be reassigned to something else. This happens all the time, so don't take the rejection personally. If you show respect for the editor's time, they will appreciate your consideration and may be more likely to cover at least some of your stories.

Why: So far, we have discussed who the news media is interested in, what news is most likely to be covered, and where and when you are going to make your pitch. Now, in looking at the "why" of your organization's story, we will address two questions. First, why did your news item come to pass, and second, why should an editor (and their readers, listeners, or viewers) find your event newsworthy? Unless there is something terribly interesting about the who, what, where, or when, "why" is the single most compelling factor available to an editor in determining newsworthiness. Why is the news important to the audience? Why do they need to know about this? Why is your particular event unusual or out of the ordinary?

Most organization's activities can be analyzed in terms of their cause and/or their effect. The more you can identify causes or effects in your story, the better chance your organization has of receiving coverage. As an example, if there is a trend of Linux being increasingly used in the enterprise, there must be a reason why. Giving the editor just a few of these reasons can make your story more newsworthy than just a simple, bland announcement. Even including some statistics to support your why will likely have a tremendous effect.

The same principle holds true for something as seemingly mundane as a new personnel selection. Why was there a vacancy? Why was this person selected to fill the spot? Adding either or both pieces of information to the release greatly increases the news interest. One of the cardinal rules of media and public relations is: "Never promote features, always promote benefits." A feature is any specific aspect that makes a product or service unique; features belong to products or services. A benefit is an advantage gained by the user in selecting a specific product or service; benefits belong to users. What a product or service does is nowhere near as meaningful as why there is some advantage or benefit to the user.

You don't need to completely ignore describing features, but you do need to present them in the context of their benefits to the end user. The reason for doing this is simple. Readers are potential users, and the better job you do of relating to the user, the more you will attract readers. Readers, as we already know, are the editor's Holy Grail. If your release is about an event, there are numerous "whys" you need to address. Why now? Why is your organization involved or being a sponsor? Why would anyone want to come to the event? Be proactive and open in sharing the causes and anticipated effects of these accomplishments. Don't leave the editor wondering: "So what?" Failing to provide answers to why your activity is news is a sure-fire way of getting your release "filed" in the recycle bin.

How: Cause and effect, and explaining why your news is happening, will very naturally lead to the "how" of your story. How did this come to pass? How are you accomplishing this? How did your organization decide to embark on this new and exciting initiative? How will this change affect people and the marketplace? Describing the hows gives color and interest to your story.

Do's and Don'ts in Media Relations

When pitching your organization's story to news editors, there are fundamental do's and don'ts that you as a public relations professional should follow.

Do's

— Do introduce yourself to different media editors, journalists, and freelancers by sending them an email note or by inviting them out for coffee or lunch. Bring along some background information or a few pages from your website to explain what your organization is all about.

— Do follow up after the meeting with thank-you note, mentioning that you will be in touch as appropriate. This is important to set the stage for future dialogue.

— Do let them know what your goals are and what special events, news, or programs you have coming up.

— Do send out news releases by email about two weeks in advance, when you have a special event planned. Send a follow-up email a few days later. Phone again at a convenient time before the event to suggest a possible meeting or interview at the event. The bigger the event, the more advance notice should be given.

— Do tailor your pitch for the needs of each medium. For example, set up plenty of photo opportunities for television media, human-interest stories for print, and interviews for radio.

— Do give them the name of someone who has a personal experience to tell. Remember that the media loves a good story. Real life stories engage readers and makes for better copy than just statistics relating to Linux and open source.

— Do ensure that you or your designated spokesperson is available for interviews at a moment's notice; otherwise much of your efforts will be in vain. Both of you, of course, should do your homework and rehearse questions and answers in advance. You should have facts, statistics, and anecdotes in your head, ready to use.

Don'ts

— Don't send out a pitch or news release with vague, general statements. Your story has to show not tell, and you must convince the editor to cover the news that promotes your organization rather someone else's. Getting editorial coverage is fiercely competitive.

— Don't ever tell the media what you want from them. Instead, ask them about the kinds of stories they're looking for, or if there are any other reporters in their newsroom who would be interested in Linux and open source. By learning what they want, you can tailor your communications to get what you want.

— Don't underestimate the importance of less prominent media like community newspapers, cable TV, trade journals, and special-interest newsletters. Look at the entire spectrum of news media for different angles.

Media Monitoring and Clipping Services

It is essential to keep abreast of the news being printed or broadcast about your organization, your competition, and the industry as a whole. A comprehensive public and media relations program must track public perception of Linux, stay informed of industry trends, and understand the impact of evolving legislation on your community. If you have time to spare, you can monitor news coverage yourself by typing key words into popular web search engines such as Google and AltaVista. However, this will track only online citations. A more reliable tracking method is to use a media monitor service or a clipping service.

Some major media monitor and clipping services are:

— AirCheck News Taping is a full-service broadcast monitor providing national and local news segments and reports.

— Advance Media Information is database of events for the next 18 months, continually updated by a team of journalists and broadly divided into news and entertainment. Each item is integrated with a press directory, listing essential information, including telephone numbers and email addresses.

- Bacon's is a public relations supplier of media directories, media software, press clippings, Internet clipping, media lists and news release distribution.
- Medialink Worldwide is a television and radio news monitoring and clipping service.
- Burrelle's/Luce Information Services is a premier monitoring service for quick and comprehensive print, broadcast, and Internet information.
- ClipGenius is a clipping service specializing in public relations news and newspaper clips as well as web and press clipping.
- ConfirMedia monitors content broadcast on radio and television.
- CustomScoop is an online agency delivering a daily customized clipping service that draws from online editions of major wires and daily papers, TV and radio stations, smaller daily and weekly newspapers, magazines, trade journals, and new media publications. Free trial available.
- Cutters is a Singapore-based press clipping service with particular emphasis on business and information technology news. Also provides tracking on electronic media.
- CyberAlert offers fully-automated Internet monitoring and clipping of content in web publications, sites, message boards, and news groups.
- E-mmediate Clipping Service offers web delivery of articles from Montana newspapers.
- JA Media Services offers broadcast television and radio monitoring, and news clipping and transcription services
- Media Source is a full-service TV news monitoring and digital video production company, offering local broadcast monitoring for 120 U.S. cities and all major national networks.
- Mediatrack provides international media evaluation, analysis, and measurement, campaign evaluation, competitor analysis, and media research nationally or globally.
- Metro Monitor is a professional broadcast news monitoring and news clipping service monitoring over 300 U.S. stations.

— Multivision, Inc. is a media monitor specializing in hard-to-find coverage and markets along with digital delivery of broadcast clips.

— News Index Delivered monitors hundreds of daily news sources, and provides keyword search-based email clippings daily.

— News Power Online provides comprehensive solutions to your information needs.

— NewsNow Digital Intelligence tracks news about your company, searching over 3500 sites every few minutes for relevant stories.

— New Media Intelligence provides research services including monitoring of newsgroups, media sites and other publicly accessible online content.

— PLCom News Services offers customized media monitoring and analysis, automated news feeds, and newspaper and TV news abstracts delivered on the web with encryption security.

— Postech is a design engineering and manufacturing firm specializing in broadcasting, data acquisition, and telecommunications industries.

— Quickscan is a software company that provides database software and technical support to professional news monitoring companies.

— SDS Media scans all U.K. newspapers and trade magazines to daily extract and deliver relevant articles to hundreds of clients.

— Smart Brief provides free, email based news summaries and other content for industry associations, professional organizations, advocacy groups, and their constituents.

— Video Monitoring Services is a broadcast information retrieval service

— Videowatch monitors news and news magazine broadcasts, maintains a 60-day archive, and sends broadcasts to you on videotape.

How to Maximize Media Coverage

Following points helps us to maximise the media coverage

1. *Have a strategy*: Tailor your strategy for each public relations opportunity. Think about the audience you want to reach and how to create excitement. An effective part of your strategy should be to enforce your organization's core messages in all news releases.

2. *Have a good story*: A news story must have a compelling beginning, middle, and end. Journalists recognize a strong story within seconds, so tell your story quickly and succinctly.
3. *Know your audience*: You wouldn't follow up on a potential business opportunity without knowing something about their business, so don't call the news media blindly. Before you pitch to any media outlet, study their work. Read the publication, watch the show, and listen to the radio broadcast. Get familiar with the characteristics of the media outlet you are targeting. Find out about their main audience and their likes and dislikes.
4. *Invest in relationships*: The more you know about the media organization and your target editor, the better and more confidently you can pitch to them. Building relationships now means editors will be more likely to take your call when you've got an important story to tell. Best of all, even if they can't offer you coverage on this particular story, they may refer you to another reporter who can. As with any relationship, building trust is critical. Keep your promises, and be on time. Be upfront about what you can and can't do. You might not be able to do everything, but reporters will appreciate your honesty.
5. *Think before you speak*: A word of caution: everything you say to a reporter is on the record, regardless of disclaimers. You are representing your organization at all times. The impression that you give has a definite impact on how the media views your organization.
6. *Monitor your media coverage*: Media coverage shows your success. As a media relations expert, the end goal is always positive media coverage for your organization. When your organization is spotlighted in major media outlets, you bring attention and respect to your business.
7. *Look for a unique angle*: Look for personal stories that can spur news media interest. For instance, if a local school board is considering Linux to save money, focus your story on the human interest angle. Unusual stories and angles that affect a media's audience are more likely to get media coverage than mundane ones.
8. *Know your story inside and out*: Research your story carefully. This allows you to revise your pitch if the editor has specific needs. You also must be able to answer any questions that the editor may have.

9. *Be persistent*: There is a fine line between being persistent and annoying, but if you have a good story and know your audience, it is fine to make contact attempts until you get feedback from a reporter.
10. *Follow up*: Many potential leads are lost because public relations people fail to follow through. If a reporter tells you to call back another time, make sure you do! Also, if a reporter doesn't answer your email immediately, do not assume they are not interested. They might not have had time to respond to the large volume of emails they receive.
11. *Be creative*: Infusing your media relations plans with innovative thinking produces stronger, more effective results, so avoid recycling the same old news releases and fact sheets.
12. *Find information*: Do you sometimes feel like you just can't write the news release? This blockage often indicates you don't have enough information. Do outside research. Interview an industry analyst. Get another perspective. This investigation can lead to the information for a great story.
13. *Study and adopt good writing skills*: Use a journalistic approach. Look carefully at how reputable publications like The New York Times or The Wall Street Journal structure a story. What is the lead? What kind of quotes do they use? Study different types of stories. Features, appointment announcements, news articles, and opinion pieces can all be useful in your public relations campaign. Often, you will see the most important information is in the lead and that the rest of the story follows. This inverted pyramid style is usually the best way to organize an article.
14. *Eliminate jargon and techno-speak*: Buzzwords are like bees-they can be highly irritating. Write with clear language, and avoid clichÃ©s, which are another sign of weak writing.
15. *Expect results*: Media coverage means increased visibility, which exposes your organization to more prospective customers. The more people you can reach, the better the impact will be on your organization.

Finally, the success of your media relations efforts means success for you in the dynamic, engaging, challenging, and creative business of public relations.

References

Carroll Bateman J. "The Path to Professionalism" , *Public Relations Journal*, Vol. 13, pp. 6- 8, 19. 1957.

Cutlip, S. M., Center, A. H., & Broom, G. H. *Effective public relations* (8th ed.) Upper Saddle River, NJ: Prentice Hall. 2000.

Dennis L. Wilcox, Phillip H. Ault and Warren K. Agee. *Public Relations Strategies and Tactics.* New York: Harper & Row.1986.

Heath, R. (Ed.). *Encyclopaedia of public relations***.** Thousand Oaks, CA: Sage Publications.2005.

Schramm, W. *Men, messages and media: A look at human communication.* New York: Harper & Row. 1995.

Toth E. & Heath R. (Eds.), *Rhetorical and critical approaches to public relations* (pp. 17-36). New Jersey: Lawrence Erlbaum. 1992.

5

Developing a Public Relations Plan

Public relations is an organized, ongoing effort to develop and maintain goodwill and support among your current and potential membership and the various segments of the community in which your club operates. The role of public relations, as it relates to your club is to convey a positive image to those persons within and outside your organization. News communicated about your club, its services, activities, and members can effectively capture the attention of potential new members of the graphic arts industry and your club. It also can reinforce positive opinions about your organization.

One of the advantages of developing a communications plan is that it allows you to assess your situation, establish your objectives and maintain greater control over your communications program and, in turn, the image you project for your litho club. In addition, by outlining the various activities you may want to pursue, you will be able to set priorities for those which can be supported within your budget constraints. This will help eliminate some of the "as you go" style of spending which can prematurely deplete the club finances.

Planning is good for public relations people, and it can contribute to the success of public relations activities. But, it takes time and effort. It can be tedious, and it's neither glamorous nor exciting. It lacks the appeal and the challenge of media relations or crisis communication and, for most practitioners, falls short of providing the satisfaction and sense of accomplishment that completing a publication or a special event does. It's generally viewed as one of those things that should be done rather than something people want to do. It's like eating broccoli instead of a hot fudge sundae.But, all public relations planning is not the same. It's as diverse as spinach, corn, and squash. Some public relations planning is like radishes. It requires very little preparation and is easy to take advantage of if you simply notice it. Other approaches to planning are more like spaghetti squash. They require much more time and effort to prepare. And some planning methods are like brussel sprouts. They're easily overdone and often become unpalatable.

Importance of a PR Plan

Planning is good for public relations people, and it can contribute to the success of public relations activities. But, it takes time and effort. It can be tedious, and it's neither glamorous nor exciting. It lacks the appeal and the challenge of media relations or crisis communication and, for most practitioners, falls short of providing the satisfaction and sense of accomplishment that completing a publication or a special event does. It is generally viewed as one of those things that should be done rather than something people want to do. It is like eating broccoli instead of a hot fudge sundae. But, all public relations planning is not the same. It's as diverse as spinach, corn, and squash. Some public relations planning is like radishes. It requires very little preparation and is easy to take advantage of if you simply notice it. In simplest terms planning is figuring out the best way to accomplish whatever you want to do or to get wherever you want to be. The basic concept is clear, simple, and straight-forward. But, over time planning has become a speciality field in its own right and has developed its own special jargon.

Traditional planners set goals, identify objectives, and define action steps to reach their goals and objectives. Contemporary planners have added buzz words like strategic, visioning, and organisational advancement to the planning lexicon. They shift into an "organisational advancement mode" to draft "strategic planning documents that enunciate organisational visions."

Public relations planning is simply identifying with whom you want to have a relationship, what you want from that relationship, and what you can do to achieve it. It seems rudimentary, but it's surprising how often such basic forethought is overlooked. Consider, for example, the Midwestern adult literacy program that printed a text-filled booklet to try to convince illiterate adults to sign up for reading lessons.

A public relations plan helps maintain self-discipline as well as being an excellent informational tool. This is especially true for public relations practitioners who have recently changed jobs or taken on new clients. Planning forces them to ask questions and review their underlying assumptions. Each successive step in the planning process sharpens their focus on how the organisation operates and where it's going, as well as clarifying public relations' role in that operation.

Despite its current overuse, the term "strategic" still has important meaning for planning, especially when it's used in the traditional sense to distinguish strategic planning from tactical planning. Strategic planning defines an overall framework, focus, and goals for a long-term or indefinitely on-going process or operation. Tactical planning is an outgrowth of strategic planning that often focuses on a specific time period, e.g., a five year plan, an annual plan, or a monthly plan, rather than the entire life of the organisation.

The best public relations practitioners are equally comfortable doing both types of planning. They work together. Think of an organisation's strategic plan as its global view of the world and its tactical plan as its local street map. The tactical plan converts the broad brush strokes and goals of the strategic plan into a series of objectives which are practical, do-able tasks involving specific campaigns, audiences, programs, or activities. Each of these tactical objective—or project—can be completed independently of the others, but they are ultimately intended to move the organisation toward its long-range goals.

At its most basic level public relations planning can be compared to the rudimentary technique Professor Harold Lasswell developed for analysing and modelling mass communication. His oft-quoted approach to studying communication boiled down to four simple questions:

i) Who says what?

ii) In which channel?

iii) To whom?

iv) With what effect?

Translating this basic approach to public relations, the critical questions become:

i) What is to be communicated?

ii) In what way?

iii) To which audience?

iv) For what purpose?

Public relations people who can't clearly and concisely answer these questions before starting a project shouldn't start it. They obviously have little idea of what they're doing or why they're trying to do it.

On the other hand, public relations people who can answer these questions can be said to have done at least rudimentary planning. Whether they did the planning piecemeal and on the fly or all at once in scheduled planning meetings is irrelevant. And, whether it was done in writing or only in the mind of the practitioner is also irrelevant. What is relevant is that the planning was done and that the practitioners who did it now have a clear idea of what they want to accomplish and how they're going to go about doing it. These observations aren't meant to denigrate formal, pencil and paper (or computer-aided) planning. There are times when such a level of planning is invaluable and absolutely necessary. But, there are also times when high level, detailed planning is not necessary or when it would be overkill. At the same time, entry level public relations practitioners need to realise that the people with whom, and for whom, they work may not always view things this way. They may not be satisfied with assurances that you have a plan in mind; they may want to see it on paper. To maintain good working relationships with them, you may have to produce a hard-copy plan even if this means doing extra, and what seems to be needless, work. Just remember, your supervisor or client may be as concerned with verifying your productivity and assuring your accountability as they are with reviewing your plan.

Development of PR Plan

Public relations plans range from single-sentence, common sense aphorisms to hundred-page, hard-bound documents, and the time practitioners devote to planning ranges from nil to nearly full-time. In a similar way, the importance they attach to planning ranges from insignificant to life-saving. There are almost as many approaches to PR planning as there are practitioners.

Mission Statement and Goals

The best starting point for public relations planning is to review the organization's mission statement and goals. These documents summarize what the organization is and what it's trying to accomplish, and they should provide the focus for every decision the organization — or any sub-unit within it — makes and every action it takes. This should be especially true of public relations efforts. Consequently, many public relations plans start with a copy of the organization's mission and goals.

The next element these plans include is a mission statement for the public relations unit which spells out what that unit does and how it assists and supports the organization in carrying out its mission. The linked page, Planning starts with mission statements. includes an example of an organizational mission statement and that organization's public relations mission statement which shows how the latter parallels and supports the former.

Target Audiences

Target Audiences can be the next focal point for planning. Beyond this point different planners structure their plans in various ways to reflect their views of what public relations is and what it does.

— Some put primary emphasis on policy research and issues management.

— Others put their emphasis on activities like publications, special events, speech writing, and media relations.

— And, those who see relationship-building as the essence of public relations often build their strategic plans around their organization's most important publics and target audiences.

The latter approach is what's used throughout the rest of this reading and the linked pages that help explain it. The approach outlined here is a fifteen-step comprehensive planning process that combines both strategic and tactical public relations planning. The first ten steps develop a strategic plan and can be used without completing the last five steps. Those last five steps, however, build upon the initial strategic plan and can be used to produce much more detailed tactical plans.

Keep in mind, however, that this is only one of dozens of different but equally valid ways of doing public relations planning. Relatively speaking, it's a moderately complex approach to planning. It's detailed enough to encompass the main elements needed to execute a successful public relations program, but short enough to avoid redundancy and not get bogged down in unnecessary and confusing minutia.

It's similar in scope to the PRSA Planning Grids recommended by the PRSA Accreditation Board and by Guth and Marsh in their textbook, Public Relations: A Values-Driven Approach. With three grids, each of which includes four columns, the PRSA Planning Grid is essentially a 12-step approach. By being just a little bit more specific and not leaving so many things to be assumed, the 15-step method presented here may be a little easier and a little less confusing for first-time planners to use.

Those with more planning experience may prefer a more abbreviated process. For the sake of comparison, note that other popular planning methods range from as few as seven or eight steps to very detailed approaches which have 25 to 30 steps. Also realize that this approach can be handled in several different ways and can use a variety of different formats for the written plan that is produced.

Take ten steps for a strategic public relations plan.

— Audience and goal identification

1. Who are the organization's key target audiences?
2. Why is this audience important to the organization?
3. What view does the organization want this audience to have of it?

— Reporting research findings

4. What is this audience's current view of the organization?
5. What issues and appeals are important to this audience?
6. Which media does this audience use and trust the most?

— Assessment and plan development

7. How does this audience's current view of the organization differ from the desired one?

   This is determined by comparing responses to items 3 and 4 above.

8. What message themes will have the greatest impact on this audience?

   These should reflect the findings from question 5 above.

9. What are the best ways of reaching this audience?

   These should be selected in light of the findings from question 6 above.

10. Who will serve as the organization's primary contact for working with this audience?

Take five more steps for a tactical plan.

— Selecting and setting objectives

11. What short-term objectives will lead to the goals of the strategic plan?

    Actions needed to reach these objectives

    Answer questions 12-15 for each objective identified in 11 above.

12. What specific actions or messages will lead to achieving this objective?

13. What resources will be needed for these tasks?

    Identify specific people, equipment, and funds needed for each item in question 12 above.

14. When should it be done?

— Specify a timetable for accomplishing each item listed in 12 above.

15. How will success in achieving each objective be evaluated?

Public Relations Plans are Rarely Finished

Having gone through this entire process and having answered all the questions, a first-time planner may be sorely tempted to consider the planning over and sit back to admire the plan and wait for accolades about it. Veteran planners and experienced public relations professionals know better. Even though a planning cycle has been completed and a document prepared, no plan is ever final and the planning isn't truly finished until all the goals are reached or acknowledged to be impossible.

Until then, a plan is a guide or a working paper, a suggestion of things to try to achieve specified objectives and a draft document that should be constantly changed and modified to fit the evolving conditions. The portion of the plan which identifies critical audiences and desired relationships may remain unchanged for years, but the rest of the plan shouldn't. It should be constantly evolving. On the tactical level, objectives will be met and new ones will emerge. The latter are added to the plan, and the former removed. Objectives which remain unmet despite the best possible execution of the plans laid to achieve them require re-evaluation and another round of planning to keep them viable.

For fast-moving, high tech organizations, plans need to be checked and revised on an almost weekly basis. For others, quarterly is often enough. And, for still others, an annual review is almost too often. The speed with which the organization and its operating environment change is a better gauge of how frequently its plans should be updated than a calendar. The critical thing is that the plans change often enough and sufficiently enough to adequately reflect the changes in the conditions they're trying to describe. If you have to blow the dust off a public relations plan to use it, the odds are it won't be worth using.

Strategic Planning o

Goal Identification

The first questions that need to be addressed—e.g. With whom does the organization need to have relationships? and What does it want these people to think about the organization?—can be answered after a little introspection and discussion with top management. Keep in mind that these are ultimately top management's decisions, not the public relations practitioners'.

The public relations people should speak out and try to influence who is included and who is excluded from this list, but they rarely make the final decision. Probably the most effective way of dealing with these first four questions is for the public relations staff to develop a preliminary list of target audiences and relationships and then meet with key managers to review and discuss them.

1 *Who are the organization's key target audiences?* Depending upon the nature of the audiences, these listings may be as short and simple as the names of key people, organizations, and communities or as long and complex as psychodemographic profiles of prospective buyers of a particular product. For most organizations the list will include a mix of short and long identifications. That's fine. Consistency isn't the goal; useful information is. Long audience identifications, if they include unique characteristics, appeals that are particularly effective with this audience, or the best ways of reaching the audience, can be very useful.

2. *Why is this audience important to the organization?* No matter how obvious it seems, each audience should be evaluated in terms of its relevance and importance to the organization. Data about the audience's abstract or general importance—e.g., how big it is, how politically influential it is, or how rich its members are—is not enough and can, in fact, be very

misleading. The critical information needed is how and why this audience affects the organization. What does it, or could it do, to help, or to hinder, the organization in reaching its goals?

Padding an audience list with people or organizations who have little or no direct bearing on the organization is a waste of time. It serves little purnpose, no matter how prestigious these audiences may be. It might even interfere with or delay meaningful planning. Be aware, however, that there is a tendency among some public relations people to become enchanted by various elite media and to make them a regular part of their media relations audience simply because of their prestige.

— Media relations specialists all over the world, for instance, dream of getting coverage in The New York Times, not because their constituents read or would be influenced by The New York Times but simply because it is The Times and reaching it is a pinnacle of journalistic success.

— Similarly, lots of promotions people for local festivals and special events spend hundreds of dollars and countless hours of time trying to get Willard Scott to mention their event on The Today Show on the morning it takes place.

A few years ago a southeastern city's special events coordinator, speaking to a public relations class, admitted that getting mentioned on The Today Show had been his number one media relations goal for two years before he finally succeeded. And, it remains one of his primary objectives today. He beams with pride each time he recalls Willard Scott mentioning his event on The Today Show even though he admits it didn't have any effect at all on attendance. "After all," he said, "how could it? — Over 99 percent of the people who watched The Today Show that morning lived too far away to even think of attending the event."

3. *What view does the organization want this audience to have of it?* Or, what kind of relationship does the organization want to have with this audience? Both of these questions boil down to essentially the same thing, a reflection of what the organization hopes to accomplish by interacting with this audience. It may be having them purchase products or services, or voting for specific political candidates, or supporting new legislation, or any number of other things, depending upon the organization and the audience.

The more clearly and concretely this view is expressed, the more helpful it will be for future planning and relationship building. Statements like "We want this audience to think of us as an asset to the community." are practically worthless for planning purposes.

Findings of Research Report

Once the target audiences and desired relationships have been nailed down, the next step is to explore the existing relationship the organization has with each of those audiences and to decide whether it needs any adjustment. This calls for more than internal discussion. Simply letting the public relations staff and/or organizational managers speculate will never yield reliable information.

You need to check with people who actually know—actual members of the target audiences. Carefully conducted research, whether it's done by the public relations staff or by hired research consultants, is the only way to get vital and meaningful information about the audiences you need to reach. It's critical to successful planning that such research be done, and that its findings then be incorporated into the plan as it's being developed.

4. *What is this audience's current view of our organization?* Or, what is the organization's current relationship with this audience? The exact phrasing should correspond to question 3 so the answers can be juxtaposed, showing where the relationship is now compared to where the organization wants it to be. This is not something to be guessed at. This question, more than any other part of the strategic planning process, requires accurate, non-ambiguous answers. Virtually all the rest of the planning process, including the setting of specific objectives and the measurement of success, is based on the information gathered at this step.

5. *What issues and appeals are important to this audience?*

6. *Which media does this audience use and trust the most?*

Some bare-bones planners consider these to be extraneous questions, and at one level they may be. They are not absolutely essential for properly assessing the organization's current relationships or for determining what can be done to improve them, but the information they provide can be extremely helpful later, during tactical planning and while carrying out a public relations campaign.

Answering these two questions helps ensure that only the most effective and efficient media for reaching the target audiences are used and that the messages the organization sends via these channels will include the best possible themes and concepts for garnering a response from the audience.

If these questions are included in the planning process, they should be asked in the broadest possible ways. Responses about preferred media or channels of communication should not be limited to the major mass media, but should also take narrower and more selective communication techniques — everything from interpersonal conversations to public speeches to telephone calls to direct mail to the Internet — into account. And the list of important or appealing issues should not be restricted only to issues which are directly related to the organization and its mission.

Plan Development

This third stage of the planning process integrates the first two stages with a series of questions that build upon and further explore the responses to the earlier questions.

7. *How does this audience's current view of the organization differ from the desired one?* Or, how does the organization's current relationship with this audience compare with what the organization wants it to be? Arriving at this answer obviously calls for comparing what the organization's managers said about the desired relationship (question 3) with the audience's responses to question 4. This comparison lets the organization know which of its relationships are moving along on track and which are most in need of adjustment. A frequent outcome of this planning step is a prioritized list of relationships which need immediate attention.

8. *What message themes will have the greatest impact on this audience?* In some instances, especially when an organization is closely tied to an issue that has a strong emotional context for its audiences, the responses to this question end up being identical to the responses to question 5. In other cases, when the issues audiences feel strongly about have no connection with the organization, there may be little correlation. However, something that has become increasingly common in recent years as organizations seek more and more ways to establish additional linkages to their constituents is that the perceived strength of an audience's feeling about a particular topic will "inspire" the organization to take a similar public stance on that issue even though it has no direct bearing on the organization and would otherwise have gone unnoticed by its management.

9. *What are the best ways of reaching this audience?*

There are some instances in which responses to this item are nearly identical to the media preferences identified for the audience in question 6. At other times, the audience's stated preferences may not be suitable or affordable for the organization to use. The means of reaching the audience which are identified here need to be appropriate, available, and affordable. In many instances, it may be most effective to list several different means of communicating with each audience, specifying which means and medium is most appropriate for various types of situations.

10. *Who will serve as the organization's primary contact for working with this audience?*

Even though public relations is concerned with all of an organization's relationships, the public relations practitioners themselves are not always the most appropriate "point persons" for working with every audience.

- Some prestigious, high-profile audiences — political figures, major business executives, etc.— may not be satisfied dealing with public relations staff members. They may expect and warrant the personal attention of the CEO or the chairman of the board.
- Other audiences may be so engrossed with technical issues that they need to dealt with by subject matter specialists and technical experts.
- Still others may not care who they deal with, just so someone from the organization pays attention to them.

Consequently, primary audience contacts can include a mix of public relations people, management executives, technical specialists, and others, all of whom are chosen for their rapport with a particular audience rather than their job titles.

Project Planning

Although some people try to do tactical or project planning without first having a strategic plan, it's rarely successful. It's far more common to view tactical planning as an extension of strategic planning. Thus, the steps discussed here are numbered as a continuation of the strategic planning process and frequently refer back to previous steps.

Objectives of Selecting and Setting

Tactical public relations objectives are developed by analyzing the organization's strategic plan, particularly responses to question 7 which reveal how each audiences' current view of the organization differs from what the organization would like it to be. In addition to identifying which relationships are most in need of attention, this analysis allows the organization to identify common threads among its various relationships and its audiences' perceptions of it:

— What do people think it does well?

— What do they think it does poorly?

— What do they like about it?

— What do they dislike about it?

— What would they like to have changed?

These findings then become the basis for developing a prioritized list of objectives—specific, short-term goals—which often include or are linked to a project, publication, special event, or other task whose achievement can be readily measured. The assumption and intent is that successfully completing these objectives will, over time, ultimately lead to the realization of the organization's long-term goals.

11. *What short-term objectives will lead to the goals of the strategic plan?*

There are any number of potentially useful ways public relations objectives can be identified, organized, and prioritized. Two of the most common are described below. Project-oriented objectives focus on specific work products (e.g., news releases, publications, etc.) or tasks (e.g., holding an open house, testifying before a legislative sub-committee, etc.) that end up on a giant "to do list" of projects that will enhance the organization's public relations. These can be either new initiatives or a continuation of current activities.

Usually the first consideration in trying to prioritize such a list is predicting how many people will be affected. The more people it will impact, the higher its priority is likely to be, although some consideration is also given to cost, ease of completion, and precedent. If it's relative cheap, easy to do, and is something the organization has been doing for a long time—e.g., publishing a monthly employee newsletter—continuing to do it may rise to the top of priority list regardless of how many people are actually affected by it.

Relationship-oriented objectives focus on the organization's various publics and the quality of its relationships with each of them. Recognizing that the ideal of having a perfect relationship with each and every public is rarely attained and that it's almost impossible to devote equal time and attention to every separate audience, this approach tries to list the organization's relationships in the order in which they should be given attention.

The priority given to any particular relationship is based on a combination of that public's importance to the organization and an assessment of how far from ideal its current relationship with the organization is. The more important the public is and the further from ideal its relationship is, the higher its priority becomes.

Generally speaking, performance or production oriented planners, especially public relations practitioners who are using a first or second phase approach to public relations, are likely to prefer the first approach and to emphasize task-oriented planning. Third-phase public relations practitioners and relationship-builders are more likely to use the second approach.

Regardless of which approach is used, the end result of this step in tactical planning is a list of objectives the organization will attempt to achieve. However, given the wide variety of tasks/relationships that may be included in this list and the differing degrees of complexity that they're likely to have, a grid format is no longer suited to reporting the plan. From this point on, it may be far more effective to use a page by page planning format in which each objective is placed on a separate page and questions 12-15 are answered in whatever length and detail is required without worrying about the fact that the plans for meeting some objectives will be longer than others.

Reach Objectives

12. *What specific actions or messages will lead to achieving this objective?*

This is a deceptively short and simple question that really requires multiple answers and may involve far more members of the organization than the public relations staff if the actions that appear to be needed involve more than communication activities, require large expenditures of time and/or money, or if they will require any changes in established policies and procedures.

Planning the communication aspects alone can be an enormous task requiring that media choices andformats be specified down to the level of identifying a spokesperson, selecting styles, tones, themes, and linked appeals, as well as message content. And, each of these decisions needs to take into account all available information about the audience's media preferences special interests, and issues or appeals that are of particular concern to them as shown in their responses to questions 5 and 6 in the strategic planning process.

13. *What resources will be needed for these tasks?*

This is another deceptively simple question that may take a lot of time and effort to fully answer. However, honest and realistic estimates of thepersonnel, time, equipment, and money required to achieve each objective let planners compare the expected effort and expense of completing the project with the likely outcome, a rudimentary cost-benefit analysis. It also helps with scheduling and work assignments when/if the project is actually undertaken. For both reasons it's important to estimate the necessary resources as accurately as possible.

Resource estimates need to include routine staff time and effort plus everyday office expenses such as postage and copying in addition to obvious and extraordinary expenses such as hiring freelancers, purchasing materials or outside services, or renting special equipment.

When appropriate, estimates should be reported on both a per instance basis and as a total cost over the life of the plan. A weekly employee newsletter, for instance, that appears to be a bargain when described as costing $800 for printing and 75 hours of staff time per issue may look very different when it's described as costing $41,600 and 3900 person-hours, almost the entire time of two full-time employees, per year.

14. *When should it be done?*

In some instances, this answer is a specific day, date, or time or perhaps a recurring, periodic response, e.g., once a year, once a month, or each pay day. In other cases, the answer may outline a contingency that may, or may not ever, occur, e.g., when the company's stock price drops below 15 times earnings or if a high level executive is indicted.

15. *How will success in achieving each objective be evaluated?*

In selecting or setting up evaluation mechanisms, public relations people need to keep a sharp eye on what it is they really need/want to measure so they're don't inadvertently end up measuring something easy to measure but irrelevant. Not everything measurable is meaningful in all contexts.

— The number of people who attend an open house, for instance, is easy to count but, in and of itself, doesn't indicate how these people feel about the organization or if their tour of its facilities changed their opinions in any way. To find out the latter, you may have to ask them. That's much more difficult than doing a headcount, but it's also much more likely to provide meaningful information.

— Similarly, some media relations people measure their success by the number or percentage of their news releases that are used by the media or by the number of inches or minutes of coverage their stories receive. Still others have a complex formula that assigns a dollar value to their each story that's run based on audience size and amount of coverage.

  While these measures may gauge the amount of media coverage an organization receives, and perhaps its success in placing stories in the media, they don't necessarily measure the organization's success in building relationships with its key audiences because they don't show how much or what kind of impact this media coverage has on the people who see it. They often don't even indicate whether the people who see the coverage are the people the organization really needs to reach.

Keep in mind that the ultimate goal of public relations is helping an organization maximize the benefits of its relationships with all its various publics. It's goal is not necessarily getting news coverage or publishing employee publications or having a large turn out for an open house or ... You get the idea. Whatever evaluation methods are used must focus on how well the organization's relationships are being handled, not how quickly or how well a to do list is completed.

Formats Planning

A public relations plan is meant to do more than look nice sitting on a desk or bookshelf. It's meant to be a working document that gets used and consulted as a day to day reference. How helpful it is and how easy it is to use are far more important than how it looks or how well it conforms to a preconceived layout. Some planners prefer to organize their information in a grid of rows and columns where each row represents an audience and each column is a different category of information related to that audience.

Other planners prefer to organize their work in terms of pages (separate sheets of paper, different displays in an electronic spreadsheet, or discrete records in a data-base file). For them, each page, or series of pages, represents a different audience and is used to organize all information related to that audience.

Grid planners say their approach does a better job of representing "the big picture" by physically showing the interrelationship of all audiences and audience characteristics at one time. Grid plans also look impressive hanging on a wall or being used in a presentation. On the negative side, grid plans can be a pain to prepare, update, and reproduce. If all that's needed is a single copy, a large wall chart may not be a problem. But, for a large work team or an organization that wants to circulate copies of its plan to all managers, reproducing a grid plan can be difficult and costly unless the grid is somehow broken down and reproduced in small sections.

The other disadvantage is that the sizes of the cells are interrelated; increasing the size of any one cell automatically increases the size of every other cell in the same row or column. For example one unusually long description of one audience will make the description cell for every audience the same size, even though much of the space in those other cells will be unused. This can waste a lot of space or pressure the planner to inappropriately shorten the long entries. The latter may look better and save paper, but it may also eliminate what would otherwise have been useful information.

Page planners counter those criticisms by saying their approach allows them to use as much room as they need for the information they have, even adding extra pages if necessary. They also claim their approach allows information to be more easily evaluated and edited on the merits of its importance rather than arbitrary space constraints or concerns that a cell looks too empty. And, the plan can be easily updated by adding, deleting, or revising pages as necessary.

On the other hand, plans organized in a page by page fashion appear much less impressive during a presentations than a large, elaborate grid. The use of separate pages for each audience may also tend to overemphasize differences among audiences rather than highlighting their similarities and the common approaches that can be used to reach them.

Combined Formats

Combined Formats may be Most Effective. By the time practitioners have developed three or four complete plans they have a pretty good sense of what works best for them and may have their own ideas of what questions to ask and which formats to use. That's as it should be. However, beginning public relations planners may find it helpful to combine grid planning for their overall strategic plans with page planning for each objective they identify in their tactical plans the first few times they do planning.

Strategic plans which provide a broad overview of what an organization is trying to accomplish often work well in grid format. This is largely because the same types of information are needed about each of the organization's publics, and the amount of information that's needed about each is also very similar and usually in a short capsule form that will fit into the cells of a grid.

On the other hand, tactical planning which addresses specific projects and tasks is much more varied and inconsistent. Some projects simply require more explanation and more planning than others. Consequently, it's more difficult and confusing to employ a grid in tactical planning. With different projects needing different numbers and types of cells (rows and columns) to adequately explain them, a standardized form becomes impractical.

Planning an executive's appearance on a television talk show, for instance, might be done in five or six cells outlining the necessary information and steps leading to its completion while plans for publishing an annual report might require 20 or more cells. Thus, starting a new page for each objective and not being overly concerned about consistency in their content or appearance makes much more sense than trying to force this information into a single uniform format.

Public Relations Implementation

Publicity and Promotion

Planned activities can be the source of considerable attention by the news media Your community, professionals in the graphic arts industry and others may be very interested in your activities. Promotion of those activities can generate a considerable amount of publicity that will benefit your club and the entire industry.

The following are just a few examples of what can be done to enhance your communication effort:

1. Participate in local community events. Try to participate in a unique and interesting fashion. Often local parades, events or shows need participants who can add color or interest to these events. Be creative.
2. Seek opportunities to address pertinent associations , schools or other community organizations. Before addressing any such group, release a news story announcing the event and your club's participation, if the host organization is not doing so. Send an advance copy of the talk to appropriate editors and/or radio and television broadcasters. Publication deadlines will vary, so be sure to give advance notice appropriate to each publication's specific requirements. Radio and television also need as much advance notice as you can give them, even if they typically deal with fast breaking news.
3. Participate in college and high school career days by setting up an exhibit or a booth. Announce such an event in a news story well in advance and don't forget to issue personal invitations to graphic arts instructors, students and appropriate editors.
4. Don't overlook newsworthy events which may be a regular part of your club's activities, such as:
   a. *News About People:*

      Appointment of new officers

      Retirements

      Participation in community activities

      Club-sponsored scholarship recipients

      Award winners, such as "Member of the Year'

   b. *News About Club Activities*

      Special events/meetings

      Scholarship sponsorship/availability

      Education support, donations, presentations

      Annual National Convention

      Social events

Editors and Newscasters have hundreds of news items competing for their attention and limited time and space to fill. Nevertheless, a legitimate local or industry news story can catch their attention. The following guidelines, along with the sample news release section in this manual, will help you in your efforts.

Publicity Guidelines

1. Use samples to guide your writing.

In the samples provided in this manual, you will notice:

The source (you) is clearly identified in the upper-left hand comer and includes a name and phone number of a person to contact for further information. Use club letterhead if you have it.

The stories are brief. They tell who, what, where, when, why and how. They tell it quickly, but with sufficient detail to satisfy reader interest.

Language is plain, everyday English. Avoid using industry terms which may not be commonly known. Even when submitting information to the trade publications, you should not become overly technical in your language.

The most important information should always be at the beginning of the story — this is known as the "lead."

Stories should be typed and double-spaced on one side of 8-1/2" x 11" paper. Use club stationery for the top page, if it's available.

Include black and white glossy photos when appropriate. Avoid the "grip and grin" handshake poses and sedentary group shots. Always try to show some action in photographs. Never write on a photo — front or back! Provide captions on a separate piece of paper, attached with removable tape, which explain the photo subject.

2. Call on local editors and media people

Research indicates that when an editor can connect a face and name with a news release, the chance that it will be used greatly increases. You might want to personally deliver an important news release. Some words of advice:

You might need to request a brief appointment in the case of daily newspaper editors. Early mornings or early afternoons are the best time to call or meet an editor because those times avoid deadline periods. Avoid calling on weekly newspapers the day before the paper goes to press; they'll be too busy to talk to you.

If you have cause to place advertisements with a publication or station, do not presume or suggest in any way that this gives you the right to have your news releases used. That is the surest way to guarantee that nothing you submit will be used.

Be sure to provide copies of stories to all appropriate media outlets.

Observe deadlines! Get "events" stories in the mail as much as two weeks to a month in advance, depending on the publication. Magazines may require as much as two to three months lead time.

If you write a story during or after an event, be sure to deliver it promptly while it is still timely.

References

Center, A., Jackson, P., Smith, S., Stansberry, F. *Public Relations Practices: Managerial Case Studies and Problems.* New Jersey: Pearson Prentice Hall. 2008.

Ewen, Stuart. *PR! A Social History of Spin*. New York: BasicBooks. 1996.

Lockhart, J. *How to Market Your School: A Guide to Marketing, Public Relations, and Communication for School Administrators*. Lincoln, NE: iUniverse, Inc. 2005.

Mayhew, L. *The New Public*. Cambridge: Cambridge University Press.1989.

6

Modern Tactics of Public Relations

"Public relations" is a fairly broad term that can have different meanings depending on the company, objective and situation. A large corporation might see it as a tactic that puts it in a good light with the public at large. A government agency or nonprofit association might see it as a direct voice to residents and members on a variety of different issues. A small business may view it as an opportunity to generate name recognition and free advertising for their products and services. Still others regard it as a response mechanism to unforeseen or unplanned news or crisis.

All of these viewpoints –as well as many others—are correct. Public relations plays an integral role in the operations of businesses and organizations of all sizes. And thanks to the Internet and Web-based services, it's become an even more valuable and versatile tool in getting your business' name in front of prospective customers and landing more of them on your Web site, Facebook page or other online property.

Before the Internet took hold in our daily lives, public relations activities were largely hit-or-miss. A business owner or staffer (or an agency, if the business had the means to afford its services) would come up with a catchy, news angle for a press release, story pitch or media advisory to send to the local media in hopes of getting some coverage. And by "send", we mean faxed or mailed, as this was the preferred method of receiving information before e-mail became standard in newsrooms and magazine production offices. This usually was followed up with a phone call to the recipient.

The topic and its appeal to readers typically determined whether a business would receive coverage. Having established media contacts was important as well. However, despite the strategy and planning in pushing an announcement or information to a media outlet, uncertainty was a given. If successful, a business could expect a few lines in the publication or perhaps even a phone interview with a reporter interested in its proposed topic. But more often than not, that mailed press release or story pitch ended up in the wastebasket instead of on the mind of an editor or reporter.

Regardless, engaging in public relations activities geared toward print publications, radio and television outlets was still important, as these were the primary means by which prospective customers got their information. This all changed when a little technology called the Internet came along and changed the way people found information. Instead of picking up a newspaper, magazine or phone book, they instead went online. This changed the dynamics of not only the dissemination of information on local, national and worldwide levels, it also significantly altered press release distribution tactics.

As the Internet expanded into our personal and professional lives, so did the number of services offered through it. These include press release distribution services, article submission sites and directories, blogs, and other venues that allow users to distribute their information online. Unlike the uncertainty that comes with sending a press release to a member of the media and not knowing if and when it will run, this method almost guarantees that information will be available to interested parties. In some instances, the copy is live and on the Internet instantly; in others, the press release distribution service may have to approve the copy first, which may take a few days.

And it's not just confined to one page of one edition of a publication. Unlike communication vehicles of the past, individuals are now actively searching out information through search engines, in which press releases, articles and blog posts can appear. Additionally, RSS feeds, other Web sites and blogs regularly pick up articles of interest and link to them or repurpose them, resulting in even greater exposure.

This new approach to public relations still relies on the fundamental strategies that have proved successful for decades, such as producing clear, concise and attention-grabbing headlines and copy. Press releases have essentially remained the same in terms of format and look. What's different is the manner and speed with which they're distributed.

In addition to building awareness and exposure, these online publications can also be a valuable component of a business' search engine optimization (SEO). Inserting key terms back-linked to pages on your Web site can not only trigger an action from the reader—such as visiting the site to learn more or purchasing or scheduling a service—it also helps build the SEO power needed to ensure that your Web site and online pages have prominence in online search results.

Today's public relations activities are no longer just a way to garner a short mention in the local daily or to promote an upcoming event. By taking advantage of online services and tactics, you'll discover an affordable (and oftentimes free) and effective way to educate your prospective customer base about your business and, ultimately, increase sales.

Changing Context of PR

Public relations is now a recognised discipline around the world; It is an industry with millions of professionals who generally apply one basic theory of practice; It deals with the way we relate to our different audiences. There is a good way and a bad way to practice public relations; The Global Alliance is there to help with establishing world-wide guidance. Today, just about every private, public or social organisation, more or less consciously, uses public relations strategies, programmes and techniques. These strategies are implemented by developing and deploying communication tools and instruments that are designed to create and manage positive relationships with influential publics. We define influential publics as those believed capable of delaying or accelerating the pursued objectives of an organisation.

It is well documented in textbooks that this practice has been going on for more than a century in Anglo Saxon countries, some fifty years in the European continent and at least thirty years in a large part of the Rest of the World. As Marshall McCluhan's- the great Canadian whose vision of a global village is now a clear reality, and instantaneous -or zero time—communication continues to blanket our globe, we are constantly reminded that we need to adapt quickly to live and communicate in a world increasingly sans frontières (sem fronteiras) Clearly, this means that our outlook on life needs to be multidimensional to accommodate the diversity of races, countries, cultures, languages, that surround us. This becomes even more pertinent when we take into account the multiplicity of social, economic and political "divides" that tend to emphasise the disparities between east and west; north and south; black and white; developed and developing worlds; men and women; children and adults; teenagers and their parents.....so, how do we close the gap between these divides?

One of the solutions is to continue to segment our communication activities so that we have a consistent message that is tailored and more relevant to the segment of the population we are trying to reach. The days of 'one message fits all' are over. Yet too many of us continue to operate in this environment. First let's start with the fundamentals. There is an emerging world theory of public relations that is based on the concept of generic principles and specific applications.

The two-way symmetrical model is largely a model that organisations aspire to use. Just like Corporate social responsibility- CSR- two way symmetrical communication is not yet a reality in most organisations. Yet, as Dr. Grunig showed, it forms the basis of the characteristics of an excellent organisation. That is very much the 'aspirational' model for all professionals to follow. It is much more effective than the traditional 'push' method of communication because it adopts a mode of operation that focuses on listening and dialogue. Within this model of practice, the RACE formula- Research-Analysis-Communication and Evaluation stills forms the basis of our work.

The theory represents the generic aspect. The 'Specific Application' represents the manner in which the RACE formula produces a different set of tactical activities. So in theory two professionals from different countries can be tackling the same problem using the same theoretical framework, but because largely of context, they will choose different solutions.At its simplest form, public relations is a way to approach the way in which an organisation wants to relate to its many stakeholders. It is as much a specific discipline with its own body of knowledge and theories, than it is a management philosophy- particularly if the organisation has adopted the Corporate Social responsibility model of operation. But even if the organisation has not adopted CSR as a model, every time an organisation makes a decision, there are four broad sets of implications that require serious consideration.

Paul Holmes who writes an European PR newsletter describes it this way: operational implications; financial implications; legal implications; and relationship or reputational implications. In most organisations, the first three sets of implications are considered routinely and formally at the highest level-there are senior executives whose responsibility it is to make sure those implications are clearly understood and fully incorporated into the decisionmaking process. Reputational implications, however, are often relegated to an afterthought. Rather than being asked for input when policy is being made, public relations people are too often called in after the fact to "spin" the selected policies, to make ill-considered decisions more palatable to a sceptical public.

Relationship implications should not override operational, financial, or legal concerns, they should be considered in tandem. This makes for a better decision. It is definitely not just an activity that supports a business line or a sub set of other activities that an organisation does. Most successful enterprises or large organisations have understood that to thrive and survive they must pay attention to their relationships with all of their contacts: employees, suppliers, clients, governments, lobby groups, etc. The Global Alliance estimates that in 2003 more than 3 million individuals were involved, in one way or another, in activities which may be defined as public relations, and it is possible to calculate, for that same year, the otherwise constantly growing annual economic impact of the profession is estimated at some 400 billion euro. Interestingly enough only a scant 10% of that 3 million are members of an institute or professional body.

If communication is the act of conveying ideas and information, and trust is such a fundamental issue in our global economy, then ethics is the glue that fosters a higher set of morals and principles by which we live. That is why, the public relations associations that form the Global Alliance have put some much emphasis over the years on ethics which culminated in the adoption of a universal code of ethics for the profession. For years our emphasis on ethics has gone unnoticed, now with Enron, Worldcom, Parmalat and others it gets the attention it deserves.

Here is a definition of Public relations that is close to universal: Public relations is the management, through communication, of perceptions and strategic relationships between an organisation and its internal and external stakeholders, for mutual benefit and a greater social order. Interestingly enough the Germans don't have a word for public relations. They call it : Offentlichkeitsarbeit -OFFEN-TLI-KAYT-SARBET- and the meaning is: working in public, with the public, for the public. As you can see the German definition is much more oriented to the impact on the 'public sphere' and this is a very noble pursuit.

Two concepts of public relations are good public relations and poor public relations. Good public relations is focused on the long range—not on crises. Cumulative effects of public relations is like a savings account at the bank to which you make regular deposits and the interest compounds. It is about building relationships and when a crisis hits. Poor public relations is primarily focused on crisis, lack of a professional public relations programme, questionable ethics and a focus on short term goals. It may look and sound good, but doesn't last. Unfortunately poor public relations examples are all around us and have been around for a long time- 140 years ago, Abraham Lincoln delivered a speech in Bloomington, Illinois declaring "you may fool all the people some of the time; you can even fool some of the people all the time; but you can't fool all the people all of time". If he was referring to public relations- sure there was some good political rhetoric behind this quote, but he might have been thinking about it!

Most politicians at all levels and in all countries are quick to deplore the lack of public confidence or credibility in their own chosen profession. This is the same world-wide. Why have we lost faith in them?: Too much cynical use of short term tactics and too little professional public relations. They might win the battles with, evasive manoeuvres, deflection or Teflon answers, and propaganda—style campaigns. But they rarely win the war for public opinion.

Politicians are not alone suffering from a lack of trust. A 1996 extensive public survey on honesty in the workplace "Shades of Grey" conducted in the United States for PRSA found that:

— 61 % say that politicians make false promises (up 9% since 88)

— 51 % believe auto mechanics misinform or overcharge clients (up 16% since 88)

— 35% believe lawyers misinform or overcharge (up 18% since 88)

You might be asking yourself if other nations would do better in such a survey. Well, the CPRS in Canada commissioned an identical survey in 1997. The results of this survey of Canadians found that Canadians are only marginally more honest than our cousins to the south. The bottom line for public relations is that communicating credibility is tough and getting tougher. The public will discount what is said in any venue, by almost any medium by a considerable amount -- 30 to 50% of the message will be immediately discounted depending on the source and the context.

For example, the Shades of Gray study found that public expectations of truth and honesty from organisations was at 65%. So the people are not expecting the truth! and are discounting more than a third of what they hear ! Scary stuff ! especially if you are trying to convince someone your product or policy is better than the next guy's or your opponents! All the more reason to practice good public relations and avoid the pitfalls of manipulation and disinformation.

But how do we get out of this quagmire? By making conscious choices to GROW trust. Without trust from within the organisation, and externally, no business strategy is going to be as effective as it otherwise could. It requires putting programmes in place that demonstrate behaviorally not rhetorically that an organisation has concern for its employees, suppliers and external audiences or clients. Actions have always spoken louder than words. And coincidently, growing trust is almost always a key public relations objective. Effective public relations starts with understanding and listening. It is rooted in complete transparency and open and frank discussion of the issues. We know that public relations works well in the following areas:

— Formation of attitudes or opinions; in other words:
— education;
— persuasion or changing perceptions and opinions; and
— changing behaviors.

We do know that public relations works most effectively when it is approached strategically, systematically and consistently. You can't do "a little public relations" and expect a lot of results. The impact of public relations builds over time, with repetition of key strategic messages in a variety of contexts. That, is using the force, the power of public relations. These good examples are not always splashy and visible—but they are highly effective and long lasting, and if they are visible the effect is even more lasting. This is important for everyone, whether your business is large or small, highly visible or less visible. Client satisfaction surveys, feedback lines, speeches, community sponsorships...these are the often the less splashy activities of a good public relations programme. Of course a good advertising programme never hurts.

accreditation. To adhere to the principles of the Universal Code of Professional Standards for the Practice of Public Relations. In most advanced democracies, these recent years have witnessed an unprecedented number of new regulations or self imposed constraints in an effort to set norms to the right of organisations to express themselves in the public arena and the public policy process.

The Global Alliance has writen a report on the state of hard regulations-legislated solutions- and soft regulations—voluntary or policy driven solutions—on the PR industry by eaxmining in detail three countries. Although full regulation of the public relations profession per se is largely absent today -save for excpetions such as the countries of Nigeria, Panama and Brazil- many of the profession's operative practices are increasingly being regulated, particularly those which have a stronger impact on the public interest: political public relations, lobbying, public sector and social public relations, health communication, financial pr, consumer pr. This trend is happening country by country, in a totally unharmonised fashion, either with the introduction of hard laws approved by national parliaments or by soft laws introduced by regulatory authorities or by other self regulating bodies.

This regulatory growth is such that, unlike in the 70's, 80's and 90's when, for example in the USA, only the legendary figure of Edward Bernays stubbornly advocated the full regulation/licensing of public relations while the rest of the professional community rhetorically invoked 'freedom of expression' and 'right to bear grievance'….respectively the first and the fifth amendment of the US Constitution- some respected figures of the professional community today are beginning to have second thoughts and wonder if a full regulation of the profession would not be a more effective as well as 'elegant' way to reassure the public interest of the fundamentally democratic raison d'etre of public relations while, at the same time, protecting the profession's overall tumbling reputation.

Of course it needs to be perfectly clear and understood, at least from professionals who have a thorough knowledge of the ups and downs of regulation because it's part of their day-to-day activity, that it is not simply a law which will change behaviours at large, and that the very policing of such law would be a highly complex matter, as at least in the three license-mandatory countries indicated above there seems to have been little if any effect on the dayto-day professional practice: it is sufficient for professionals to call themselves communicators or something else rather than public relators to avoid compliance with the law.... However it would make a great difference within a professional community to be able to publicly 'call foul' if someone, even a non member, committed a criminal offense because a universal regulation was violated, rather than balking, as is the more frequent case today, in the fear of being sued for libel every time. We are too often silent on matters within our own backwyard.

We can now see very clearly is the proliferation of pervasive communication channels. These are beginning to have a potentially detrimental impact on individuals. With everyone empowered 'to have a voice' the competition to be heard has the effect of diminishing individual attention and concentration capabilities—evidenced by one recent study which purports that in 2003 each human-being received and distributed 800 million bytes of information. The recent phenomenon of blogging is a case in point. Now everyone who has something to say can set up a blog and let people read their thoughts on everything under the sun. Of course it did not take long for specialisation to take hold here and we now have several blogs about PR.

Then there is the CSR- Corporate Social Responsibility trend. An entire cottage industry supports this new dogma of management. The United nations has adopted a Global Compact as a way to guide governance issues. This CSR phenomenon has accelerated awareness within the public relations community of today's most reputed theoretical approach to the profession—the Grunig model- which in 2004 marks its 20th anniversary as a framework theory by which public relations is taught/understood.

Another trend that is the increased interest in accreditation- or professional certification programmes. Now that certified education programmes, the idea that individuals should obtain a professional credential- like the APR which is in use in at least nine countries around the world- is gaining ground. The Global Alliance has decide to explore the creation of its second world- class standard in the area of professional certification. A benchmarking process is now underway to determine how much commonality we have between the various accreditation regimes. Professional associations are there to help practitioners get better by offering conferences like this one and other workshops, knowledge as well as to offer a network of contacts. Above all, these institutions are there to promote professionalism and standards in our industry. Employers need qualified, ethically minded and preferably accredited professionals who take their profession seriously on their staff.

Public relations is part art, part science. It is up to public relations professional to use the power of listening, to find out what the public is thinking and relay that to management, formulate a public relations programme.

Dimensions of Public Relations Orientation

A general theory of the public relations (PR) behaviour of organisations remains an elusive goal of scholars. Attempts such as four models developed by the researchers fall short of a PR theory of orga nisational behaviour, since most organisations practice each of the models at different times. For this reason, it is not yet possible to classify organisations by their practice of PR, to predict the type of PR an organisation will use, or to explain the effect of different types of public relations on organisational performance.

Some of the organisational scientists believe theories of organisational behaviour must begin with a "classification of the species" in order to identify homogenous populations within the species about which falsifiable hypotheses can be formed and tested. A preliminary classification system, or typology, of public relations behaviour based on a new construct called public relations orientation is shown in Figure 1.

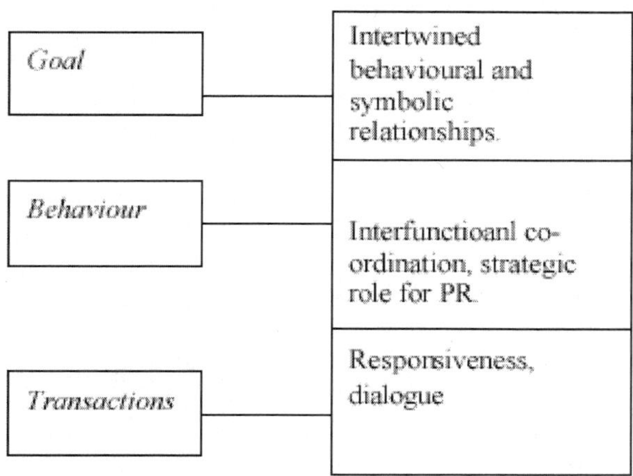

Figure 1: The Dimensions of Public Relations Orientation

The constructed types presented here describe what type of organisation practises what type of public relations, and what organisation level outcomes may be expected from pursuing public relations strategy through a given type. Classification is an essential prerequisite to good science because it identifies homogeneous populations within the larger species (in this case, organisations) about which falsifiable hypotheses can be formed. By specifying the diversity inherent in the species called "organisations" organisational behaviour can be explained and predicted. Types are "constructed" by ordering or synthesising a complex set of variables for comparing and measuring objectively probable phenomena. Typologies meet the criteria for theory building because they contain constructs or variables on which a theoretical system can be built, they specify relationships between the constructs, that is, they generate hypotheses, and they are empirically testable.

Good typologies should specify the dimensions of the type and how they are measured and describe the logic underlying the configuration of dimensions. Additional criteria include terminological clarity, essentiality, extensiveness, inclusivity, systematisation, power, theoretical productivity, logic, and prescriptive utility Mitnick. With these guidelines in mind, begin the task of constructing a typology of the public relations behaviour of organisations, based on our construct, "public relations orientation".

The term "orientation" is used to describe the possible philosophical stances of an organisation towards public relations (Figure 1). Orientation involves

a) a specific goal (direction),

b) a description of the way one acts as a consequence of the goal, and

c) the response one adopts when dealing with things external to one's self.

Thus, an orientation can be described in terms of the characteristics of the goal, the goal directed behaviour, and the transactions with the environment and parties threatening or enabling the achievement of the goal (stakeholders). Explication of public relations orientation is based on five dimensions grouped under the three categories of goal, behaviour and transactions. Each of these dimensions will now be described and its underlying variables deconstructed. Each is also generally measured as "high- low".

Goal Dimension of Public Relations

The goal dimension of public relations has two axes: the quest for positive images (symbolic relationships) and the quest for substantive behavioural relationships between organisations and publics. PR people can set short term objectives to improve symbolic relationships with publics, but over the long term public relations should "examine behavioural relationships with publics relationships that directly affect the ... ability to accomplish organisational goals".

High PRO occurs when behavioural and symbolic aspects of relationships are "intertwined". When they are separated, public relations practitioners offer little value because "they suggest that the problems in relationships with publics can be solved using the proper message disseminated through publicity or media relations to change an image of an organisation". The disconnection of symbolic relationships from behavioural relationships represents low PRO. The two sub-dimensions, each specified as high or low, lead to four possible cells, which form the foundation of the proposed PRO typology (Figure 2). The four cells are high behavioural relationships/high symbolic relationships (HBR-HSR), named "integrated"; low behavioural relationship/high symbolic relationship (LBR-HSR), named "promotional"; high behavioural relationship/low symbolic relationship (HBRLSR), named "technical"; and low behavioural relationship/low symbolic relationship (LBRLSR), named "restricted".

Public Relations Behaviour

The PR behaviour category is based on two dimensions: interfunctional co-ordination, and a strategic role for public relations. These dimensions are considered the foundation of effective public relations behaviour of organisations.

Interfunctional Co-ordination: Constraints on information collection and dissemination, which is call interfunctional coordination, limit public relations effectiveness. Interfunctional coordination is a term borrowed from the marketing literature, to indicate the integration of efforts by all parts of the organisation to achieve the PR goal (integrated symbolic and behavioural relationships). It includes the systematic generation, analysis and dissemination of intelligence across functional boundaries about relationships with publics or stakeholders.

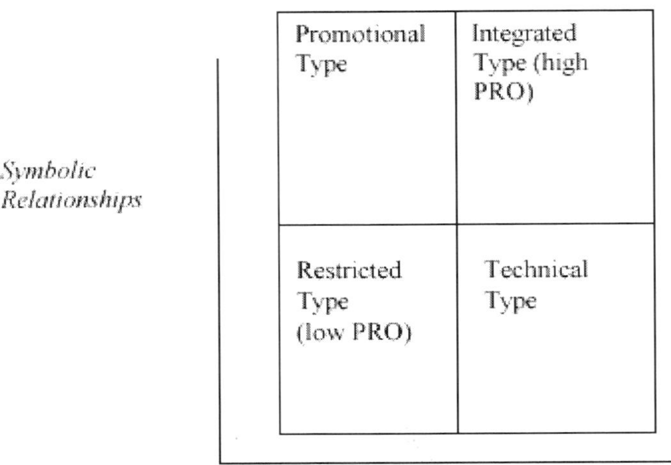

Figure 2: A Typology of the Public Relations Behaviour of Organisations

Strategic Role: Scholars have identified the presence of a strategic role for public relations as a requirement of public relations "excellence" and its lack as a constraint on public relations effectiveness.

Transactions with Environment

The third category of PRO dimensions is the transactions of the organisation with actors in its environment (publics) who threaten or enable achievement of the public relations goal (high, intertwined symbolic and behavioural relationships). This category has two dimensions, responsiveness to stakeholders and a dialogic approach to stakeholder relationships.

Responsiveness

Responsiveness is implicit in much of the public relations literature. However, the concept of responsiveness adopted here is based on the results of the grounded theory study. The responsiveness atom has two axes, one being the intensity of activity ranging from "do little" to "do much", the other being the nature of activity, ranging from "adversarial" to "collaborative". The twoby-two structure of this dimension leads to four possible cells, which conform closely to the responsiveness modes. The do-much/collaborative cell is named "proactive" (lead the industry); the dolittle/ collaborative cell is named "accommodative" (be progressive); the domuch/

adversarial cell is named "reactive" (fight all the way); and the do-little/ reactive cell is named "defensive" (do only what is required).

Dialogic Approach

A dialogue process is necessary to fully and accurately identify stakeholder needs and to negotiate effective responses. Dialogue is a precondition for ethical public relations. Dialogue in this model is composed of respectful attitudes towards the dialogic partner, mutual agreement about the structural attributes of communication, and mutual satisfaction with the rules of communication. Effective, ethical dialogue also requires openness and a willingness to disclose information that is critical to the relationship.

Integrated PR Organisation

In the integrated public relations organisation, the public relations goal synthesises high symbolic and high behavioural relationships with publics. The public relations function has a strategic, managerial role and its manager is most likely to generate valuable outcomes for the organisation. The organisation effectively utilises public relations intelligence to adapt itself to its changing stakeholder environment, which may be both complex and dynamic. The integrated PR organisation is proactive in that it actively seeks collaborative solutions to conflict with publics or stakeholders.

Dialogue and openness are key relationship maintenance strategies, providing an ethical framework for decision making. This organisation is likely to hold a symmetrical worldview for public relations and is more likely than the other types to use symmetrical public relations strategies, although mixed mode strategies will be used. Among the four types, this organisation is most likely to practice "excellent" public relations. The integrated public relations type is expected to be most frequently associated with the "analyser" strategic type. The analyser organisation tries to exploit new product and market opportunities (requiring attention to symbolic relationships that can signal quality or other attributes to prospective customers) while maintaining a firm base of traditional products and customers (requiring attention to behavioural relationships aimed at improving customer loyalty, repeat purchase and so on).

The ability of public relations managers to develop measurable, strategic public relations goals and strategies that support the overall business goals will lead to influence within the dominant coalition. The major problem faced by public relations managers in integrated organisations is the tension between the need for innovation in relating to new or changing publics and the need for efficiency without staleness in relating to traditional publics. When executed well, the organisation level public relations outcomes for this organisation are likely to include a good reputation, legitimacy (license to operate), and reduced conflict with stakeholders.

Promotional PR Organisation

The promotional PR organisation pursues high symbolic relationships with publics, but does not place the same emphasis on behavioural relationships. Therefore, the organisation's actions do not always match its rhetoric. While intensely active, the organisation's asymmetrical worldview for public relations leads to behaviour aimed at persuading publics that it is right, which is an adversarial, rather than a collaborative, type of responsiveness. Interfunctional co-ordination is moderate as the type of PR information exchanged within the organisation relates only to the organisation's ability to promote itself and not the full stakeholder environment.

In the promotional public relations organisation, public relations may contribute to image making strategy, but not to overall organisation strategy. The organisation selectively attends to stakeholder groups important to its image, such as customers. It does not seek dialogue, although it may seek feedback in order to more scientifically persuade its publics that it is right. It is moderately open, insofar as is required to promote itself to various publics. The correlates of the promotional type are, therefore, an assymetrical worldview for public relations and a managerial role for public relations.

The managerial role is posited because the manager is likely to have control of an adequate budget for promotio ns and use research to ascertain the effectiveness of promotional programmes. The promotional type of organisation may be most closely associated with the Miles and Snow "prospector" strategic type. The prospector is continually modifying its productmarket domain to take advantage of perceived opportunities and therefore has a high requirement for both marketing and promotions. Its requirement for speed to market means that attention to long term collaborative relationships with stakeholders takes a back seat to the requirements for symbolic, image making activity. Creative approaches to public relations will flourish in this organisation when the top communicator is able to enact a managerial role.

However, the inherent inefficiencies of the prospector's rapidly changing, diverse operations may be a trap for the public relations function, which typically requires a long term focus for maximum impact. The organisation may have an active PR department and be well recognised because of its intense image making activity, but its failure to attend to substantive behavioural relationships puts it at risk of stakeholder cynicism, and ultimately, loss of reputation.

Technical PR Organisation

The technical PR organisation pays a lot of attention to maintaining good stakeholder relationships but places little emphasis on image, believing that actions speak louder than words. The organisation is not well known except among those it has a direct relationship with. Long term relationships with key publics are likely to be collaborative rather than adversarial; for example, the organisation may be a supplier of customised components to long term customers in a stable industry. While responsive, the organisation takes little initiative and routine communications predominate. PR interfunctional co-ordination is low because public relations generates little valuable intelligence for the organisation. In this organisation, the worldview for public relations is technical, and public relations plays a technical role rather than a strategic role. Public relations will use little or no research, set output rather than outcome goals, and make little contribution to the achievement of business goals. The transactional dimensions of public relations orientatio n, namely responsiveness and dialogue, are moderate because even though public relations has little input, the organisation as a whole has an accommodative approach towards its long standing stakeholders. This organisation is most like the Miles and Snow "defender" type, which has a relatively stable environment, with few changes to its product market domain. This organisation is focused on efficiency to defend its narrow market domain. Because the product market domain is stable, and public relations enacts a technical role, life for the public relations staff is predictable and routine. Changes in its business environment or business strategy put this type at risk unless it develops a proactive communication plan to keep emerging and existing stakeholders well informed.

Restricted PR Organisation

The restricted PR organisation places little value on either symbolic or behavioural relationships with stakeholders. It is least likely to have a discrete public relations function, thus it is the most restricted organisational environment for public relations. When publics intrude into the operations of the organisation, the response is to do as little as possible (defensive). Because publics are not valued, neither is the public relations function, and all of the dimensions of public relations orientation will be low. If the organisation has a public relations person, the person's tasks are likely to be technical, or even clerical, in nature, such as distribution of statutory reports or product samples.

Such an organisation may be successful with a low public relations orientation if it is has few and undemanding stakeholders. However, low attention to stakeholder relationships is an unsustainable strategy for most organisations. The strategic impotence of the restricted PR type makes it like the "reactor" type defined by Miles and Snow. This type represents a failure of an organisation to use any of the other strategies to adapt to its product market environment. Miles and Snow suggest that reactors, which are inherently unstable, fail to adapt to their environment. A public relations manager is unlikely to be able to perform well in this organisation.Thus far, described a new construct called public relations orientation and developed a typology of the public relations behaviour of organisations based on its dimensions. The typology meets Mitnick's essential criteria for a good typology because it includes all relevant entities (all organisations whether they have a public relations function, or not), captures important features of public relations behaviour in a systematic way and has a clear logic.

Typology of Power

A powerful typology is one that subsumes other typologies. Several typologies have been developed in public relations theory. For example, worldviews for public relations have been identified as symmetrical and asymmetrical. Our integrated type is symmetrical, while the other three types are asymmetrical. The technical type, however, may well emulate the technical worldview. Public relations roles have been typified in the literature as managerial and technical. Managerial roles are more likely to predominate in our integrated and promotional types, and technical roles are expected to prevail in our technical type. Our restricted type may not have a discrete public relations function.

Another PR typology is the four models of public relations. Each of the models may be practised in all of our types except the restricted type, although symmetrical public relations will be practised more in the integrated type than in any of the others. Use of the models in each type is more likely to vary by intensity. In other words, the integrated type uses all the models more than the promotional type, and the promotional type uses all the models more than the technical type. Public relations environments have also been classified as complex/simple and turbulent/static. Relating the public relations types to the Miles and Snow typology addresses aspects of the product market environment. However, public relations is also concerned with publics in the non market, or social and political environment. The addition of non market environmental variables to the types suggests a further research direction.

Finally, structure of the public relations department has been classified in relation to the Hage-Hull typology with limited success. The typology addresses structure via linkage to the Miles & Snow typology, which is based on the variables of structure, strategy and process. However, more remains to be explained about the contribution of the structure of public relations to organisational performance. Nevertheless, even at this preliminary stage of development, a typology based on public relations orientation has considerable power.

Each of the types can be considered a midrange theory that explains how public relations works within a particular type of organisation. However, types are most useful in theory development when they are treated as independent variables in a grand theoretical assertion, that is, that variation in the types predicts something. By linking our typology with the Miles and Snow typology, suggesting that variation in the public relations types explains some variance in organisational performance. The pathway by which public relations contributes to performance is by managing behavioural and symbolic relationships with publics.

Symbolic relationships may influence reputation, which in turn impacts performance. Behavioural relationships may reduce the level of conflict, which contributes to performance by lowering costs. Behavioural relationships may also engender co-operative behaviour from publics, which leads to outcomes such as legitimacy (license to operate) and loyalty. Thus, the types contribute to a general theory of the public relations behaviour of organisations, by hypothesising how each type contributes to performance (or not).

The multi-dimensional construct, public relations orientation, clearly has prescriptive utility as managers can use it as an organisational diagnostic, to make changes to the public relations mission, behaviour or stakeholder transactions. Prescriptive utility also arises because each type relies on a public relations strategy that is more or less likely to produce particular outcomes, such as reputation or reduced conflict with stakeholders.

PR, Relationships and Reputations

Public relations helps an organisation and its publics adapt mutually to each other. Business schools teach profit maximisation, transferring wealth from customers to owners, because that is what business does. Commerce is unlike medicine where lifesaving is at the core of what doctors do, or engineering where improving mankind's lot is at the heart of calculations. Commerce is about exchange of goods, services and wealth. There needn't be any ethic other than completion of a transaction. One can complete business transactions with illegal and injurious products and services as well as with offerings that are for the betterment of mankind. It is up to company leadership and to governmental and societal regulators to make sure companies remain within the boundaries of accepted societal ethics. On the other hand, PR teaches relationship and reputation building in ways that lead to profits.

PR assumes a business has vested interested in ethics. We know, of course, that this isn't true. And, concerns for reputation and relationships can be addressed as easily in illegitimate businesses as in legitimate ones. A madam can run a whorehouse with an eye to treating customers well, so they return often, and a drug dealer can protect product from harmful contamination that might kill users and diminish cash flow. As PR practitioners, we advocate reputation and relationships to company leadership that sometimes listens and sometimes doesn't. We point to societal pressure, often expressed through governmental action and news stories, that can revoke a company's permission to operate if it steps too far over the line of what society deems acceptable behavior. But a direct link to revenues and profits is missing unless a company is in a disaster scenario. There is even more conflict.

Under financial assumptions, money now is more important than money later. Reaping the greatest wealth today from customers for shareholders is better than doing so tomorrow. Under PR principles, money later is as valuable as money now, if one wants an enterprise to which customers return repeatedly and stand by loyally. In a business school view, one maintains reputation and relationships to produce revenues and earnings.

For public relations, reputation and relationships lead to revenue and profits. The points of view appear identical, but practically speaking they aren't because business people, like business school professors, forget part of the equation. Business school professors tend to abstract profit from the business context, while public relations holds that the business context is essential-profit comes from flesh-and-blood people engaging in transactions. Put another way, in business schools, there appears to be more emphasis on mathematics than on messy details of customer, vendor and employee relationships and reputations.

Finance Tyranny

In fairness to business schools, many offer real-world experiences to students in to give them a better feel for the totality of business. But too often real-world courses are optional and attendant lessons in leadership, communications and ethics are good things to do but not essential. Communications or public relations courses in business schools are not mainstream, and perhaps never will be. Finance professors are often first among equals and financial theory and calculation are considered more important than organisational theory and psychology. Students manipulate numbers without reference to people who turn numbers into facts. Too often, financially trained MBAs become quantitatively oriented consultants unskilled in leadership, communications and ethics necessary for making products, completing sales and serving customers for the long term.

Few ever run stores or factories, even though these can be large enterprises. A big-box, do-it-yourself store can produce $50 million in annual sales with all the problems attendant to retailing including staffing, logistics, shrink, training, communications and customer service. But, it is not uncommon that managers running these stores and responsible for a business' primary relationships are not college graduates. Relationship and reputation management are at the core of marketing but even so, academic discussion often turns on abstract considerations and mathematical models rather than practical considerations of how to handle a customer who has just purchased $20,000 of kitchen cabinetry and finds it doesn't fit. However, what business schools teach is responsive to their market-large corporations, consulting firms and Wall Street financial houses that hire business school graduates. A gauge of a business school's success is the number of graduates employed by prestigious companies at high starting salaries. These businesses want the analytical skills of MBAs and reward them proportionately. It may be that businesses hiring MBAs do not understand the need for reputation and relationships (which is unlikely), or they assume business students, as well as businesspersons, come equipped with ethical skills. But the problem turns quickly into one of focus, especially on Wall Street.

Pursuit of wealth is at the heart of investors' participation in markets. They prefer money now, although they can be suckers for a story that profits will come later - as happened during the Internet Bubble. Capital is impatient and institutional investors demand return. They are not shareholder loyalists, if a company fails to perform, and they rarely focus on the totality of a business or consider reputation and relationships when reviewing portfolios. Investors are angry when scandal and fraud diminish the value of investments, but they are not necessarily upset by how a company relates to other target audiences, such as employees, customers and vendors, even if there are violations of human rights.

Governments pass laws, such as the Sarbanes-Oxley Law of 2002, to forbid practices that penalise shareholders and institute reforms that reduce the possibility of fraud. These reforms barely extend beyond investors to employees and others who are part of a universe of reputation and relationships that comprise a business. Other laws apply to them, but investors may not take such laws into account except in how they affect a company's revenue and earnings potential. Sharp focus on the bottom-line assumes, or forgets, too much. Companies in highly competitive environments with driven CEOs tend to forget the wider context of ethics, reputation and relationships in pursuit of revenues and earnings that "keep the Street happy." Business schools teaching profit maximisation also tend to forget that numbers are not isolated abstractions.

There is an irony that a foremost proponent of reputation and relationship principles was the senior PR person at a monopoly - AT&T -- , which wasn't subject to real-world competition when Arthur W. Page developed public relations philosophy and principles. And as a consequence of his actions and example, as well as his many speeches, letters, and presentations, he fashioned a model of public relations and public relations performance that today remains the ideal to which all of us aspire. American Telephone & Telegraph. Page's philosophy centered about understanding and communicating corporate and individual character. He emphasised humanism and freedom as preconditions for capitalism. He stressed that a "successful corporation must shape its character in concert with the nation's. It must operate in the public interest, manage for the long run and make customer satisfaction its primary goal".

"Real success, both for big business and the public, lies in large enterprise conducting itself in the public interest and in such a way that the public will give it sufficient freedom to serve effectively." Open most finance and accounting books, and you won't find that view expressed. A company in a benign monopoly is concerned about keeping captive customers happy and not just keeping customers. And indeed, when AT&T lost its monopoly, it faded to a shadow. Companies fighting in tough marketplaces prefer sales-oriented communications and push messaging, and they are numbers driven with a short-term focus that coincides with Wall Street's demands. The long run is a quarter, and strategy is how Wall Street bids the price of the stock.

Public interest is an abstraction and in an era of multinational corporations (MNCs), it applies to many publics in many countries at the same time. MNCs leverage the wage and price structures of one country against another to maximise profits. Their views of humanism and freedom are tempered by the opportunities to reap profit in societies where neither are a high priority (e.g., China). Page's view was that of an American nationalist, but we compete today in a global environment where pursuit of wealth allows indifferent treatment of publics that do not have the power or will to remove a company's freedom. MNCs are skilled at using differences between societal expectations and regulations as profitable opportunities.

Consider China. There, pursuit of profit has created factories with low paid workers churning out goods that have made competitive manufacturing in the US and elsewhere unprofitable. What to the US worker is shockingly bad pay is to a Chinese worker better than nothing. A company's pursuit of profit benefits millions of Chinese even as it disadvantages millions of American labourers. MNCs note there is no rule that business must be nationalistic.

We can examine some principles against the same background.

— Tell the truth. Let the public know what's happening and provide an accurate picture of the company's character, ideals and practices.

— *Prove it with action.* Public perception of an organisation is determined 90 percent by what it does and ten percent by talking.

— *Listen to the customer.* To serve the company well, understand what the public wants and needs. Keep top decision makers and other employees informed about public reaction to company products, policies and practices.

— *Manage for tomorrow.* Anticipate public reaction and eliminate practices that create difficulties. Generate goodwill.

— *Conduct public relations as if the whole company depends on it.* Corporate relations is a management function. No corporate strategy should be implemented without considering its impact on the public. The public relations professional is a policy maker capable of handling a wide range of corporate communications activities.

— *Remain calm, patient and good-humored.* Lay the groundwork for public relations miracles with consistent, calm and reasoned attention to information and contacts. When a crisis arises, remember that cool heads communicate best.

One can place numbers against these principles, but they would be irrelevant. If the leaders of a company do not have a truth-telling ethic, it takes a law like Sarbanes-Oxley to compel them, but compulsion does not relate to whether a business is successful. Plenty of profitable businesses have lied and will lie and get away with it. Plenty of profitable businesses have ducked responsibilities to act on what they have promised customers and regulators. Plenty of profitable businesses manage for today and not tomorrow.

Many have no public relations arms and the notion of remaining calm, patient and good-humored during a crisis is foreign. They might not engage with the public at all if they can get away with it. When a businessperson or business school student focuses on profit and profit maximisation, relationship and reputation considerations have little bearing. Is it any wonder the two sides cannot talk to one another without translation? Page had an answer for this, but his answer hasn't percolated into any business school text. Here is an excerpted letter he wrote to the executives of the Continental Oil Company. The Continental Oil Company was chartered by public authority on the assumption that it would serve the public's needs for petroleum products. The theory was that its self-interest would insure its activity and competition would keep its products and services and its prices satisfactory. That is still the main basis of Continental's relation to the public. It is still a fact that the company was set up under pubic authority to benefit the public, and public authority can at any time limit its functions, its methods or abolish it altogether. "So we, like all other companies, live by public approval and roughly speaking, the more approval you have the better you live. This is the fundamental reason for seeking public approval. The fundamental way of getting it is to deserve it. As a management function, public relations encompasses the following:

Anticipating, analysing and interpreting public opinion, attitudes, and issues that might impact, for good or ill, the operations and plans of the organisation. The free flow of information to aid informed decision-making, integrity, honesty and accuracy in all communication and openness that builds trust and credibility. But in pursuit of profit, free flow of information is beside the point and often deleterious to the completion of economic transactions. Business need only supply sufficient information to complete a transaction - e.g. basic characteristics and price of a product or service. It is often the case that missing information includes limitations on products or services that make them useless to the buyer.

In other words, deception is part of the transaction. Deceptive techniques of marketing are and will be used as long as there are buyers and sellers. The Latin phrase, "Caveat Emptor (Let the buyer beware)" applies in an environment where making a profit is proof of business success.

Recent incidents such as paying journalist commentators to promote political agenda is close to what early publicists PR did when they paid reporters and editors to write favorably about products and services. The notion of arms-length persuasion of the news media and conferred credibility of impartial journalistic evaluation were later developments in modern PR. They are principles that many businesspersons dislike because they lack control over communications outcomes. That is why advertising and promotion command the lion's share of expenditures, even though advertising agencies have moved close to a time-billing model and away from commissions. The largest PR accounts today appear to be in marketing as well and consist more of push messaging - publicity placement and promotion -than of mutual adaptation between a company and its publics.

Relationship and reputation management must remain a concern for any business that plans to be around for the long term, but it might not be a priority where profit is the difference between success and failure. That said, there is room for idealism that PR practitioners bring to the corporate environment. Practitioners, however, must be prepared to defend their principles and to suffer defeat. The tougher the competitive environment, the more likely it is that rulebending will occur and PR principles will be less important, unless the CEO personally takes up the cause. Few companies today have the sanctuary of a monopoly in which to focus on relationships as much or more than on return.

Public Relations Consultancies

Good public relations raises share-prices, catapults products into brand-leadership and turns enemies into allies. Incompetent public relations destroys products, careers and investor support overnight. Securing the very best public relations services must be high on any organisation's agenda. The public relations consultancy sector in the UK is world-class but surprisingly small. Professional procurement executives are increasingly involved in selecting public relations consultancies and managing their terms of engagement.

Public relations practitioners operate across a wider range than any other business or professional service from briefing a Government Minister to writing a press release to negotiating with a Non-Governmental Organisation -and this can make it hard to determine exactly what they do, what they can be expected to do, and what they should be paid. The Public Relations Consultants Association (PRCA) has produced to help clarify some of these questions. The first part tries to explain what public relations consultancy is and does; the second part concentrates on the more technical aspects of selecting consultancies and negotiating contracts.

Greater involvement and support on the part of procurement professionals will add rigour to the process of selecting public relations consultancies, setting their terms of reference, negotiating their remuneration and monitoring their performance. It will help to focus effort on desired business outcomes rather than just PR activities. In this way we will be able to work together to make tangible the value delivered by PR consultancy.

Public relations works exceptionally well in UK, which has led to rapid growth and a high degree of specialisation. There are now 200 substantial public relations consultancies in this country—many managing global or European programmes on behalf of UK clients—and 2,000 small partnerships or individual practitioners. The services they provide to client organisations are diverse:

Financial communications and investor relations: corporate communications, which may include Corporate Social Responsibility, issues & crisis management and liaison with stakeholder groups; public affairs at local, national and EU level; product support, including retailer relations, launches and promotions; sponsorship in arts, sports and the community; internal communications and change management... Most consultancies have a strong core competence in media relations—preparing editorial material for broadcast, web and print outlets and managing relationships between clients and their key media; and nearly all are expert at event management -staging meetings, writing speeches and presentations and maximising the impact of a corporate event or a client's participation in a public occasion.

The common factor in this varied landscape is skill in communication. A good public relations consultancy will be able to master a brief rapidly, design a communication programme to achieve the stated business result, create original materials to attract attention and change opinion, and report on the degree of change which has been achieved. The business model of most public relations consultancies resembles that of a legal or accountancy practice. The role of management is to balance client demand—usually expressed in hours or days per assignment per senior/junior specialist/ generalist consultant—against available resources. Most consultancies invest in talent ahead of known demand. Consultancies' overheads are largely fixed and are allocated over the coming fiscal year on a straight-line basis.

A percentage of every consultant's hour or day charged is therefore accounted for by rent, IT systems and office support costs. Management exercise discretion in the level of investment they make in knowledge acquisition and maintenance and in training and professional development. Most consultancies seek to improve margins by offering services which are visibly better, often in specialist areas, and therefore able to command a premium in the marketplace. Awards, publications, research and the hiring of "star recruits" all contribute to the looked-for differentiation between a consultancy and its competitors. A strong track-record in a particular field, a name for exceptional creativity, or possession of a good international network, are also clearly apparent methods of establishing points of difference.

The majority of consultancies' account teams are made up of an account director, who will be the focal point of the relationship with the client, and one or more account managers and account executives. A board director, usually with a named deputy, will provide overall guidance, advice and knowledge based on their greater experience. In many cases specialists—in, for example, political or internal communications—will be assigned to the team on a temporary or part-time basis.

Value of Public Relations Consultancy

The importance of maintaining a good corporate reputation, and the desirability of securing more than a fair share of attention in the marketing arena, are generally accepted by most organisations in the UK today. This is good evidence for the effectiveness of the practice of public relations. Yet three questions continually confront clients:

— How much of our public relations work should be undertaken in-house, and how much is best out-sourced?

— How can we determine the optimum amount to invest in public relations?

— How can we reliably assess the relative value offered by consultancies, both before an engagement begins and at review?

The answer to the first question varies according to the size and complexity of the client organisation and according to the inclination of the in-house communications director or public relations chief. Most consultancies will have advice to offer on all three questions, and this is one of their most valuable contributions at the strategic level. Consultancies can help in four principal ways:

— A good consultancy can offer exceptionally expert people, usually with a diverse range of experience, who can complement the knowledge and ideas of the in-house public relations team.

— Consultancies will usually be able to bring experience from other industries and possibly other countries to bear on the issue at hand, thus exposing the in-house team to ideas cross-fertilised from completely different business areas.

— Consultancies are designed elastically, so are ready and able to provide many-handed support, at a moment's notice, in times of emergency or peak demand.

— Because they exist outside the corporate structure, consultants can offer observations and advice which are objective and impartial.

Calculating the right amount to invest in public relations is extremely difficult. Companies in the same industry sector can be seen allocating widely differing budgets to public relations, sometimes in the order of 500 per cent. Much depends on whether the client organisation sees itself as a "challenger", in which case—ypically—higher than average investments in profile and marketing will pay back as market-share increases, or as a "defender" of an existing market position, in which case expenditure may be minimised in order to favour margin.

In most instances, the client organisation will have an existing involvement in public relations. So there will be benchmarks against which to review budget adjustments. Clients frequently invite the consultancy market to help determine the optimum budget by soliciting tenders based solely on (a) a commercial objective, or (b) a tightly-defined scope of work, sometimes expressed as a set of deliverables or as a specific improvement across a range of existing benchmarks. When a client wishes to take a completely fresh look at public relations investment, it is usually in tandem with marketing and communications expenditure across the board. A number of analytical tools exist to help allocate budgets between the various communications channels.

Procurement professionals can help their colleagues achieve value by ensuring that every assignment has a framework of deliverables, milestones, key performance indicators and essential measures of success, and that the consultancy commits to this framework as the core of its proposal. Comparing relative value offered by public relations consultancies at the outset of an engagement, or at a competitive review, is necessarily a combination of objective and subjective judgements. Research shows that experience, creativity and chemistry are normally the three key factors in consultancy selection. Value for money is generally recognised as being difficult to gauge. Yet this is, perhaps, the key focus of procurement professionals. The PRCA recommends a series of questions which may help to determine comparative value in a consultancy review:

— Recent and relevant experience in the client's industry sector and/or in a communications programme similar to the brief.

— The presence on the engagement team of individual practitioners with relevant experience and demonstrable insight into the communications challenges and solutions.

— Capacity to devote sufficient time and expertise to the assignment without over-stretching resources. For example: how many clients, and what size of programmes, does each team-member handle?

— Ability to bring specialist communications skills to bear on the problems: for example, experts in NGO liaison, crisis preparation, sponsorship, webcasting, product placement, guerrilla marketing, internal communications, community relations… as appropriate.

— A track-record of long-established and successful relationships with organisations of your type and culture. —emonstration of better-than-average staff retention, and evidence of serious commitment to training and career development.

— Cost-effective proposals for measuring the success of the programme—either in its entirety or via selected key elements which can be isolated and evaluated. Most consultancies use measurement tools authenticated by the PRCA and IPR, or have developed proprietary systems, or recommend the involvement of an independent evaluation specialist.

— Overall… an understanding on the part of all team members of the contribution which public relations can make to the business objectives of the organisation.

For over thirty years in the UK the public relations industry has made a consistent effort to determine and publish professional standards of behaviour, performance and accountability. There are two principal bodies involved in this pursuit: The Public Relations Consultants Association (PRCA), whose focus is consulting firms, and the Institute of Public Relations (IPR), whose members are individuals working in-house, in consultancies or in the academic world as teachers or students. Members of the PRCA have all obtained the Consultancy Management Standard, independently audited by Det Norske Veritas (DNV). They must also abide by the PRCA's Professional Charter and Codes of Conduct. Members of the IPR must satisfy a range of criteria to join and progress from "associate" to "member" to "fellow".

Some consultancies have earned Investors In People accreditation, ISO certification or other independent marks of professional and commercial competence. Specialist consultancies in public affairs or healthcare, for example, may belong to the Association of Professional Political Consultants (APPC) or the Healthcare Communications Association (HCA), while financial and investor relations specialists may belong to the Investor Relations Society (IRS). Many large client organisations now require that rostered public relations consultancies must demonstrate appropriate certification, in particular the PRCA's Consultancy Management Standard.

Most public relations consultancies base their charges on the hourly rate of the individuals comprising the client's account team, multiplied by the number of hours each person devotes to the client's programme. These hourly rates tend to be similar between consultancies for the same kind of consultant (experience, track-record, degree of specialist knowledge). The value and cost differential between one consultancy and another lies in the quality of the practitioners they employ and the quality of the support—knowledge, research, IT systems, training, career development, leadership, management—they deploy. Public relations consultancy contracts are normally of four types:

— A set fee for a specific project with a beginning, middle and end.
— A taximeter system for engagements where the level of service is likely to vary widely— including no requirement at all from time to time.
— An annual retainer based on a pre-determined work requirement and a set schedule of deliverables.
— A retainer with an agreement for over-hours to be charged when unexpected demand occurs.

Many public relations assignments start on a project basis and evolve into retainer-plus-over-hours once trust and an appreciation of good value have developed. Most consultancies will charge a standard price for work carried out during the normal working week but a premium price for services provided after-hours, at weekends and during public holidays, or in emergencies. Costs in other countries vary considerably, from 200 per cent of the UK average to 25 per cent in developing markets. Expenses and office costs may be charged item-by-item, or may be charged as an all-in percentage of the budget, or may be absorbed within the overall service fee.

Purchases (photography, print, events and so on) may be charged to the client after consultancy sign-off, or may be paid and re-billed by the consultancy with an agreed additional handling charge. Many consultancies propose an element of payment-by-results within their overall compensation. This is often the case in financial communications, where success fees are a frequent component of inter-firm agreements, and also in engagements where the looked-for result is solely attributable to the consultancy. The PRCA and the ISBA have developed a standard contract, which is available from either organisation.

Negotiating with Public Relations People

Public relations consultancy managers may be entrepreneurs, but that they are first and-foremost public relations practitioners. Only at the largest firms will you encounter trained negotiators or professional counterparts to yourselves. The PRCA offers the following signposts in the hope that they will help conclude a mutually successful agreement:

- Ascertain and compare the hourly/daily rates charged by each consultancy for each "rank" of practitioner. Determine how each firm defines its "ranks"—executives, managers, account directors and so on —so as to be sure that you are comparing like with like. Similarly, how will the team be put together? Will the consultancy need to recruit additional people? For a large programme this is inevitable.
- Enquire how each consultancy handles purchases made on your behalf. Is a handling-charge levied? If not, and suppliers' bills are submitted to you directly, does the consultancy take responsibility for checking quality, cost and timely supply?
- How will the consultancies invest in the success of the relationship? For example: will they absorb all or some of the costs of the learning curve? Will their most senior people be available to advise? Most public relations firms are hoping for long-term engagements with new clients: how will the contenders for your account go about building a partnership with your organisation?
- What Key Performance Indicators and what core deliverables do the consultancies envisage as being crucial to the success of the programme? How do the consultancies propose to monitor client team satisfaction -how often, and by what methods?

— Do you see the assignment as routine, important or business-critical?
— Is it clear to the consultancies how you will make your selection?
— Which methods of measurement and evaluation do the consultancies believe are most suitable to the assignment? Have you set aside a separate budget for this function?
— Are the consultancies ready to negotiate a proportion of their compensation on a payment-by-results basis? Are you prepared to offer a bonus for exceptional performance? The PRCA's Consultancy Management Standard The PRCA's Consultancy Management Standard was the world's first independently-audited quality certification scheme for public relations consultancies. Introduced in the UK in 2000 after three years of development, it is being adopted in ten other countries and is the model for similar schemes throughout the world.

The Standard was designed to give clients the assurance that a certified consultancy is financially stable, well-managed, adheres to best practice in all dimensions of client service, invests in training its staff, has a convincing strategy for the development of its business, abides by the principles of the PRCA's professional charter, and adheres to the PRCA's Codes of Conduct. Member consultancies are re-examined every two years by DNV.

Framing Applicable to Modern Public Relations

Public relations can be examined from a variety of frameworks, including systems, critical, and rhetorical perspectives. The rhetorical approach focuses on how public relations is engaged in the construction of messages and meanings that are intended to influence key publics important to an organisation.

Rhetorical theory encompasses a wide range of approaches, including argumentation, advocacy and persuasion, corporate communication, dialectics and discourse, dramatism and storytelling, information, organising, public opinion, and reputation management. Yet, none of these approaches represents a comprehensive foundation for fully understanding the processes or consequences of public relations.

Another theoretically rich approach that offers the potential of subsuming and tying together many of these seemingly unrelated approaches involves framing theory. Framing has been used as a paradigm for understanding and investigating communication and related behaviour in a wide range of disciplines. These include psychology, speech communication (especially discourse analysis and negotiation), organisational decision making, economics, health communication, media studies, and political communication.

Framing theory provides a potentially useful umbrella for examining what occurs in public relations. In addition to a rhetorical approach that focuses on how messages are created, framing is conceptually connected to the underlying psychological processes that people use to examine information, to make judgments, and to draw inferences about the world around them. This linkage is missing in many of the other rhetorical frameworks.

Moreover, framing phenomena operate across levels of analysis, making framing theory applicable at the intrapersonal, interpersonal, group, organisational, interorganisational, and societal levels in which public relations influence attempts operate.

It is important to recognise that public relations work fundamentally involves the construction of social reality. The constructivist approach to communication draws on ideas from the symbolic interactionism school of sociology. Symbolic interactionism rejects attempts to examine human behaviour in terms of instinct, external forces, or the structural-functional explanations that predominated early sociological thinking.

Instead, human behaviour is thought to result from how people interact and their use of symbols to create meaning. Constructionists contend that representations of objects or problems in people's minds vary from the corresponding actual objects or conditions on which they are based. More important, constructionists contend that people act based on these perceptions, or what Lippmann deftly described as "the pictures inside our heads," rather than "objective reality".

Public relations workers have been referred to pejoratively as "imagemakers" and "spin doctors"-labels that only partially portray their important role in constructing social reality. Indeed, public relations counseling involves defining reality for organisations by shaping organisational perspectives about the outside world-a process also termed enactment. Similarly, outbound public relations communications involve attempts to define reality, at least as it relates to client organisations, for the many publics on whom the organisation depends. This construction process might be dismissed as manipulation. However, because defining reality is the very essence of communication, constructionists would argue that the process is neither inherently good nor bad.

Framing is a critical activity in the construction of social reality because it helps shape the perspectives through which people see the world. Although public relations practitioners commonly refer to framing effective messages in the same way that a builder frames a house from the bottom up, the framing metaphor is better understood as a window or portrait frame drawn around information that delimits the subject matter and, thus, focuses attention on key elements within. Thus, framing involves processes of inclusion and exclusion as well as emphasis. The essence of framing processes with the following:

Framing essentially involves selection and salience. To frame is to select some aspects of perceived reality and make them more salient in the communicating text, in such a way as to promote a particular problem definition, causal interpretation, moral evaluation and/or treatment recommendation for the item described.

Frames, then, define problems – determine what a causal agent is doing and costs and benefits, usually measured in terms of cultural values; diagnose causes – identify the forces creating the problem; make moral judgments – evaluate causal agents and their effects; and suggest remedies – offer and justify treatments for the problem and predict their likely effects.

Implicitly, framing plays an integral role in public relations. If public relations is defined as the process of establishing and maintaining mutually beneficial relations between an organisation and publics onwhomit depends, the establishment of common frames of reference about topics or issues of mutual concern is a necessary condition for effective relations to be established.

As a property of a message, a frame limits or defines the message's meaning by shaping the inferences that individuals make about the message. Frames reflect judgments made by message creators or framers. Some frames represent alternative valencing of information (i.e., putting information in either a positive or negative light, or valence framing).

Other frames involve the simple alternative phrasing of terms (semantic framing). The most complex form of framing is storytelling (story framing). Story framing involves

— selecting key themes or ideas that are the focus of the message and

— incorporating a variety of storytelling or narrative techniques that support that theme.

Framing can be evidenced in a series of structures within a message. These include syntactical structures, stable patterns of arranging words and phrases in a text; script structures, the orderly sequencing of events in a text in a predictable or expected pattern; thematic structures, the presence of propositions or hypotheses that explain the relations between elements within a text-including the presence of words such as "because," "since," and "so"; and rhetorical structures that subtly suggest how a text should be interpreted. Rhetorical devices can include metaphors and similes, familiar exemplars and illustrations, provocative language and descriptors, catchphrases, and visual imagery.

Framing operates by biasing the cognitive processing of information by individuals. At least two mechanisms to explain the process are found in the literature. One suggestion is that framing operates by providing contextual cues that guide decision making and inferences drawn by message audiences. Drawing on their earlier work on the concept, Kahneman and Tversky suggested that the simple positive-versus-negative framing of a decision operates as a cognitive heuristic or rule-of-thumb that guides decisions in situations involving uncertainty or risk.

Negative reactance to losses or risks is consistent with other findings in the impression formation literature that suggest negative information is weightedmoreheavily than positive information and is more attention-getting. It is also consistent with motivational theories that people act to protect themselves. More recent evidence for this heuristic explanation was provide. The elaboration likelihood model to suggest that negative framing might serve as a peripheral cue in processing. Specifically, negative framing might prompt people to think more about a message.

This finding is consistent with research that suggests that message framing effects vary by level of involvement. The second mechanism through which framing operates is priming. Knowledge is thought to be organised in human memory in cognitive structures or schemas, which operate as constraints on the arrangement and interpretation of situations and events. Alternatively, schemas have been conceptualised as categories (hierarchial structures), as prototypes (idealised representations of objects within particular classes), and as scripts (expected scenarios for events). Although the schematic organisation of memory has been challenged, the notion jibes with at least three of the major models that describe memory in terms of associative networks, storage bins, and distributed memory models. Regardless of the specific model, researchers agree that schematic processing entails people using association and expectation to make inferences about events and to impute meaning not manifested in the message itself.

Significantly, some researchers use "frame" synonymously with schema to delimit which memory nodes are associated with a particular topic in memory. Framing affects cognitive processing by selectively influencing which memory nodes, or sets of memory traces organised as schemas, are activated to interpret a particular message. Priming effects can be conscious, such as when a person purposefully uses message cues to attempt to retrieve stored knowledge from memory.

Priming effects also can be unconscious or automatic, such as when a person categorises a topic or message during the pre-attention phase of processing and then processes information using rules that are considered appropriate in the situation.

Framing Models

Although a theoretically rich and useful concept, framing suffers from a lack of coherent definition. An exhaustive literature search suggests the existence of more than 1,000 citations about framing in the academic literature. Framing has been adopted as a textual, psychological, and socio-political construct.

Depending on the circumstances, the meaning of framing varies based on the research question, the level of analysis, or the underlying psychological process of interest. Framing's ostensible weakness also is one of the concept's inherent strengths. Framing's emphasis on providing context within which information is presented and processed allows framing to be applied across a broad spectrum of communication situations.

An examination of the literature across disciplines suggests at least seven models of framing that have potential application to public relations. By examining these alternative conceptualisations, it is possible for researchers and practitioners to understand the usefulness of the framing concept, to apply it in practice, and to pursue a systematic research agenda about framing as it might be applied to public relations. The seven models involve the framing of situations, attributes, choices, actions, issues, responsibility, and news.

Framing of Situations

Researchers from anthropology and sociology were the first to examine communication using a framing paradigm. Their legacy of using framing to describe how reality is constructed through language and the structure of interactions among people can be labeled as relational or situational framing. A psychological frame as "a spatial and temporal bounding of a set of interactive messages".

The participants' understanding of the interaction in which they engage – including their roles and the rules to be followed – operate as a form of metacommunication. The notion and described framing as "the definition of a situation built up in accordance with principles of organisation that govern events – at least social ones – and our subjective involvement in them".

A frame as a "schemata of interpretation" that provides a context for understanding information and enables individuals to "locate, perceive, identify and label". Of these, three of the most important were keying, bringing into focus particular aspects of everyday life by recreating past interactions; anchoring, the rooting of ideas in deeper frames of meaning; and fabrication, the recasting of certain dimensions of experience so they are made salient within a situation or interaction.

Two of the most important research domains relevant to public relations in which situation framing has been investigated involve organisational behaviour and negotiation. Framing as the process by which managers at all levels attempt to impose their version of reality on situations. Normative framing has facilitated acceptance of once-disdained business practices, such as hostile takeovers. In the same way, organisational framing (i.e., the use of frames by organisations in its discourse) has been used to examine contemporary problems.

Examples include sexual exploitation and concealment of sexual harassment. Economists similarly have employed framing concepts. Social norms, or unconscious rules of social exchange behaviour, have been used to contrast actions in different types of economic systems. They suggested the business contexts in which individuals work provide important cues that frame understanding of problems and lead to distinct behaviours.

In the negotiation arena, Bargaining is defined through the processes of framing and reframing that occur throughout the deliberations. Other researchers have examined the linguistic patterns used by bargainers to frame negotiations and the critical role of mediators as framers and reframers of issues.

Framing of Attributes

Separate from defining and describing overall situations found in everyday life and literature, a second and distinct form of framing involves the framing of attributes (i.e., the characterisation of objects, events, and people). Semantic framing is used to focus on particular attributes that might be flattering or derogatory and, thus, be advantageous or disadvantageous to message sponsors in persuasive communications.

Consumer behaviour researchers are the most active in attribute framing research and use the term in at least four distinct ways. Picture framing describes ads in which captions accompany a photo and are used to prime the cognitive processing of visuals by calling attention to particular attributes depicted. Problem framing refers to the deliberations used by decision makers, particularly novices, to structure a preference judgment task.

Advertising has been shown to influence judgments by altering key aspects of the decision process by refocusing consumer attention away from certain attributes or choice rules in favor of others, thus defining (framing) the criteria on which decisions should be made and the schema that should be used. Advertising framing of product experience, drawing on William D. Wells's notion of transformational advertising, suggests that promotional messages transform how the consumer perceives and judges the subsequent consumption of a product.

Finally, experience – frames – advertising effects have been identified. These involve how a consumer's prior experiences and satisfaction using a particular product bias the salience of particular product attributes in a commercial message and, thus, influence the criteria used to judge messages and featured products. Product positioning is another term commonly used by marketers to describe attribute framing. Positioning as the "act of designing a company's offerings and image so they occupy a meaningful and distinctive competitive position in the customer's mind".

Positioning heightens product expectations and enables consumers to differentiate people, objects, and brands. Although they do not use the term "schema". People rank products and brands using "little ladders" in their heads; the ladders are product categories, and the ladder rungs represent brands. Framing also has been used to describe alternative presentation of product claims or attributes.

Alternatives examined include whether the product is described (framed) based on price versus benefits, product connections to political concerns (pro-environmental "green marketing") versus instrumental qualities, and the alternate anchoring (framing) of price references. Finally, framing also is central to research about comparative advertising that examines claims made about a particular product's attributes relative to others in the same category.

Attribute framing has received increased attention in media studies from Maxwell McCombs and his colleagues. Media are effective in not only raising the salience of particular topics, issues, or objects but also can create specific knowledge of attributes related to issues and people, such as political candidates. The media's ability to create general top-of-mind salience about a topic is known as agenda-setting.

McCombs labeled the media's ability also to frame attributes as second-order agenda setting or frame setting. The extension of the familiar description of agenda-setting thus suggests, although media are not necessarily effective in telling people what to think, media can be strikingly effective in telling people what to think about -and how to think about it.

Beyond marketing and communications, attribute framing has been used by economists to explain economic behaviours. The theory of institutional framing suggests that perceptions of fairness (i.e., an attribute of an institution involving whether it deals fairly with others) accounts for aberrations not explained by standard economic models that emphasise self-interest. Other economists reject classical notions of economics that presume people use a single absolute zero-base as the starting point for making economic decisions.

Instead, people are thought to use multiple reference points in decision making; each of these reference points represents a distinct frame of reference that is used to assess attributes or values when making comparisons. Finally, still other neoclassical economists reject the notion that people are rational in making decisions and only seek economic benefits (utilities).

These economists contend that nonrational economic behaviour can be explained by the fact that individuals seek a variety of different benefits (utilities) and that any of these can dominate decision making at a given time and can thus focus judgments on different attributes. In examining research in psychology related to decision making. Attribute framing involves individuals making evaluations of particular attributes of an object. They assume no risk is involved.

In general, attribute framing relies on semantic differences related to making what is fundamentally the same choice, such as a describing beef as "75% lean" or "25% fat". Attribute framing also can involve effects from alternative descriptions of the success-failure rate of a particular procedure (i.e., whether results emphasise a 60% success rate or a 40% failure rate), or win-loss rates (i.e., whether a team won 30 games or lost 20 games). Positive framing of attributes consistently leads to more favorable evaluations of objects and attributes than negative framing.

Framing of Risky Choices

A third important area of framing for public relations involves the framing of risky choices, wherein individuals must not merely evaluate attributes but must make a choice between two independent options when some level of uncertainty or risk is present. (The framing of risky choices can be distinguished from framing where no independent choice is at issue and only one course of action is involved.

The framing of choices is one of the most extensively researched areas of framing, based on the classical work of psychologists Daniel Kahneman and Amos Tversky. A frame as a decision maker's perception of "the acts, outcomes, and contingencies associated with a particular choice". In particular, they argued that human decision making is inherently nonrationale because the prospect of a loss has a far greater impact on decision making than does the prospect of an equivalent gain.

In developing their prospect theory of decision making, the psychologists began with an expected-value model wherein it was assumed, in a linear fashion, that an individual who finds $1 would happy and that a person who finds $100 should be 100 times happier. Conversely, they theorised that a person who loses $100 should be proportionately more distressed than a person who loses only $1.

Instead, the researchers discovered an S-shaped curve of responses wherein the prospect of greater gains was perceived as less valuable but that the prospect of even a modest loss far outweighed the prospect of a comparable modest gain. People tend to avoid risks when a choice is stated in terms of gains but will take greater risks when choices are stated in terms of losses. Prospect theory's revelations about the predominant influence of loss-prevention has been a topic of ongoing interest among researchers. Although a variety of moderating factors have been suggested, framing effect has largely withstood testing.

Most studies of prospect theory have involved hypothetical, experimental situations. Original question involving how people would respond to an Asian disease. However, research about the framing of choices has been conducted in a wide range of applied domains as well. For example, health communicators have found patients are willing to select greater risks if the decision means saving a life or reducing suffering.

The same phenomenon has been observed among health care professionals. Findings consistent with prospect theory are reported in the negotiation literature. Mediators have been found to favor bargainers who frame issues in terms of losses rather than gains. Mediators also propose settlements of higher value when both parties frame decisions in loss terms.

A programme of research on the effects of framing on negotiations spearheaded by Margaret Neale suggested that how a negotiator's role is framed influences the negotiator's task orientation to seek the greatest possible concessions, that positive framing of a negotiator's self-confidence leads to more concessions, and that framing can moderate the effectiveness of even expert negotiators.

Organisational behaviour researchers have found that individuals in businesses are willing to take greater risks to avoid losses rather than to seek gains. Marketers similarly have used prospect theory to examine purchasing risk behaviour. Finally, economists have examined the influence of framing on the risk tolerances among auditors and financial planners and the effect of framing persuasive messages related to taxpayer compliance.

However, the effect varies by the domain of the choice. For example, People are more willing to take risks to save human lives than to preserve public property or save personal money. This is consistent with research in health communication that suggests that the context of the decision influences willingness to take risks.

Framing of Actions

Closely aligned to prospect theory's emphasis on the influence of framing gains versus losses, other research related to decision making has focused on the best way to describe action that might be undertaken by individuals to achieve a desired goal. This idea can be labeled framing of actions.

The framing of attributes involves focusing attention on inherent qualities of an object, and whereas the framing of risky choices focuses on willingness of individuals to take risks, framing of actions focuses on persuasive attempts to maximise cooperation in which no independent options or choices are involved. For persuasive communicators, the concern is how to frame actions necessary to achieve compliance with a desired goal.

A familiar example illustrates the idea: Some universities allow students to pay tuition early in a lump sum or to pay a slightly higher amount in installments. Assuming that a university wanted to improve its cash flow, the desired action of paying money earlier can be framed as a discount (a gain), whereas the installment plan might be framed as a surcharge (a loss). The two explanations are different semantically, but the options are the same.

Framing of actions is similar to purevalence framing as used by economists and to goal framing. The latter researchers explain that positive action (goal) framing involves focusing attention on obtaining a positive consequence (gain), whereas the negative frame focuses attention on avoiding the negative consequence (loss) resulting from not taking a particular action.

A specific applied domain in which action framing is especially pertinent is in the effort by health practitioners to promote healthy behaviours and communicate the dangers of risky behaviours. Framing studies have been conducted in the context of preventing automobile accidents, cancer, Downs syndrome, HIV, sexually transmitted diseases, and weight control problems, among others.

People's willingness to engage in particular health-related actions have been shown to be influenced by how risks and alternatives are framed, although various moderating factors have also been suggested. Research in economic psychology similarly suggests that individuals differentially will make choices about the same personal benefits derived from society as a whole, based on whether the issue was framed as an action involving a social dilemma or a public goods problem.

Findings from research involving the framing of actions is somewhat similar to the results obtained in research obtained in the framing of risky choices but differs from findings pertaining to the framing of attributes. Framing of actions in terms of negative consequences appears to have greater persuasive impact than framing that emphasises positive consequences or gains.

Positively framed messages might be more persuasive when people engage in little detailed processing of messages and that negative framing of actions only applies when people engage in higher levels of cognitive elaboration. Aalthough the presence of negatively framed arguments might prompt more elaborate message processing, the effects also might be moderated by an individual's expectations about the type of framing found in a persuasive message.

The effect is also moderated by an individual's perception of self-efficacy (i.e., whether a person believes that following a particular action will lead to the desired outcome). Individuals with high levels of self-efficacy are less inclined to engage in effortful processing, in which case positive and negative frames are equally persuasive. Other factors that influence the framing of actions include the level of consumer expertise and the presence or absence of social interaction.

Framing of Issues

Framing has received increased attention among sociologists and others as a way to examine alternative interpretations of social reality. This approach can be labeled the framing of issues. An issue is a dispute between two or more parties, usually over the allocation of resources or the treatment or portrayal of groups in society. Issues frequently result in extensive public discussion and frequently require resolution within a public policy forum, such as a legislature or the courts.

Issues are the bases around which publics are organised and public opinion is formed Issues can be constructed by as few as two individuals but also can emerge at the group, organisation, interorganisational, or societal levels. At the heart of most issues is the question of interpretation. Disputants involved in an issue often vie to have their preferred interpretation predominate so that others will see the dispute from a perspective similar to their own (i.e., using similar schemas).

Framing has been employed as a tool for analysing public debates on issues and as the focus of still other research in the arenas of negotiation and bargaining. Legal theorists also have recognised the importance of effective issue framing as a key strategy in persuasively communicating with jurors. Organisational behaviour researchers have employed issues framing as variable to understand why and how decisions are made and actions are undertaken.

Applications range from ethical decision making to emergency response planning and employment practices. Framing similarly has been used to examine people's judgments of the fairness of allocation of economic resources. Studies in economics have focused on issues such as income equity, tax equity, willingness to pay for public goods, and social conflicts pertaining to environmental and public health risks.

Framing plays a pivotal role in defining social problems and the attendant moral actions in dealing with them. Investigators outside media studies have used a variety of methods to study the framing of controversies involving politics, gender rights, race, property rights, the threat of religious cults, and the marginalisation of various groups in postmodern society.

In a similar vein, public health issues have been shown to be dramatically influenced by the way they are represented. For example, AIDS has been framed alternatively as a disease involving "high-risk groups" and resulting from "risky practices". Sympathy for AIDS victims varies considerably depending on whether AIDS is described as a disease affecting hemophiliacs, intravenous drug users, or homosexuals.

Social researchers who adopt a constructionist approach argue that social problems are best understood as issues that are constructed by claim makers. Advocates for issues engage in a process of agenda-building that involves mobilizing support, building coalitions, manipulating symbols, and actively seeking publicity in public media. Agenda-building involves pushing issues from the arenas of public discussion, onto the media agenda and ultimately to the public policy agenda, in which issues and social problems can receive official acknowledgment, validation, and the fullest possible hearing.

However, not all issues fully attain public visibility. Among factors that determine the success of issue advocates is the limited carrying capacity of the system as well as the frame enterprise and the effectiveness of frame sponsorship by issue advocates. This process also can be conceptualised as frame building. Framing plays an integral part in the process of agenda-building as advocates attempt to communicate with members of affected or sympathetic groups, either directly or indirectly using the media.

In the latter case, social identification theory suggests the goal is to signal uninvolved group members about how they should think or act in regard to an issue. Frames operate in this definitional process as "devices embedded in political discourse, invented and employed by political elites, often with an eye toward advancing their own interests or ideologies and intended to make favorable interpretations".

In doing so, claims makers try to influence which schematic representations of issue are invoked by politicians and media workers and, most important, by media audiences.Social movement organisations have theorised extensively about the importance of framing. Snow and Social movements engage in three distinct framing processes. Diagnostic framing involves the identification of an event or aspect of social life as problematic or in need of alteration.

Prognostic framing proposes a solution to the diagnosed problem and outlines what needs to be done. Finally, motivational framing represents a call to action as well as the rationale forengagingin ameliorative or corrective action. Elsewhere, the researchers define framing as a device for mobilisation wherein groups attempt to create linkages amongotherwise disparate individuals through a process of frame alignment.

Four strategies identified by the researchers are frame bridging, frame amplification (clarification and crystallisation of beliefs and values held by followers), frame extension (reaching out to include other constituencies), and frame transformation (in which frames are altered in the wake of changing conditions).

Framing of Responsibility

Beyond matters of definition, most issues and social problems entail questions of cause and responsibility (i.e., who should be credited or blamed for events). Whether because of instinct or experience or for self-protection, individuals engage in what Heider termed "intuitive factor analysis" to understand why events happen. Attribution of an event to either personal or environmental factors determines the extent to which an individual is held responsible.

However, the attribution of responsibility does not always reflect the objective facts of a situation accurately and can be distorted based on how events are described. This accounts for yet another type of framing relevant to public relations, the framing of responsibility. Attribution processes, or how humans explain events and human behaviour, have received extensive attention from psychologists.

Theory of causal attribution identified three distinct types of attributions: to an actor, to the object or entity acted on, or to the environment or circumstances in which an event occurs. When individuals have multiple opportunities to observe events, Kelley suggested that attributions are based on patterns of covariation involving three factors: distinctiveness, the extent to which different entities evoke similar behaviour; consensus, the extent to which different actors behave in a similar way; and consistency over time and modality, the extent to which the behaviour is similar in different contexts.

In situations in which only one opportunity to observe is possible. People will tend to give less credence to the role of a given cause if other plausible explanations are also present. Similarly, his argumentation principle suggested that facilitative causal explanations of events are judged more plausible than inhibitory casual explanations if both are considered.

Later attribution research suggests that actions can be labeled (framed) as controlled or uncontrolled, internally or externally originated, or as a result of stable or unstable conditions within a person. Ability, for example, represents an explanation for success that combines internal and stable factors within an individual. Luck or fate, on the other hand, entails external, unstable factors. Attribution processes are easily biased as a result of a variety of factors. These include a lack of effort to find the "best" explanation, the salience of alternative explanations, prior knowledge and extant schemas, and personal needs and motivations.

Fundamental attribution error refers to the tendency to attribute other people's behaviour to stable personality factors or dispositions rather than situations or external causes. Actor-observer bias is the tendency to attribute other people's behaviours to stable dispositions, whereas people attribute their own behaviour to situational factors. Self-serving bias involves self-attributions of success or failure: People tend to attribute their own successes to stable dispositions and their failures to situational factors.

Personal control bias suggests that humans assign blame for disastrous occurrences in proportion to the perceived severity of the consequences.

Finally, the just-world hypothesis suggests evaluations of a victim's suffering become increasingly negative to the degree that the victim's suffering is seen as unjustified. All these ideas suggest that the way an event is portrayed can lead to different conclusions about responsibility. Although some events occur for unidentifiable reasons (so-called "acts of God"), most individuals are unwilling or unable to accept such a simple explanation.

Most people seek to identify the cause and assign responsibility. Americans frame issues to portray the overall social system as fundamentally sound and prefer to attribute problems to corrupt, inept, or irresponsible individuals. The result is to ignore systemic problems related to social organisation or societal resources available to deal with a problem. As a result, events that might have been prevented through intervention simply are dismissed later as accidents due to human error.

Various problems – AIDS, alcoholism, child abuse, cigarette addiction, drug abuse, and overeating – have been framed as problems of individuals rather than society. The solution often involves the medicalisation of problems, wherein emphasis is placed on treatment of individuals rather than on prevention or elimination of the root causes at the societal level.

Efforts to assign responsibility for issues and social problems is referred to as diagnostic framing – a process that can be at work among individuals as well as groups. Diagnostic framing plays a central role in investigative journalism. News workers often begin with a single incident and then work inductively to identify other cases or individuals who might be affected. After sensing the inherent dramatic values in a story, investigative reporters conceptualise a story by placing it within a broader context through framing.

Stories are identified as part of a particular investigative genre and typified as an example of a particular well-known problem, such as political corruption, corporate exploitation, or government waste and inefficiency. As the drama unfolds further, roles inevitably are assigned to victims and villains. Attribution processes are evident in the way that media subtly frame stories and assign responsibility.

News coverage is predominated by the episodic framing of stories to exclusion of thematic framing. Episodic framing involves storytelling from the perspective of people and individual events. Audiences are believed to be more interested in people and more responsive to portrayals involving concrete events and actions (episodes). By contrast, media engage in comparatively little thematic framing, where stories are told more broadly from a societal perspective using abstract concepts instead of case studies or exemplars.

An unintended consequence of the preponderance of episodic framing is that audiences feel absolved of responsibility for social problems because responsibility is so readily attributed to the people portrayed in the news, whether or not the newsmakers depicted are culpable. The desire to attribute responsibility has lead to an emphasis on victimisation in modern society, although stories about victims suffering at the hands of villains can be found in literature across cultures over the centuries.

The seemingly natural tendency is for victims to attribute responsibility for their misfortunes to misdeeds of others, rather than assume any responsibility for their own plight. Although production-of-action is one element of responsibility, causality and responsibility are distinct concepts. Responsibility can subsume causality but also can incorporate notions of legal accountability and moral accountability. Significantly, legal culpability is addressed in courts of law, whereas moral accountability is debated and framed in the court of public opinion.

Framing of News

The final model of framing relevant to public relations deals with news framing (i.e., how news stories are portrayed or framed by the media in an effort to explain complex or abstract ideas in familiar, culturally resonating terms).

Framing has received considerable attention in the past decade as an approach to understanding news processes and effects, although the role of public relations as sources in news framing has been largely overlooked. To recognise the integral role that framing plays in news gathering by media workers and news processing by audiences. News workers use frames to construct social reality for audiences and thus give meaning to words and images.

News workers as "symbol handlers" who use frame selectivity to shape the way news is defined using dominant social frames. The ideas that appear in news are best understood as media packages that feature a central organising idea for events and employ various symbolic or framing devices that support the main idea of the story. The task of media workers thus is to arrange random events into a meaningful, organised interpretive package.

Later media theorists have paid increased attention to framing as an alternative formulation of issues such as bias and objectivity. Hackett observed framing is not necessarily a conscious process on the part of journalists but is the result of their unconscious assumptions about the social world. Although frames are not unique to journalism, they are central to journalistic work and serve as "mental maps" that can be activated quickly and can reduce journalists' efforts.

The ability of media to raise the salience of attributes and to frame values. Strong effects that go beyond simple agenda-setting. Separately, considerable discussion has ensued about how to measure framing effects and role of framing as both dependent and independent variables in media research.

The topics of news framing studies have spanned a wide range of social problems, including abortion, America's "drug problem", Cold War criminals, child mistreatment, fathers' rights, labour strikes, and welfare. Framing also has provided a useful perspective from which to examine portrayals of occupational groups such as artists, as well as ethnic minorities.

The media's portrayal of scientific issues and processes, including issues such as climate change, cold fusion, ozone depletion, and memory recovery. Of particular interest has been the role of framing in the reporting about risk. Specific topics examined within the domain of risk communications involve environmental issues and disputes as well as issues pertaining to public health and the availability of public health services.

References

Friedman, Marsha. *Celebritize Yourself: The Three Step Method to Increase Your Visibility and Explode Your Business*. North Carolina: Warren Publishing, Inc. 2009.

Grunig, J. "Two-way symmetrical public relations: Past, present and future" . In R. Heath (Ed.), *Handbook of public relations* (pp. 11-30). Thousand Oaks: Sage. 2001.

Hall, Phil. *The New PR*. Mount Kisco, N.Y.: Larstan Publishing. 2007.

Kruckeberg, D. & Stark, K. *Public relations and community: A reconstructed theory*. New York: Paeger.1988.

Ledingham J. & Bruning S. (Eds.), *Public relations as relationship management: A relational approach to the study and practice of public relations* (pp. 3-22). New Jersey: Lawrence Erlbaum. 2000.

7

Public Relations and Marketing

Public relations and marketing are essential for companies aiming to get in the public eye and keep a positive image once they are there. When practiced correctly, they gain trust and loyalty from consumers. These practices are intertwined yet can be studied and performed independently. Students studying public relations need to understand both fields to offer more services to potential employers and in result, to consumers.

Public relations is usually encompassed in university communication programs; marketing programs are generally located in business schools. Not all universities require public relations majors to take marketing classes as part of their degree, but it is a good idea to be well versed in both.

Public relations' main concern is that of building positive relationships with publics, crisis and image management, and gauging public opinion on issues relevant to specific companies. It strives to keep the company trustworthy, reliable and current, whereas marketing is involved more with prices, sales and productivity.

Both marketing and public relations went through such dramatic growth and evolution during the first half of the twentieth century that at least one business historian has referred to this period as their "teen-age years." They both experienced surprising growth spurts and, as they gained increasing influence in the business world, they experimented with new strategies and frequently flexed their muscles as they adjusted to what they were becoming and tried to project a positive and confident self-image.

As marketing and public relations expanded their spheres of activities and as they became more aggressive in communicating with more and more and ever-larger publics, they often ended up talking to the same publics, and they sometimes used the same techniques to do it. But, even when their actions appeared to be similar to outsiders such as the consuming public, the practitioners themselves knew that their two disciplines were conceptually very different. Many took pride in these distinctions and were quick to explain them to anyone who asked. Ray Simon, for instance, expressed them very concisely in his second edition of *Public Relations: Concepts and Practices* when he wrote:

> "Marketing and public relations ... both are major external functions of the firm and both share a common ground in regard to product publicity and consumer relations. At the same time, however, they operate on different levels and from different perspectives and perceptions.
>
> The traditional view ... is that marketing exists to sense, serve, and satisfy customer needs at a profit.
>
> Public relations exists to produce goodwill in the company's various publics so that the publics do not interfere in the firm's profit-making ability."

The future is undoubtedly going to be a need for closer relationships between PR and marketing. Indeed, those with PR competencies should be best placed to take advantage of the need for greater flexibility and maturation of communications beyond the traditional one-way advertising approaches. But we won't capitalise on this opportunity for strategic generalists by denying the reality of specialist PR practice. Surely it is time for reverse encroachment with PR people embracing and adopting the best from marketing alongside their own assets.

Advertising and Publicity

Advertising and publicity are two very different communication tools, even though both employ the mass media as a vehicle for reaching large audiences.

— Traditionally, most marketers placed heavy reliance on advertising and only occasionally used publicity.

— On the other hand, public relations practitioners have primarily relied on publicity—or, as they sometimes prefer to call it, media relations—and only rarely used advertising.

This does not mean that advertising should be seen only as a marketing tool and that publicity should be seen only as a public relations tool. Thoughtfully used, both tools are valuable for both functions.

An advertiser purchases air time on a broadcast medium or page space in a print medium and then uses that media time/space to deliver whatever persuasive messages the advertiser chooses to the media's audiences. Presumably, a smart advertiser will purchase ad space in only those media whose audiences are known to be consistent with the target audiences the advertiser wants to reach.

- Most often, advertising messages are inducements to purchase a product.
- However, advertising space can be used for non-product oriented messages.
  - "Adver-torials," for instance, are advertising messages which take sides and present a specific view or opinion about public issues.
  - "Image ads" are those which provide favorable information about an organization and its policies that would not normally be considered "newsworthy" enough for the media to report it of their own volition.

The biggest advantage of advertising is that it gives the organization total control of the message that will be presented to the audience. The advertiser, not the media's editors, control the content, the timing, and the amount of time/space given to the advertising. The biggest disadvantages are the high price of advertising and the skepticism with which audiences sometimes view advertising that they know is unedited opinion of the advertiser.

Public Relations Can Benefit from Advertising

Advertising which had previously been used almost exclusively by marketers trying to sell specific products began to show promise for broader, less sales-oriented messages. Some of the first were so-called image ads that tried to polish or "sell" the reputation of ad's sponsor. Then, despite initial skepticism and, in some instances, strong opposition from traditional journalists and the media companies themselves, public relations people began experimenting and having great success using "issues advertising" to get their views to an otherwise unaware public.

It was a strategy that had previously been used by social and political activists, including the civil rights organizers of the 1960s, to garner support for their causes. It had also been occasionally used for corporate comment on pending public referenda or elections, but it had never been used, or at least not consistently nor successfully used, by corporate public relations practitioners to achieve the business goals of their organizations. By purchasing full-page newspaper ads and using the space to run thoughtful explanations of pricing, tax impacts, and other oil company concerns instead of product ads, Mobil was able to present its perspective to the American public at a time when the predominant popular sentiment was anti-Big-Oil.

Considered an aberration in the early 1970s, these efforts were mocked as "adver-torials," a coined term for paid advertisements which tried to present editorial-like opinions. And, at the time, unlike today, that term carried an almost universally negative connotation. Today, the term "advertorial" is much more neutral than it used to be, but the practice is still most often called issues advertising, a term and a tactic that is fully accepted and respected by the media, the general public, and the public relations profession. It's become a mainstay of many corporate public relations programs.

Publicity is presented by the media because it's "newsworthy.": A publicity-seeker tries to "make the news"—i.e., to convince reporters/editors to present news coverage about a particular person, organization, or event—by saying or doing something that the news media will choose to report of their own volition as part of their usual task of informing the public. The publicity-seeker's intent is to gain free and hopefully favorable editorial coverage. Other people and organizations who are fearful of receiving negative or harmful publicity will employ public relations practitioners to try to suppress or counteract negative media coverage. Publicity-seekers are entirely at the mercy of the media's editors and other staff members.

The editors, not the individual or organization who wants the publicity, decide whether or not anything will be reported in the media. And, even when something is reported, it's the media staff who decide how it will be reported and how much attention it will be given. It's very possible that information which an organization offers the media in a positive and flattering news release could show up in a news story that casts a negative or critical light on the organization that supplied it. For years the conventional wisdom was that the biggest advantages of publicity were the lack of direct cost and the apparent "third-party endorsement" effect.

— It's not necessary to buy media space/time, but publicity is not totally free. There are salary and production costs involved in having someone prepare news releases or perform other publicity work.

— Media audiences often give information presented as publicity more credibility than if the same information were presented in an ad. That's because they know that presumably objective editors decide what's included in the news whereas self-serving organizations decide what to put in their ads.

Integrated Marketing Communication

Integrated Marketing Communication may be a fine term, and an even better concept, but let's not become so enraptured with IMC or any other new terminology that we lose our perspective. Marketing communication, regardless of its parentage, is a reality in many companies..." but then came the punchline: "Employers don't care what integrated communication calls itself as long as it gets the job done." Perhaps, public relations practitioners shouldn't be overly concerned about what their profession is called either.

Public relations has never been the unanimous choice for what to call the process of managing organizational relationships, but in recent years, O'Dwyer's Directory of Corporate Communication has noted, "The number of companies that identify their internal unit for communicating with their constituents as public relations has dropped off dramatically." This is more fully discussed in a linked reading.

Whether integrated marketing communication, corporate communication, or one of the other popular buzzwords will ultimately overshadow public relations as the name of choice remains to be seen. They may all turn out to be short-lived fads. What will be far more important is whether the underlying integration of communication functions that these terms purport to represent will actually be realized and, at this point, the projections are anything but unanimous.

Nonprofit Public Relations

Communicating with the public is an extremely important aspect of any non-profit organization. Through creative and consistent public relations, nonprofit organizations are able to create and present an image to their community. With careful planning and lots of time and effort, an organization can create a public relations plan that will be beneficial for the life of the organization. PR includes ongoing activities to ensure the organization has a strong public image, helping the public to understand the organization and its products and services.

Public Relations defines the term as "...the deliberate, planned, and sustained effort to establish and maintain mutual understanding between an organization and its public. Public relations are the key to how the public perceives, its programs, and its services." Central to effective pubic relations work is design and implementation of a well-designed public relations plan that defines what you want to convey to whom, how you plan to convey it, who is responsible for various activities, by when, and a budget to fund these activities. Some nonprofits have treated public relations as a draining of resources from more mission-critical activities.

However, nonprofit organizations of every size, shape, and mission statement have had to take a crash course in the world of public relations. They need PR to advance those mission-critical services. In today's nonprofit world where competition between organizations can be fierce, we must rely heavily on public relations to convey our messages. The nonprofits that are most successful make public relations planning an integral part of preparing for every activity. What the organization needs is more publicity. We've all heard that assertion. In fact, it's the only real job description many of us ever get. The natural reaction is to start trying to get more publicity. But first things first: you need to answer some important questions before you begin planning a publicity campaign.

Organization Goals: Developing a clear statement of the organization's mission is the essential first step. When this is accomplished, a set of short-term goals will enable you to direct the organization's energy toward achieving your mission successfully. Development of goals leads to questions related to publicity:

- Why do we need publicity?
- What is the nonprofit trying to accomplish that would benefit from other's awareness?
- Who-specifically do we need to talk to in order to succeed?
- Who is the audience?
- What do we want to say to them?

— What is the message?

— What are the best vehicles for our message?

— How can I get the word out in the most direct, efficient way?

Think first about who you need to communicate to. Most nonprofit groups have at least two target audiences; the people who use their services and those whose contributions of volunteer labor, cash, or in-kind contributions enable the program to survive. The most effective communications with each of these groups may be very different. Making sure the potential users of your services know how to gain access to the important message of the nonprofit.

Another form of communication is your effective use of cash contributions which can produce a tangible benefit for the community and for the donor. Still another might be that your nonprofit provides meaningful opportunities for volunteer involvement. The overall objective should be to ensure a steady flow of information to your constituents through a variety of channels. This means integrating your media activities with other public relations/communications tools to keep your visibility high among consumers, volunteers, current and potential contributors, public officials, and other groups or agencies which might lend support.

Planning Process

The most common pitfall in the practice of public relations is the vain hope that one newspaper story or one all-purpose brochure will create all the public awareness that you're nonprofit will ever need. Successful communication is an on-going process that reinforces a few key messages. It's taking every opportunity to seek out potential customers or supporters and tell them why your nonprofit's work is important to them and how they can be involved. The more specific your public relations goals, the more effective you'll be. If your organization needs to increase ticket sales by 20 percent, for example, your public relations plan needs to focus on media and other communications channels most likely to reach potential ticket buyers.

You need to define who those ticket buyers are and what message, carried in what format, has the greatest likelihood of persuading them to buy tickets. A big feature story on your play's "star" in the Sunday paper probably won't cause them to place an order. But if you copy the clipping and send it to your "potentials" list with a personal note and a ticket order form, you'll get better results. Once you've defined who you need to talk to and what you want to say, you're in a position to make the best choice of a communications medium. Next, it's important to try to accomplish only one objective per promotional message. If you want to increase program use, don't also try to raise funds for your program and recruit volunteers in the same promotional piece. It's also important to create separate promotional activities for each distinct target audience and message.

Finally, be alert for opportunities to create working relationships with other groups that reach consumers, volunteers or even contributors to your program - and vice versa. For example, programs for adolescent boys might be of great interest to the high school guidance counselor, Parents without Partners, even juvenile officers. When you're defining "who" to talk to, be as inclusive as possible. Count as potential supporters all the professionals who regularly deal with your target consumers, the organizations which share an interest in them or serve them in some other way. Perhaps you can strengthen each other. Among the most useful elements or tools for creating a solid public relations campaign are these:

Mailing lists are worth their weight in gold if they are broken into constituent categories and if you keep them updated. Gather names and addresses from every possible source within your organization-items like checks from donors, subscription forms from newsletter subscribers, and sign up sheets from volunteers. Enter those names and addresses in your database that can sort them by postal or zip code. At the beginning and end of an event, make a brief public pitch explaining why it is so important for people to respond to the surveys.

Make pencils and pens available. Create incentives for completing the form, like a free museum membership to be given to a person whose survey will be drawn at random. Newsletters you produce can cover the good news that's interesting to your constituents but not necessarily to the mass media. Your newsletter is the place to include consumer profiles, salute volunteers and contributors, outline upcoming activities and thank the repairman who fixed your office equipment at no charge. Thanking such supporters publicly encourages further support.

And it's impressive to potential donors, who often not only want to see that other companies underwrite your activities but also, that you generate grassroots support. Brochures are greatly favored by any organization, and they have their uses. But funds should be allocated for a newsletter first because it's an on-going communication whereas a brochure appears only once. "Go for reach and frequency" is an advertising principle that underscores the importance of consistent, targeted communication. "Reach" refers to the number of members of your target audience that will be exposed to your message. "Frequency" refers to the number of times your message is repeated.

Thus, the brochure targets a single message—one time. The newsletter allows you to change the message frequently and continuously. Audio-visual presentations of five minutes or less can prove useful in many settings: as part of community service fairs, fundraising calls, at presentations to clubs and organizations. Always keep duplicates in case of loss or the need to be represented in two places at once. Speakers bureaus can bring a representative of your group before clubs, churches, service organizations and professional groups that might share an interest in the service you provide.

Poll your members and professionals working in the field to determine their willingness to speak to your group. Then contact groups whose support would be beneficial to your organization to see if a speaker might be scheduled. Follow up on the bookings, keep a list of equipment and power requirements, make sure your speaker is certain of the time, place and directions and ask for feedback after the talk. Exhibits can be assembled from photographs, clippings, existing audio-visual presentations and memorabilia from your group and used at a variety of public gatherings.

Special events, open houses and tours, especially if demonstrations are incorporated, allow old friends and potential new ones to see your organization in action. Billboards and bus cards can often be arranged free or at lower non-profit rates. Contact the billboard company or transportation agency's public service director. Flyers and posters can be placed in homes, stores, community centers, libraries and spots with public bulletin boards. Cleverly designed, they can also serve as mailers to patrons, or, with the addition of a wooden stake, they become yard signs. Certificates and plaques you give to supporters, special volunteers and helpful officials are likely to be displayed if they're attractive. And they'll further spread your fame... as well as your reputation for practicing good public relations.

More and more nonprofit organizations feel that having a presence on the Web is as important as being listed in the telephone book. A basic

Website need not be difficult to create. A nonprofit website should be designed as a resource. Brief description of the nonprofit's history, past projects and activities and long-standing relationships with other organizations may give the browser a positive impression of the nonprofit. Like the newsletter, information for constituents shouldn't just inform, it should also encourage involvement and develop enthusiasm.

The mass media reach large audiences and can, indeed, give your group a shot in the arm that's unequaled. But many newspapers have a rule of thumb limiting feature stories about any group to once a year. Hard news coverage, which includes events and openings of new performances, isn't included in the once-a-year limit. Hard news is what you should strive to create for the greatest mass media exposure. But just because your organization is doing wonderful things doesn't make it automatically newsworthy.

While imagination can increase your success rate enormously, there are some events that are meaningful to you and you alone. They're wonderful. But they're dull to anyone not intimately involved in the organization, no matter how much creativity you apply. You want media to open envelopes bearing your logo and not automatically pitch them because "these people never send me anything interesting."

Contacting the Media

Getting to know the area media contacts is key. It is essential to know who writes the stories, so you know who to contact when you have a worthwhile event taking place. By having a relationship with a particular member of the media, it can increase your chances of getting your story covered. Building positive relationships with the media is an example of how important external communications really are. A personalized letter sent alone or with a press release can point out a specific angle or suggest story ideas or good interview subjects.

A fact sheet or news advisory ticks off the WHO, WHAT, WHEN, WHERE and WHY IMPORTANT in very concise fashion—often with times and places underscored to catch a busy editor's eye. A press kit may be necessary, if you have several related stories to tell; a number of related events, like a month-long series of speakers or demonstrations; or a new programming season to announce. In addition to a fact sheet and general release, a press kit may contain photos, a calendar of events, biographies of key individuals involved and brochures. Calendar Items, if your meeting or event is open to the public, should be in one paragraph detailing the program, place, time and ticket cost (if any) and sent to calendar editors of magazines, newspapers, radio and television stations.

Public service announcements (PSAs) are non-paid "commercials" on a nonprofit organization's upcoming event or its on-going services which many television and radio stations will run free-of-charge. Contact the station's public service director to see if the station requires:

— a written script for a 15 or 30 second spot (type it double spaced in CAPS),
— a pre-recorded spot (which you must produce on your own),
— whether the station will record it for you either in its studios or at your site (usually without charge).

Sometimes radio and television stations assemble basic media lists and make them available to non-profit groups. But if you have to start from scratch, begin with the phone book and organize your list in categories. Radio, television, magazine and newspaper assignment and feature editors deserve a category apiece, as do talk show producers. Another for calendar editors and one for public service directors may also prove useful, depending on the kind of programming your organization does.

Be prepared to update the names on your list with regularity as assignments can change fairly frequently. It may be helpful, in addition, to make two copies of your list: one set up to create labels and another which carries telephone numbers and notes about insertion deadlines. Follow-up phone calls are often helpful in placing stories. A good way to start the conversation is to identify yourself immediately, briefly state your reason for calling and ask if this is a good time to talk. If the reporter says "no," ask when you could call back.

Sometimes reporters or editors are relaxed and chatty, but it's still best to be well prepared with what you want to get across and to make it as succinct as possible. Making a placement on the first try is terrific (and exhilarating). More often, perseverance and many calls will have to be placed before a firm interview is set. On the other hand, if someone is clearly not interested, it's best to take "no" for an answer. If you push too hard, chances are you'll never place anything with that particular reporter. Don't be discouraged if you get minimal or no interest in a given story. It is extremely rare for 100 percent of the media to be interested in a story; and even if they're interested, sometimes a reporter just can't be available at the right time.

Finally, every PR person's recurring nightmare is that a spectacular fire will erupt 30 minutes before his or her "good news" event is set to begin. If that happens, kiss the cameras goodbye. Remember, reporters do file releases for future use in "round-up" stories. And even if you can't sell your first story, you will have made a valuable media contact and have improved your chances for the next time!

Scheduling Publicity

Scheduling distribution of press releases and PSAs(Public service announcements) can make the difference between getting media coverage, and wondering what happened to the crowd you expected.

— *Four weeks in advance*: For Immediate Release. Especially important for long- range print media (magazines and special sections of the newspapers), and television.

— *Two weeks in advance*: For Immediate Release. Follow up releases to weekly/daily print media and radio/TV.

— *One week in advance*: Media advisory. General summary information only that generates media interest and reminds them of the project. Limit to one to two paragraphs including your highest priority information.

— *One day in advance*: Media Alert: Fax or email typically works best, so make sure that your media outlets will accept fax or email formats of press notifications.

Where long-range planning is possible, you should prepare items for community calendars, Chamber of Commerce publications, etc. Lead time on these outlets is often very long; six months or more, so check to be sure you are providing the information in the posted time frame.

E-Mail Campaigning

An email campaign is an excellent way to build interest in an event, promote attendance, solicit volunteers, and even solicit donations. Like all other aspects of marketing and PR, you need to consider timing, potential interest and providing complete and accurate information. The e-mail list is the most critical aspect of planning this part of a campaign. If your organization produces an on-line newsletter or regularly updates its website, then you can use both to solicit interest in signing up for email information. If you purchase your email list, make sure to do so from a reputable organization, and keep in mind that no matter how current your list, some addresses are going to be out of date. When constructing an email for mass distribution, consider the following:

— Subject line should be succinct, eye-catching and complete so that people scanning their mailbox will be less likely to delete without reading
— Contents should provides the answers to the (Who, What, When, Where, Why, and How)
— Not all email readers work the same way, and not all email recipients use the same format. Consider an HTML version and a plain-text version.
— Provide links to websites with more information, and other means of contacting the organizers.
— Provide a means for the recipient to unsubscribe.
— Insert addresses in the BCC: box, not the TO: box. This reduces the opportunity for spammers to harvest e-mail addresses, and alerts the recipient that you recognize the value of their privacy.

Flyers and Postcards Designing

— Use standard sizes whenever possible for flyers and posters
— Postcards: Use USPS standards for postcard sizes to keep postage costs to a minimum.
— Web pages: Contact the webmaster for information on how your event web page can be included on the chapter site. Sponsoring organizations should be linked, and you should get links from their sites. Basic layout will be similar to poster or flyers.
— Provide the basic 5Ws (Who, What, Where, When and Why) and 1H (How) information and use the PR worksheet to determine what needs to be included.

Design flyers/postcards/posters with:

— No more than two fonts
— Adequate white space to prevent cluttering

— Appropriate and well-designed borders, clip art or photos
— Eye-catching but not distracting layout of elements
— Short, pithy and entertaining text.

Once you know what you will produce, then get it done and get it out. Work closely with vendors to determine what they need-electronic files, or camera-ready hard copy, transparencies, etc. and what formats are acceptable. Have someone other than the person creating the piece proofread it carefully. Printing vendors will usually provide a proof copy and will ask you to sign off when it is ready.

Distribution of flyers and posters is critical. In person visits to local businesses are a great way to get flyers posted. Some businesses may even be willing to include a small flyer when bagging purchases. Always ask permission, and thank the businesses even if they cannot post a flyer for you.

Public relations can make or break a new product launch: To have a successful new product launch, one needs more than a good product. Good public relations can be part of that "more." In fact, it can sometimes produce a successful product launch, while the lack of public relations may contribute to the failure of a launch. The type of public relations (PR) usually used in new product launches, especially with consumer products, can be defined as "enhanced persuasion."

The formula for success in this type of PR as shown in the box to the right is to target the right people and generate word-of-mouth buzz. In practice, a PR product launch plan may include items such as selecting appropriate launch messages, preparing company representatives for public presentations, getting non-disclosure agreements signed, identifying and using third-party advocates, pre-briefing analysts and reporters, getting media coverage, and arranging public speaking engagements.

The first company introduced their product line with a minimal launch effort. Although the product line was a technical success, it was withdrawn from the market after five years because of poor sales. The customers that had standardized on this product line had to re-invest to incorporate alternative products into their processes. The second company launched their product line with the support of their senior technical staff and other respected industry experts.

Their product line had over 700 part numbers and the market was convinced of their commitment to the new technology. Within 18 months, the PR campaign and product advertising helped this product line achieve an annual run rate of $5 million in sales. The product line's success ensured that it would continue to be sold for many years and provide revenue to the company to enhance technical support. Firms that lack the resources or the will to mount a PR campaign in support of a new product should seriously consider whether it even makes sense to invest in product development in the first place.

PR played a major role for the winner for the best hi-tech campaign. The winner was OutCast Communications along with Good Technology. They won for Good Technology's enterprise solution which provides a desktop-like experience from a mobile device. This device enables two-way communication for messaging and information access for handheld devices.

Increasing Awareness

Good Technology's pilot program promised that if an enterprise gave them two hours with their Microsoft Exchange Server administrator they would provide hardware devices, software, and service for 30 days. Good Technology worked with partner organizations such as cellular providers, equipment manufacturers, and software developers, and made strategic alliances with companies such as Dell to demonstrate wireless corporate messaging and information access solutions to a wide variety of industries. Each success enhanced their credibility to provide a solution for new customers.

Good Technology focused on their core competencies. They have a customer-centric product development process. They identified and implemented important features such as cradle-free synchronization to provide convenience and fresh information; standards-based components to provide a greater choice in the selection of supported hardware and software; and bulletproof security. They had to have a great product because the competition was the established market leader. The sales and support groups were prepared to customize solutions for new clients.

How can successful PR be measured?: One primary success metric - besides press clippings - is the number of highly motivated inquiries that a product receives. In addition, marketing synergy is improved when the PR assets can be re-purposed for use in the company's web site or promotional materials. Begin by inventorying your internal capabilities and capacities in marketing, public relations, advertising, branding, event management, and analyst relations. If you need an external PR agency, identify teams that have had success with existing clients in the same industry. Talk to colleagues.

Look on the web sites that list public relations pros the Public Relations Society of America, and the International Association of Business Communicators (IABC). You will find there are advantages - and disadvantages - in working with large PR agencies versus boutiques. Typically, a PR agency should not be used for strategic development or for most of the marketing portion of a new product development effort. Traditionally, PR agencies engage in the new product development process when product prototypes are available and they have maximum visibility at the time of product announcement.

To gain fullest value, the PR agency should become part of your launch management system. Typically, it is better equipped to handle communications problems - such as production delay or some other negative publicity - than you are, or even your in-house PR people.

Public Relations as a Management Function

Public relations help our complex, pluralistic society to reach decisions and function more effectively by contributing to mutual understanding among groups and institutions. It serves to bring private and public policies into harmony. Public relations help organisations manage change, something they must do to stay competitive and efficient. But since change is threatening and often resisted, smooth transition through a necessary change guided by public relations professionals is a real dollar-saver. As a management function, public relations encompass the following:

i) Anticipating, analysing and interpreting public opinion, attitudes, and issues that might impact, for good or ill, the operations and plans of the organisation.

ii) Counselling management at all levels in the organisation with regard to policy decisions, courses of action, and communications, taking into account their public ramifications and the organisation's social or citizenship responsibilities.

iii) Researching, conducting, and evaluating, on a continuing basis, programs of action and communication to achieve the informed public understanding necessary to success of an organisation's aims. These may include marketing, financial, fund raising, employee, community or government relations, and other programs.

iv) Planning and implementing the organisation's efforts to influence or change public policy. Setting objectives, planning, budgeting, recruiting and training staff, developing facilities-in short, managing the resources needed to perform all of the above.

Public relations does seek to persuade people. It can influence what you buy, how you use a product, and what you do to improve your health. Yet the average person may have no real idea of how omnipresent public relations is in their lives. In fact, most people do not know what public relations really is. Critics warn us that the hidden public relations industry is a danger and that stealth is a strategic choice. Public relations is unseen largely because people choose not to see it. News outlets do not announce a story was the result of a news release or pitch letter. However, if you look closely at the news you can determine which stories are likely to have public relations origins. Do some research and you will quickly learn about nutrition labels and the efforts to shape their content, the groups pushing for bans on trans fats and companies changing their products, and what efforts are underway to promote "No Dirty Gold" and who is doing the promoting.

Public relations is just below the surface in our daily lives. We can realise its existence and potential influence on our lives if we critically examine the messages generated by public relations. Public relations should be able to survive thoughtful interrogation. Those who would abuse and misuse public relations should fear public relations literacy. The tricks of these charlatans could and should be exposed.

Periodically in the public relations literature there are defences of the use of persuasion. For those from a communication studies background, such defences appear to be an unusual and needless exercise. Of course a communication-based activity such as public relations would involve persuasion. Most, if not all, communication has a persuasive dimension. However, some in the field of public relations try to divorce the field from persuasion and claim public relations is objective and neutral. They contend public relations, like the news media, just presents the facts to people. They see public relations as a mechanism for carrying information from organisations to publics.

The objectivity of the news media has always been a myth. Journalists select what to report and how to report it. These selections involve subjectivity. The same holds true for public relations. Trying to argue there is no persuasion in public relations denies the fact that public relations does promote self-interests. That is not inherently a bad thing. Moreover, public relations as a field looks naive and even deceptive to people outside the field when it claims to be objective and simply a conduit for the facts.

Corporate-centric View of Public Relations

Public relations is about influencing behaviours, knowledge, and attitudes. The practice must accept the implications that accompany the use of influence including issues of power and its abuse.

Public relations can be as the management of mutually influential relationships within a web of stakeholder and organisational relationships. The term "stakeholder" is used because it captures the idea that entities have some connection to one another for some reason. They are interdependent. These connections are why actors are enmeshed in a web of relationships. In addition, stakeholder theory does denote some consideration of power. Stakeholders are people, groups, organisations, or systems that can affect or can be affected by an organisation.

Managers look beyond shareholders and financial stakes to a broader range of stakes or connections to an organisation. Stakeholder theory, rooted in the work of R. Edward Freeman, seeks to identify and to understand the various stakeholders in an organisation. By better understanding stakeholders, managers can decide who deserves their attention and time. Managers then work with the more important stakeholders with a hope of advancing organisational interests. Stakeholders can shape organisational practices through their giving or retracting of stakes (support). If it is important for stakeholders to grant an organisation a license to operate, they do have some power. However, critical scholars have expressed some concerns over using the term stakeholder.

The concern is that the term stakeholder has been co-opted by corporations and reflects the continuing corporate-centric bias in public relations. A corporate centric view of public relations emphasises how corporations use public relations to achieve economic success. True, Freeman's work does place the organisation at the centre of his explanation of stakeholders. Originally, stakeholders were conceptualised as groups whose support was essential to the survival of the organisation. Later, stakeholders were seen as those who were affected by or could affect the organisation. Ultimately, the term stakeholder today can legitimately be viewed as a way that organisations, especially corporations, evaluate groups jockeying for their attention. There is compelling evidence to support the critical claim that "stakeholder" is tainted by its corporate use and an emphasis on the centrality of the organisation.

Alternatively, some have argued for the use of the term "public." However, the corporate-centric taint also plagues "public." A public forms "when stakeholders recognise one or more of the consequences as a problem and organise to do something about it or them". The consequences centre on the connection between the organisation and stakeholders. Hence, publics form in reaction to organisational actions. Publics develop when they realise they share a concern over an organisation's action and join forces to address that "issue." Publics are aware they are connected to one another and choose to take action. Stakeholders may realise others share their stake but are not an active entity. "Publics ... organise around issues and seek out organisations that create those issues".

Grunig's situational theory of publics tells public relations practitioners to engage those publics most likely to communicate on an issue. The situational theory of publics uses surveys to determine which people are aware of a problem and interested in doing something about it. The surveys assess public interest by determining the extent to which people perceive a problem (problem recognition), the amount of concern they have for the problem (level of involvement), and extent to which they perceive factors limiting their ability to address the problem (constraint recognition). Situational theory makes value judgments and is used to prioritise publics—who will receive an organisation's attentions. Clearly, the organisation is still at the centre of how public relations theorists have conceptualised "public." The terms stakeholder and public both use organisations as a reference point in their conceptualisations.

Perhaps the term "constituencies" is a better choice than stakeholders and organisations. Constituencies can be defined as groups of people in a similar situation. By this definition stakeholders are constituencies and organisations are constituencies. Stakeholders share a stake while people in organisations share an affiliation with that organisation.

People engage in public relations largely from self-interest and self-advantage. Even those entities engaged in social marketing—the application of traditional marketing principles to solving societal problems and benefiting the recipients of the message– have an interest that drives their public relations effort. Public relations is about advocacy and power. Too often, those who write about public relations use the guise of informational efforts to hide intent but should acknowledge they are engaged in persuasion. Influence is a type of power when one constituency can alter the behaviour of another. Rarely do two parties in a relationship have equal influence/power. In most instances, corporations and government agencies are the constituencies with the most power in the web of relationships. Still, any constituency has some power when it can remove itself from the web of relationships. Constituencies use public relations to compete with one another in efforts to influence the other players in the web of relationships.

Frequently, public relations textbooks treat each relationship between two constituencies in isolation from the others. Generally, the textbooks are corporate-centric. So students learn about media relations or community relations as distinct units and processes. This creates the impression that the relationships are independent rather than interdependent. When constituencies take action (communicate with others), it has the potential to affect more than one relationship. Therefore, it is important to remember the web of relationships.

Another feature of the web of relationships is the connection to social capital. Social capital is the aggregate of the actual or potential resources which are linked to possession of a durable network of more or less institutionalised relationships of mutual acquaintance or recognition. Constituencies want to manage the web of relationships because of the social capital generated by that web. Social capital makes it easier for constituencies to achieve their goals. This can include advocacy efforts to improve the health of a community, reduce greenhouse gases, or reduce impediments to corporate profitability.

Modern public relations has attempted to re-energise the term relationship. This reclamation includes an emphasis on building strong relationships with constituencies and ways to measure the strength of those relationships. The relationship-oriented public relations research reflects the corporate-centric view. Organisations are said to derive benefits from close relationships with constituencies. The rationale for the relationships clearly is grounded in the benefits the constituents provide the organisation. Customers are a prime illustration. Corporations want customers that have close ties to the corporation and perhaps even become advocates or evangelists for the brand.

Consider an alternative view based on Simon's Empty World Hypothesis. The Empty World Hypothesis holds that most things are weakly connected to one another, what Weick terms *loose coupling*. People or entities often benefit more from their weak ties than from their strong ties. The typical example is that weak ties are the most common route to finding employment. Weak ties extend a person or entity's reach and supply them with unique information they are unlikely to find in their close relationships. Research across a variety of fields supports the value of weak connections/ loose coupling/weak relationships.

More recently, activists have begun to recognise the value of weak connections/ relationships. Instead of creating large organisations that have a strong central structure, some experts argue that activists should be net-centric. Net-centric activists are collections of weakly linked activist groups that form a loosely connected coalition. When action is needed, the activist groups are mobilised through tighter/stronger links, but then return to their loosely connected structure once the action is completed. Weak links create communication channels that are used to reach and to mobilise the various activist groups and form a tightly connected coalition for short periods of time. Moreover, the weak ties help to build social capital that can be spent on activist efforts.

Constituencies can be heavily interconnected. The web of relationships is rather fluid. The links that are active and relationships that are close will vary over time and situations. In addition, no one constituency is monolithic. Each constituency can be subdivided into smaller units. Coalitions shift in the relational web as different constituencies and subgroups form temporary strong ties and may even conflict with other constituencies in the web.

Perhaps corporations should take a lesson from the activists. It could be unrealistic to expect most or even a larger percentage of a corporation's constituencies to have close relationships with an organisation. Weak links/ relationships may be sufficient. Weick's idea of partial inclusion is helpful here. *Partial inclusion* holds that people have connections and affiliations with a wide range of groups, not just one. As a result, people have divided loyalties. People are invested in a variety of constituencies, not just one—

they are partially included in the various constituencies. It forces people to choose between the conflicting groups. So which constituency is favoured when issues are contested? A person typically selects the group in which she or he has invested the most or rejects those in which they have minimal investments. The investment is a type of social capital. However, investment is not a perfect predictor of which constituency a person will select when there are conflicts. If the investments in conflicting constituencies are small, the outcome is difficult to predict.

The weak ties provide avenues for staying connected and building social capital, but do not have to be overused. The role of public relations may be to build and maintain links, not to obsess over the relationship quality. Those links need to be two-way. All constituents need to be open and responsive to communication from others in the relationship web. Responsiveness could be the hallmark of an effective link. Ccorporations and other entities should not think all ties must be strong ties with all constituencies all the time. A more likely scenario is that most constituencies have weak ties to entities. It is the maintenance and utilisation of those weak ties that will make the greatest difference when self-interests collide in the web of relationships.

Public relations utilises various communication tools in its efforts to influence constituencies and to shape the web of relationships. It is one mechanism for attracting and retaining constituencies in the web of relationships and those efforts are an exercise in influence.

The term public relations does not always bring out the most favourable reaction when it is used. Too often, the media and people in general use the term as a derogatory comment, such as "It's a public relations move." The insult involves the belief that public relations is all about style and not substance. Clearly, people who have been through a public relations course know—or should know—differently. Public relations must be rooted in actions to be effective.

Public relations often is equated with spin and publicity. Spin doctors make sure only the positive information about an organisation or individual is communicated to others and reported in the news media, or they reinterpret information to cast it in a more favourable light. Public relations practitioners are roadblocks to people being truly informed. The public assumes public relations is a mechanism corporations use to polish their images by hiding their true selves. Again, an introductory public relations course should correct that perception. The problem is that the vast majority of people who encounter the term public relations never had and will never have had a public relations course. Instead, the term public relations is victimised by its own past that leads many to treat it as a pariah in society.

Many writers, especially public relations historians, claim that public relations was born from corporate reactions to the muckrakers and reformers of that time. This choice gives rise to two of the common criticisms of public relations. Journalists left newspapers to become public relations practitioners for corporations. First problem, public relations is a tool of corporations. Second problem, public relations is just a simplistic form of media relations (attempts to place information into the news media) or spin.

Corporations are not inherently evil; some just choose to act that way. However, for many social critics, being a "corporate tool" is a scathing indictment. From their perspective, public relations has been used to oppress workers, exploit consumers, harm society, and ravage the environment.

Today, public relations becomes an important device in civil society. Civil society is composed neither of business nor government, but is essential to the operation of a democracy. Non-governmental organisations (NGOs) and private voluntary organisations (PVOs) are part of civil society. Civil society allows people to come together and to debate issues of the day and petition the government for change. Public relations is a tool for social reform. It is born from activists desiring to improve the human condition and was a tool of public advocacy.

Public relations would be rooted neither in the corporate realm nor journalism/media relations. It would be a valued tool in social reform. When corporations and their journalist cronies began using public relations in the 1900s, it would be treated as the spread of public relations to the corporate sector, not its birth. The roots of public relations would be firmly planted within reform and civil society rather than corporations and the news media.

The concept of public relations literacy, the ability to identify, analyse, and evaluate public relations messages, can help us to wrestle with these larger issues. Public relations literacy is inspired by and derived from media literacy. In general, media literacy helps people develop a critical understanding of the media, the techniques used by the media, and the effects of those techniques.

Public relations is primarily a mediated enterprise and does have effects on individuals and society. Therefore, media literacy is relevant. In fact, some public relations issues do appear in discussions of media literacy. Public relations literacy is more specific and warrants consideration in its own right although it is informed by media literacy. In addition, public relations literacy is not a criticism nor a condemnation of public relations. The point is to create critical consumers of public relations actions who understand the effects of those actions. The point is not to create people who will simply bash public relations as a profession.

Public relations literacy is the application of critical thinking skills to the examination of public relations techniques and the effects of those techniques on individuals and society. Public relations literacy skills include the ability and willingness to understand public relations messages, an understanding and respect for the power of public relations messages, and the ability to critically evaluate a public relations message regardless of its source. Public relations literacy demands an understanding and interrogation of the public relations process. Just as the media have various genres or forms, public relations has various disciplines. To be critical, a person needs a working understanding of the various disciplines of public relations. Understanding the target for the public relations action is insightful because it reminds us who is considered relevant and irrelevant.

As with most fields, the future of public relations is bound to technology and globalisation. Today, technology refers to online communication. Constituencies have many more and improved options for communicating with one another than they did ten or even three years ago. Consider the availability of interactive video, instant messaging, blogs, vlogs (video weblogs), and other communication tools.

The public relations move to the online world is viewed as rather aggressive by some critics. Public relations is corrupting the independent exchange of information spirit of the internet. Public relations practitioners now pitch or even buy bloggers to write favourable comments about an organisation. Under the banner of public relations, actions have been taken to suppress fair comment and free speech to comment on corporations. The word *flog* (fake blog) was created to cover public relations practitioners posing as "independent" bloggers. Granted, these are isolated examples for the most part and do not reflect all public relations activities on the web. Still, these abuses by those claiming to practice public relations serve to pollute the online environment and cast additional criticisms on the field.There are favourable trends developing from the online application of public relations as well. Activist groups can use various online technologies that are comparatively inexpensive ways to reach potential constituents and build their power. Online resources are used to recruit and mobilise supporters, pressure decision makers, generate media coverage, and raise money for other public relations efforts. But some activist groups have abused that power by trying to silence the voices of others.

Ethics always will remain a concern because of public relations' role in influencing others. Consider how the professional associations have and continue to wrestle with ethics. Visit any popular public relations blog and you will read postings about ethics. Public relations is influence and influence is dangerous when abused. Concerns for ethics remind practitioners to honour their responsibilities to society.

Business Advantages of PR

If you have all the business you will ever want and are rich beyond the dreams of avarice, you may not need public relations. A crisis is an obvious exception. Even if your sales are skyrocketing and you don't need to promote yourself, you may want to engage in PR activities to avoid negative publicity or correct any bad press that comes your way. Other reasons a business or person may want to use PR are:

i) To grow the business

ii) To make more money

iii) To increase sales

Doctors, lawyers, dentists, chiropractors, therapists, and other professionals can promote their practices with public relations. PR is used with virtually every product category, from construction equipment and industrial goods to food, health and beauty products, healthcare, travel, tourism, real estate, and investments. In high-tech industries, everyone from hardware manufacturers to software companies, e-commerce websites, and service providers has benefited enormously from the power of PR. So one perspective of PR concerns a person's goals, where she is now, and where she wants to be. Good PR can turn marginal businesses into profitable ones and ordinary folks into millionaires.

Another perspective of PR has to do with resources. If a business has an advertising budget that approaches infinity and it won't miss the money if it's spent, the business can probably get its message across without relying on the subtler medium of PR. That doesn't mean it *shouldn't* use PR as part of its marketing mix, however: Many clients find that a relatively modest investment in PR greatly extends the reach of their total promotional program.

Cost is one of the great appeals of PR to both small businesses and large corporations alike. Small businesses with limited budgets simply can't come close to matching the ad budgets of larger competitors. PR can help them level the playing field and get the same or better promotional bang for a lot fewer bucks. As for the big corporations, if you work for one, you know that getting more money in the marketing budget is always an uphill battle. With PR, you can achieve the objectives senior managers want even if they don't give you the money you think you need to do it.

The real value of PR is using it to solve a real-life marketing situation for a real product, service, organisation, brand, or image. PR can work for any and every industry, from florists to funeral directors, software to soft ice cream. Any organisation or individual with a message to deliver or a goal to achieve can benefit from a PR effort.

Creative PR, with proper execution, can work wonders for manufacturers, wholesalers, distributors, retailers, resellers, agents, service companies, and professional practices in any industry. PR is perhaps the best means of getting your message out on a continual basis and eliminating periodic sales slumps.

Public relations can connect you with anyone who reads a publication, listens to radio, watches TV, or rides the internet—in short, anyone who is exposed to the media, which in the United States means just about everyone. PR, therefore, has the broadest reach of perhaps any element of the marketing mix. Websites and banner ads reach only those people connected to the internet, which amazingly is fewer than 5 percent of the world's population. Direct mail reaches only people whose names are on mailing lists, and in many countries, mailing lists are not available for rental.

But almost everyone, everywhere, reads a newspaper or magazine, or watches TV. That's why PR is effective at targeting both business and consumer audiences. The best publicity outlets for reaching consumers are radio, television, newspapers, and consumer magazines. For business, use these as well as business magazines, associations, and the internet. If you want to appeal to a particular industry or profession, target the trade publications they read.

Employees are a well-defined audience and reachable at any time. One of the best PR vehicles for employee communication is a company magazine or newsletter. Some large corporations even have in-house TV stations that broadcast the latest company news and information via closed-circuit TV. Investors and members of the financial community are an important PR audience for publicly traded corporations, and press releases are the way to reach them.

Public relations is more than just pitching stories to the media or mailing out press releases. The PR umbrella covers a number of related activities, all of which are concerned with communicating specific messages to specific target audiences. If you're the PR person at ABC Enterprises, you're responsible for managing communications between your company and your public.

The label public relations typically encompasses the following:

i) *Research:* You have to thoroughly understand not only your company but also your customers and potential customers.

ii) *Strategic planning:* Define each target audience, your marketing objectives for that group, and the messages you must communicate in support of those marketing objectives.

iii) *Publicity:* For most small businesses, the central public relations activity is publicity—getting visibility for your products, the company, and the owners in print and broadcast media.

iv) *Community relations:* The PR professional's job is to find a favourable solution that will get the store built while preserving the store's goodwill with the citizens.

v) *Government relations:* Community relations often involves relations with the local government, and PR people are often called upon to help companies improve their relationships with local, state, federal, and even foreign governments.

vi) *Internal relations:* Employees are the internal audience. With the unemployment rate at an all-time low, good employees are hard to find, and a good public relations program job can help improve loyalty and retain more of them.

vii) *Investor relations:* With the incredible stock market volatility of 2000, or more recently, the events of September 11, 2001, and the Indian Ocean Tsunami in 2004, we've all seen how emotion and public perception have the power to send stock prices soaring or plummeting. Investor relations is the aspect of PR that communicates the company story to stock analysts and other financial professionals.

viii) *Stakeholder relations:* A stakeholder is anyone or any organisation that holds a stake in how well your company performs. A key vendor is a stakeholder; rumours that you are financially shaky may cause them to restrict your credit terms. Other key stakeholders can include top consultants, board members, your bank, suppliers, sales representatives, distributors, and industry gurus.

ix) *Charitable causes:* When a company gives to charity, it wants to help the cause, but it also wants to be recognised for its contribution. PR specialists can help you get maximum publicity and goodwill from the time, effort, and funds you donate.

x) *Communications training:* In large corporations, PR specialists may spend a lot of time coaching senior executives in dealing with the media and other communications skills. The specialists may also advise the executives on strategy for day-to-day PR as well as PR crises.

Effective Use of Public Relations

Public relations is such a flexible communications tool that it can be used as part of almost any marketing strategy. However, it is a discipline that relies on having an interesting story to tell about your product or service. The more interesting it is, the more you can expect journalists to write about it, key opinion leaders to want to have an opinion about it, and consumers to want to know about it.

If your product or service isn't inherently interesting, then you'll need to spend more on your public relations to make it so. If you don't, your PR efforts will fail. It really is as simple as that. A couple of examples to illustrate the point. Let's say your company has just launched a brand new product. It's the first of a kind. It could be used by millions. It'll save people lots of time and money. That's a story. In this case, a well-crafted press release might be all you need to generate media coverage worth hundreds of thousands.

Most people think of PR as a tool primarily for generating offline media coverage. In that sense, it's sometimes seen as an alternative to traditional advertising. On internet, however, it's a very different story. On the net, advertisers have essentially just one choice: banner advertising. There are two problems with banner advertising. Firstly, they are by definition limited in size and 'presence'. You just can't create the same impact with a banner as you could with a page in a tabloid newspaper. Secondly, there is growing evidence that the more time we spend on the internet, the more we condition our brains to ignore banner ads, and indeed any other extraneous information that we aren't looking for. PR, on the other hand, integrates your message right where it needs to be: within the actual text of the information the reader is looking for. With that in mind, here are a few examples of when and how to use public relations. This list is by no means exhaustive:

When to Use Public Relations

— To launch and establish sales of a new product or service.
— To maintain awareness about and drive sales.
— To directly increase traffic to a website and drive online sales.
— To increase a website's search engine rankings.
— To get key opinion leaders to influence others about your product.
— To get distributors or retailers to influence others about your product.
— To secure more favourable terms from your suppliers.

To minimise the impact of a crisis relating to your product or service.

How to Use Public Relations

— By generating editorial coverage in the traditional trade or consumer media.
— By generating coverage in the online trade or consumer media.
— By placing advertorials (paid for editorial), in the trade or consumer media.
— By hosting or sponsoring an event.
— By carrying out a public stunt or guerrilla marketing.

— By sending a direct mail piece.
— By contributing to online discussion e-mail groups.
— By triggering word of mouth discussion, on or offline.

Those are just a few of the ways that you can communicate your message using PR. There are many others.

Selection of PR Consultants

Your choice of PR consultants is critical to the success of the project. The tips for selecting a public relations agency is given below.

Judge the People

Public relations agencies will usually field a team of their most senior staff to pitch for your business. Nothing wrong with that. Certainly you need to have confidence that the people in charge know what they're doing. But they're rarely the people that will be representing you to the outside world. So don't just talk with the organ grinders, go and spend some time with the monkeys.

Scrutinise the Quality

Passion and enthusiasm—make sure that the person who will be talking to journalists on your behalf is as excited about your business as you are. A charming and easy manner—hard to define, but you're looking for someone who is easy to warm to. They may have only seconds to make an impression over the telephone, so they'll need to be enthusiastic without being annoying; confident without being arrogant.

Grasp of the facts—sector experience can help, but it's not the be all and end all. What's really important is that your PR grasps the facts quickly, and can answer a journalist's questions promptly.

Common sense and a can-do approach—public relations is often unpredictable. So whether a project throws up a completely different outcome to that expected, or a journalist sets a seemingly unmeetable last-minute deadline, your PR needs a problem-solving attitude.

Don't be Over-impressed

It helps to know people in the media. But only inasmuch as it helps a PR company get the job done quicker. What matters above all to a journalist is the story. That's all. If the story is good, they'll take it from a stranger. If it's not, even their best friend won't persuade them to run it.

Size Matters

When you select the agencies you want to pitch for your business, make sure you include a big and a small agency on your shortlist. Bigger agencies may have access to more resources, and offer economies of scale. But the bureaucracy associated with bigger agencies can stifle individual initiative. Smaller agencies may also be hungrier for your business and offer a more personal and accountable service.

Don't be Impressed by Jargon

On the contrary, the more jargon an agency uses, the less likely it is able to 'connect' with the public, or its intermediary, often the tabloid hack.

Watch for Hidden Costs

Many public relations agencies charge extra for things that you might presume would be included in a retainer fee or project costs, such as photocopying. Some also charge substantial mark ups on expenses. Be clear from the start exactly what you're getting for your money.

Maximising Media Coverage

Almost every story presents multiple opportunities to secure media coverage. So, once you have written your main press release, identify any other categories of journalists that might be interested, and tailor the release for the different needs of each category.

If your story was initially targeted at the national media, is there an angle for local or regional media? If there is, prepare additional releases that lead on the local angle. For example, you've organised a national competition—you should be able to secure media coverage in the home towns of each of the finalists. If, on the other hand, your release was originally targeted at a local newspaper, consider whether it might be strong enough for the nationals. If the story is that you're opening a new store, probably not.

There may be many different angles to your story. Say you've just commissioned research that has proven that children from pet-owning households are healthier than children that don't have a pet. That's a national news story. But you've also got obvious angles for the parenting media, the pet press, and children's magazines. Whilst you're there, don't forget to submit your press releases to internet-based news services. They are becoming more valuable in their own right, and your story may get picked up from the internet by an offline journalist.

Want bucket loads of media coverage with the least amount of effort? Then don't forget to submit your story to a regional or national news agency. Get your story in with them, and it could get picked up by all the nationals for the next day.

Write your radio press release to read more like a script. Make it sound like something you'd expect to hear being read on the radio. Offer an interviewee and include, say, five proposed interview questions that the broadcaster can ask your interviewee.

Television is the hardest nut to crack. Broadcast media is governed by very tight regulations concerning how and if commercial products can be mentioned. Your story needs to be very strong and very visual. You'll have to be very inventive in finding ways to get your product mentioned or seen.

Contacting Journalists

If there's one thing that really annoys journalists, it's being telephoned when they're in the middle of writing something, by someone who wants to know whether they got a press release.

Afternoons are never much good for daily newspaper journalists, as they're rushing to meet deadlines for the next day's edition, and won't appreciate your call. Also, never ring a national newspaper when there is big news breaking.

Introduce yourself and ask the journalist if they've got a couple of minutes to hear your story. Then tell the story as if you had never sent the press release in the first place. If the response is: "Ah yes, I saw a press release on this", you can ask whether they think they'll be doing anything with it. If the response is: "Do you have a press release", you can say you've already sent one. It's obviously gone missing; can they give you an e-mail address to re-send it to. Either way, you've made contact, elicited some sort of reaction to your news, and all without asking whether or not they received it.

Writing of any sort requires concentration and undivided attention. Journalism probably requires these things in greater measure, as in addition to the requirement for good copy, there are deadlines to meet. So, don't expect to be met with a warm response from every journalist you ring. Most are helpful and polite. A small minority, usually the ones under greatest pressure, will just tell you to bugger off. Don't let the rude ones colour your opinion of journalists per se. Just take it on the chin, and move along to the next one.

Unless your press release has been met with a hugely positive reaction, or you know the journalist well, don't expect them to commit to publishing your story. Chances are that it's not their decision anyway, and the best you can hope for is a broad indication of whether they liked it.

By all means have a laugh with a journalist to get them to warm to you, but don't forget that you are on record, and off-the-cuff remarks may be taken down and used against you. If it happens to you, and some unfortunate remark is reprinted, put it down to experience. Learn from it. Complaining, in most cases, is a complete waste of breath.

Sending Press Releases

If your press release is being distributed on a small scale, then it's easy enough to get the telephone numbers of the targeted newspapers, radio and TV stations, ring and find the named journalist you should address it to. Often, you'll be told: "send it to the newsdesk." Don't let that stop you from asking for a name.

If you're sending your press releases to a much wider audience, your best bet will be to use one of the distribution agencies listed in the recommended links directory on this website. Regardless of whether you have an agency distribute your press release, or you send it out yourself, there are only a limited number of ways it can be delivered on a normal budget.

Certainly one method of press release delivery, even in these days of e-mail. Traditional post gives you the greatest flexibility as regards presentation, and what you include with your press release. In addition, a letter demands more of the addressee's attention, even if it's only to open the envelope and look inside.

E-mails suffer from the fact that they are such transitory things. They are fast and cheap. But if the journalist is using Outlook, your e-mail could 'fall' off the bottom of their screen after just 12 e-mails, never to resurface.

Evaluation of PR

Whether you are doing your own public relations, working at an agency for a client, or working in-house, you will need to measure and evaluate the effect of your efforts. Doesn't matter whether that's because you're genuinely interested in knowing what's worked and what hasn't, or because you just need to justify your existence to the board.

Reading editorial is usually just one of the factors involved in the consumer's decision to buy, and PR is usually just one of a number of different and simultaneous marketing initiatives. The problem isn't restricted to measuring the value of media coverage. How, for instance, do you put a value on changing a key opinion leader's mind about something? In some cases, it could transform sales. In others, it'll make bugger all difference.

This issue is hotly debated within the profession, and there are two schools of thought. The first argues that accurate measurement and evaluation of public relations activity is achievable using various tools at our disposal, and that this task should account for a significant proportion of a PR practitioner's day. The other argues that there are simply too many subjective variables for evaluation to provide anything meaningful, and any time spent evaluating is time not spent getting on with the job. Both extremes are wrong, of course. Measurement and evaluation is possible, and necessary. But the time it takes needs to justified by the quality of information it provides.

Ask the Audience

Ultimately, the only truly accurate way to quantify the effectiveness of public relations, irrespective of the platform used to communicate a message, is to survey the target audience. Ideally before and after a public relations campaign. But that can be expensive and/or time-consuming, and the reality is that few marketing managers are prepared to invest in something that isn't directly contributing to sales.

Valuing Media Coverage

In the absence of a target audience survey, public relations is usually judged by the amount and value of editorial media coverage generated. However, this can only be a measure of how effective you've been in placing the story, not how effective the story was in generating sales.

Given this limitation, it is simply not worth spending huge amounts of time and effort using complex media analysis software to work out the financial value of coverage achieved. So far, we have yet to find a piece of media analysis software that doesn't make the job more time-consuming than doing it by hand. And since software relies on the same subjective human inputs, the results it produces are no more accurate.

If you want to ascribe a value to media coverage, calculate the amount it would have cost to place an advert of the same size or duration. Then rate each piece of coverage on the tone, strength and prominence of the message, and apply a multiplier of 1.2, 1.4 or 1.6 accordingly (and if you're reporting to someone else, make sure they agree the multipliers).

So, if the coverage is 'on message', multiply advertising value by 1.2. If the point is strongly made, implying editorial endorsement, then multiply the ad value by 1.4. And if it is in the first paragraph, prominently on the page, multiply the ad value by 1.6. Apply the same in reverse for negative media coverage. This still provides an arbitrary value. After all, it is still subjective, and what proof that people are 1.6 times more likely to act on a prominent, strong editorial call to action than an advertisement? But logic dictates that editorial does carry a premium over advertising, and if you can justify a different multiplier, then work with that instead.

Record and Report Everything

A good PR campaign will often generate a spontaneous reaction from a wide cross-section of different people: members of the public, journalists, the sales-force, customers, even the CEO. Record any and all reaction to your media coverage, wherever it comes from. It won't be as scientific as a survey of the target audience, but it does go some way towards measuring the effect PR is having, and not just the output.

PR: New Perspectives

Advertising dollars in media products from corporations like News Corp. and Dow Jones are under rapid decline in favour of direct advertising products offered by search engines and other tools. Traditional media publications are laying off journalists, consolidating beat reporters, shrinking their print editions, and many publications are shutting down entirely.

Blogs have lower over-head costs than traditional media and are often said to provide better news coverage and analysis. Blogs are increasingly sprouting to replace traditional media with a more sustainable low-cost business model and are gaining more of a following.

The advent of social media is the most pre-eminent trend in PR today. It's important to note, while social media is on the rise, traditional media is yet to be taken over by the trend as of January 29, 2009. Social media releases, search engine optimisation, content publishing, and the introduction of podcasts and video are other burgeoning trends.

The need of public relations personnel is growing at a fast pace. The different types of clients that public relations people work for include, but are not limited to: the government, educational institutions and outlets, nonprofit organisations, specific industries, businesses and large companies, athletic teams and entertainment companies, and international opportunities.

Many of the techniques used by PR firms are drawn from the institutions and practices of democracy itself. Persuasion, advocacy, and education are instruments through which individuals and organisations are entitled to express themselves in a free society, and many public relations practitioners are engaged in practices that are widely considered as beneficial, such as publicising scientific research, promoting charities, raising awareness of public health concerns and other issues in civil society. However, a number of strong criticisms of public relations have been made over the years.

One of the most controversial practices in public relations is the use of front groups—organisations that purport to serve a public cause while actually serving the interests of a client whose sponsorship may be obscured or concealed. The creation of front groups is an example of what PR practitioners sometimes term the third party technique—the art of "putting your words in someone else's mouth." PR Watch, a nonprofit organisation that monitors deceptive PR activities, has published numerous examples of this technique in practice.

Public relations is often misused in day-to-day conversations, even by experienced business people and by the news media. Sometimes they define it too narrowly. Sometimes too broadly. Sometimes they attach undesirable, negative connotations to it. Even public relations practitioners who are performing public relations for a living and who should, therefore, have a pretty clear idea of what it is often encounter other practitioners whose definitions and interpretations are dramatically different than their own.

According to Edward Bernays, the three main elements of public relations are practically as old as society: informing people, persuading people, or integrating people with people and the means and methods of accomplishing these ends have changed as society has changed. The introduction to the third edition of *The Dartnell Public Relations Handbook*, one of the oft-cited bibles of the industry, notes: "Every organisation, institution, and individual has public relations whether or not that fact is recognised. As long as there are people, living together in communities, working together in organisations, and forming a society, there will be an intricate web of relationships among them."

In its most basic form, building that intricate web of relationships is what public relations is all about. The fact that human beings live together forces them to think about their interactions and organise their relationships with one another. In a primitive society the relationships are fairly basic and the organisation is minimal, but as the society advances and becomes more complex, so do the relationships.

On an individual level, when you wash your car inside and out before you pick up a date, you're practising public relations. When you comb your hair and wear a conservative suit instead of cut-offs and a T-shirt for a job interview, you're practising public relations. Any time you consciously act in a particular way in order to influence how someone perceives you or thinks about you, you're practising public relations.

Organisations have the same basic need to interact and establish relationships with others that individuals do. As described by Todd Hunt and James Grunig in *Public Relations Techniques*, "Organisations, like people, must communicate with others because they do not exist alone in the world. (They) must use communication to coordinate their behaviour with people who affect them and are affected by them." Their size and complexity, however, generally require them to have somewhat different relationships than individuals. Instead of person-to-person relationships, they rely on a combination of organisation-to-individual relationships, organisation-to-group relationships, and organisation-to-organisation relationships.

Public relations is for any and all kinds of organisation, from a neighbourhood club to the Home Ministry, from a local hospital to the All India Institute of Medical Sciences, from a small business to Hero Honda, and from a small agency of county government to the United Nations. The size of the organisation is irrelevant. The organisation's motivation is also irrelevant. Whether it's driven by a desire to make money, have fun, or enslave the world doesn't change the fact that it has to relate to and interact with other people, both individually and collectively, in order to succeed.

Managing Personal and Organisational Encounters

In any human encounter, how the participants react to one another, and whether they respond positively or negatively, is affected by the interplay of five factors.

— New information participants gain about one another during an encounter is usually presumed to be the most influential factor in determining the outcome of the encounter.

— Any previous interactions with one another will have already shaped their feelings and predisposed them to react to one another in certain ways.

— Participants' beliefs and value systems affect what they'll be able to agree or disagree upon, as well as affecting their willingness to deal with one another.

— Images the participants project to one another, whether intentionally or unintentionally, are also influential, especially during first encounters. Initial impressions set the stage for a long-term relationship whether it's love at first sight or a bitter feud.

— The circumstances that surround the encounter also affect its outcome.

Since these are the five primary factors influencing the outcome of human interactions and public relations is about managing relationships or, in the words of the Public Relations Society of America (PRSA), "help(ing) an organisation and its publics adapt mutually to each other," most of what public relations practitioners do focuses on managing these five elements of their clients' interactions with others.

Managing information is so fundamental and pervasive in public relations that there is no need to belabor it here. Numerous techniques for managing, presenting, and disseminating information will be treated more fully in other readings and by other sources throughout the semester. Past history has to be accepted as a given, and even the most aggressive and inventive public relations person has to accept that it will always have some influence on an on-going relationship and any future interactions. If the past history has been positive, the public relations person will most likely want to emphasise that and may frequently remind the participants of how positive their past dealings have been. On the other hand, if the past history has been less than positive, but not terrible, it may glossed over or "politely" ignored by all parties. Sometimes, however, it may be necessary to admit the "sins" of the past and take steps to address the consequences of a negative past history.

In public relations, just as in personal relationships, it is possible and sometimes desirable to try to reinterpret or explain past actions, especially those that have or that could cast a negative pall over a relationship. Announcing a change of heart, whether it's in the form of a personal opinion or a company policy, can often eliminate the recurrence of previous differences of opinion or failed business ventures. And, sincere apologies can often mend fences and minimise, albeit never totally eliminate, the negative effects of previous encounters.

While it's theoretically possible to change someone's beliefs, modern psychological theory and lots of practical experience indicate that most adults' core beliefs and value systems do not change significantly over the course of their adult lives. They may shift from a moderate to a more extreme position, or from an extreme position to a somewhat more moderate one, but they are rarely transformed from one extreme to another, for instance from opposition to support of a given position. And, short of clinical brain-washing, any changes that do occur, take place gradually over time and are not in response to the kinds of short-term persuasive campaigns public relations people are able to conduct. Consequently, honest and ethical public relations people readily admit that they cannot control or change anyone's basic beliefs or values.

Skilled public relations people can help others shift their perspectives and see the world in a new light, preferably a light that's more advantageous to the practitioner's clients. These same practitioners can also help their clients identify new publics that haven't previously been addressed but whose values are already compatible with theirs and who might, therefore, be potentially valuable allies.

In some instances, they're able to resolve situations in which participants initially appear to have fundamental conflicts in values, not by changing anyone's basic beliefs but by getting them to look at their particular situation or at the world in a different way. What looks like a conflict from one angle, can appear quite peaceful from another angle. They might, for instance, even be able to convince two apparently disparate special interest groups that it's not inconsistent nor a conflict in values for a group that opposes the death penalty to cooperate with another group that favours assisted suicide.

In part, the participants' images and the situations and circumstances involved in an encounter can be managed because they're here and now and still subject to change, unlike past experiences. And, they can be manipulated because they're more tangible and concrete than abstract beliefs and values. They're inherently more malleable, and managing them is something we've all grown up doing as part of our everyday life.

Such things as using deodorant, dressing up for special occasions, or minding our manners in mixed company or when guests are present are all examples of how we manage our personal images. Similarly, cleaning the house and bringing out the "good china" when company comes for dinner, turning down the lights and turning on soft music when we want to encourage romance, or waiting until our spouse has enjoyed the great dinner we fixed before mentioning the dent we put in the fender of the car are examples of how we routinely manage the circumstances of everyday personal encounters.

When they're performing public relations, practitioners do exactly the same sort of thing for their clients or their employers. Sometimes it's done on a much larger and grander scale so it affects an entire company's interaction with millions of customers instead of one person's interaction with a few others.

Another reason images and the circumstances of an encounter are malleable is because they're essentially sensory experiences rather than intellectual ones. They're physical happenings, not abstract thoughts. In managing an image or an encounter, the immediate concern is what the participants see and hear rather than what they know or what they believe. In other words, what's really being managed are the participants' perceptions.

Insofar as public relations practitioners can influence people's perceptions, they can affect how those people will respond to another person or an organisation. And, like it or not, the bottom line is that what we see, hear, feel, smell, and taste can be controlled, adjusted, and manipulated in countless ways over a wide range of intensities.

Public Relations and People's Perceptions

Insofar as public relations practitioners can influence people's perceptions, they can affect how those people will respond to another person or organisation. And, like it or not, our perceptions can be manipulated in countless ways. When another person is physically present with you—e.g., he or she is standing in front of you and conversing with you—you're having a direct, first-hand, and personal experience of that other person. Some people call it a "real" or "actual experience." But, whatever it's called, you're forming your own direct perceptions of that other person without having to rely on anyone else's impressions or interpretations.

Historically, direct perceptions and personal experiences were the most common way of knowing about other people or organisations. Unless you directly interacted with people, you knew very little about them. And you knew of very few living people with whom you didn't interact.

If someone is not physically present with you—e.g., if you're watching that person on television or reading about them in a magazine—you're having an indirect or second-hand experience of that person. Instead of experiencing the actual person yourself and forming direct perceptions, you form mediated perceptions of that person because your sensory impressions have been filtered by and through other people and communication mechanisms before you ever receive them.

The adjective "mediated" wasn't given to these perceptions because they involve the mass media, although they often do. They're "mediated perceptions" because one or more third parties (mediators) are interposed between us and the people or events we're encountering. Public relations is involved in this because its practitioners often create mediated realities to trigger favourable perceptions of their clients.

We shan't debate whether direct perceptions are better than second or third-hand mediated perceptions. Sometimes they are; sometimes they aren't. When you have a face to face meeting with a Member of Parliament (MP), you form direct perceptions of that MP. This is true whether she planned and prepared for your meeting or not. However, the more she planned for it, and the more she talked it over with her advisers, the less "pure" it may be in terms of giving you a glimpse of what's really on her mind and in her heart. Even though your perceptions are direct, they may well have been manipulated and intentionally pushed in one direction or another. And, although it confounds philosophers and would astound earlier generations, it's not at all unusual for modern citizens to give greater credibility to their mediated perceptions than to their own direct perceptions.

In video or motion picture films the camera operators and the director determine not only what is seen, but how it's seen, and this can have tremendous impact on how viewers perceive and ultimately feel about the people and events on the screen.

Beyond the basic impact of which visual content is chosen for the cut-aways, the choice of camera angles and focus make an added difference in how the person and event are perceived by viewers. Whether the audio is crisp and clear or "muddy" and hard to understand also affects the listeners' perceptions of the speaker. It may seem overly simplistic, but research has repeatedly shown that clear, properly modulated audio that is easy to hear and understand leaves the impression that the speaker was clear and forceful in his/her thinking.

The addition of lead-in or background music can also have a dramatic impact. Music that is well known to the audience and emotionally evocative can predispose the audience to a speaker, in favourable or unfavourable ways, before he/she even begins to speak.

Today we use the term "image" to convey what a person or an organisation appears to be, which is sometimes very different from who/what they actually are in private. Some personal or corporate images seem to be "more real," or to be a more honest reflection of the subject's "actual personality." This may be because such people/organisations are without artifice and feel comfortable being themselves in public, or it may be because they became public unexpectedly or by accident and had no time to prepare a different sort of image. Other images are obviously public personalities that are very consciously and carefully projected.

The mere fact that images can be constructed and can be manipulated doesn't necessarily make them bad. Modern life depends upon artificially constructed realities of all kinds. If the person who creates an image has an evil or deceptive purpose, then, depending upon how well he/she does in constructing the image, the image may end up being evil or deceptive. If the person who creates an image has a noble purpose, there's more likelihood, albeit no guarantee, that the image will be good and noble. The greatest reason for being concerned about images shouldn't be their artificiality or the fact that they've been constructed. It should be how much correlation exists between the constructed image and the underlying reality that it's presumed to represent.

Originally, the degree of correspondence between an image and its underlying reality was the primary factor in distinguishing a good image from a bad image. Plato, for instance, compared an image to a shadow cast on the wall, and Walter Lippman in Public Opinion said images were "pictures in our heads." Both believed that the more closely and more accurately an image portrayed external reality, the better and more meaningful it was.

Today, when we label an image as good or bad, its correspondence with reality may not even be considered. When we refer to someone having a good or bad image, we're hardly ever implying anything about how well their image reflects their real personality or their actual behaviour.

The terms "good image" and "bad image" as used today rarely reveal anything about the relative amounts of fact or fiction in an image. They don't even represent an ethical or moral value judgment. They simply reflect how positively or how negatively people who are exposed to the image respond to the person or organisation represented by the image. Insofar as public relations is able to help people or organisations project "good images," it can help them receive favourable public responses whether they deserve them or not.

PR: Emerging Opportunities

Many types of organisations virtually and physically interact and communicate with publics and/or audiences outside their own country of origin to build a dynamic set of relationships. Trade, direct foreign investment, political coalitions, worthy global causes, information flow, and social networking, among other phenomena, are increasing the complexity of these relationships dramatically. Moreover, this complexity results in greater interdependence and inter-connectivity among societies, groups of ideology-driven or cause-driven individuals, and organisations worldwide.

This reality parallels the evolution of public relations as a profession, practice, and field of study in every corner of the planet.

The growth of the world's interdependence and the role that public relations and communication management play in this dynamics have motivated the creation and development of several institutions that advocate for, represent, and contribute to the profession and professionals. In addition to the public relations institution representing the global industry and practice, national associations are growing in importance and making valuable contributions to the documentation of the practice in specific countries or regions. For instance, Sweden has a professional association with one of the largest proportional representation of the total number of professionals of various industrial sectors of any other public relations trade group worldwide, and South Africa counts as an institute with one of the world's most elaborated systems of accreditation recognised by the country's higher education authority.

It is estimated that there are anywhere from 2.3 to 4.5 million public relations professionals globally. They are assisting their organisations not only in building and maintaining multiple relationships at home-where organisations have their headquarters, but also constructing and keeping those bridges abroad in other host locations and transnational environments-especially with activist groups, global media, and international non-governmental organisations (INGOs). Interactive communication technologies and the activist groups that use them, also known as "globalutionaries," are increasing the complexity of global public relations practices. Thus, corporations and other mainstream entities are compelled to respond to global competition and to interest groups who can band together across borders and apply pressure in a given country or globally.

At times, the idea of a home or host location may be difficult to capture because there are situations and active actors who are transnational in nature; they function as a global network or matrix with communication flow in every direction. In other words, many organisations are no longer limited to interact and communicate with home publics, but additionally with host and transnational publics.

Global Public Relations

Global public relations (GPR) professionals would be likely to succeed in and to pursue further international assignments when acquiring adequate preparatory background or cultural competency. Alan R. Freitag conceptualised an ascending cultural competence model, which includes: Initial preparation in relevant course work or training in culture, political and economic aspects, and foreign languages; international assignment seeking behaviour; international assignment itself; perceived success and satisfaction; increased cultural competence; and further international assignment seeking behaviour. Each component is a condition for the achievement of a higher stage of the model. Thus, the author concluded: "The ascending cultural competence model posits that increased preparation will result in commensurate increases in levels of perceived satisfaction and success in international assignments and in the desire to seek those assignments". For instance, cumulative foreign travel appears to be positively associated with the perception of success in international assignments, and also likely job satisfaction and the desire for additional international assignments. This professional behaviour seems to characterise successful GPR professionals.

Any multinational organisation with operations in several countries faces particular challenges to practice public relations as it is conducted in its home country. These challenges are imposed by a unique set of geographical, cultural, political and legal, socioeconomic, and communication media environments. In 1993, Hugh Culbertson and three former students published a book with a series of applied studies to understand an organisation's or client's social, political, economic, and cultural contexts, as well as to analyse the theoretical foundation needed to articulate these contextual environments.

Scholars then studied the association between public relations models and the organisational and societal contexts faced by all kinds of organisations. This was a component of the Excellence Project on Public Relations and Communication Management sponsored by the International Association of Business Communicators (IABC) towards the end of the 1980s. "The extent to which each of the six [public relations] models [i.e., press-agentry, public information, two-way symmetrical, two-way asymmetrical, personal influence, and cultural interpreter] is practised seems to be a function of management worldview or definition of the nature of public relations, the education and knowledge of practitioners, and the extent to which the culture and political system in which an organisation exists is participative or authoritarian". The latter aspects consist of the contextual or environmental framework multinational businesses and organisations face in the countries where they operate.

To effectively perform in given society, public relations professionals and their organisations need to understand the following aspects associated with the three major sets of contextual variables:

— The value of public opinion and pluralistic views, which are closely related to the level of sophistication of the practice;
— political ideology present in the government and the classification of the political system, as well as its respective policies of economic development;
— types and number of competing groups seeking legitimacy and power through public opinion and elections;
— the acceptance and lack of alternative views, which in emergent democracies may be only encouraged in theory;
— covert or overt forms of self- (including professional), social, government censorship;
— level of economic freedom and level of centralisation of economic decision-making, and consequently the extent of entrepreneurship, which allows for a dynamic public relations industry;
— private sector power to influence economic decisions, as well as the relationship between private and public sectors; moreover, vast public sectors become primary publics for organisations;
— level and availability of technological development relevant to the practice;
— national rates of poverty and illiteracy, which determine the complexity of the communication mix;
— history, types, and extent of activism, knowing that activists force organisations to be socially responsible and fulfil societal expectations;
— power and independence of the judicial system, as well as the interaction between the judicial and executive branches of government;
— legislation that regulates public relations, any of the specialised sub-practices, and/or related communication activities and professions, including legal versus social and religious codes;

— corporate culture as a distinctive corporate personality of an organisation, including leadership type, years since its foundation, industry type, and size;
— how people in a given country behave toward and perceive organisations;
— characteristics and dimensions of societal culture, including idiosyncrasies and traditions;
— media infrastructure and level of professional standards of journalists and editors, including media control;
— the level of media outreach; that is the ability of media to diffuse messages to different audiences according to their patterns of media consumption;
— and the level of access to the media for organisations, agencies, and activists, as well as the value of information subsidies, such as news releases, news conferences, face-to-face interviews, etc.

MNCs and Public Relations

The transnational or multinational corporations (MNCs) can be effective and succeed in historically resistance host environments through culturally attuned involvement, intervention, and respect for local publics, proven through socially responsible performance and actions over time. These are the questions facing all MNCs: (1) where should decision-making power reside? (2) How should foreign operations report to headquarters? (3) How can the company ensure that it meets its global objectives? The answers to these questions require new ways of thinking or a transnational mentality composed by worldwide learning, multinational flexibility or national responsiveness, and global efficiency. The new paradigm ought to account for a more comprehensive approach that creates thinking and acting at both the local and global levels of the organisation. Some conditions to achieve excellent GPR management are listed below:

— Being globally effective
— balancing the global and the local
— public relations in one unit or single coordinated department
    — "They will create global strategies to preserve the entity's reputation, to retain consistent messages and identity, and to participate and handle problems that might cross borders".

— horizontal and team-oriented structure

— consideration of agencies

The balance between the global and the local is achieved via coordination and control mechanisms. Martinez and Jarillo defined a mechanism of coordination as "any administrative tool for achieving integration among different units within an organisation". Control is defined as management's planning, implementation, evaluation, and correction of performance to ensure that the organisation meets its objectives. The aim is to keep a MNC's direction and strategy on track. Management's toughest challenge is to balance the MNC's global needs with its needs to adapt to country-level differences.

These are examples of control and coordination methods: Corporate culture; reports; visits to subsidiaries; management performance evaluation; cost and accounting comparability; evaluative measurement; information systems; global, cross-functional, and virtual teams; advisory personnel; management rotation and socialisation; training programs; assemblies and special global or regional meetings; and keeping international and domestic personnel in closer proximity.

Concerning the extent of centralisation or decentralisation in the establishment and execution of GPR policies and procedures, shareholder relations appears to be the most centralised function and community relations the most decentralised practice. Media relations, government relations, and consumer relations show a medium level of centralisation, and internal communication or employee relations a low level of centralisation. Integrative communication devices are used to achieve a glocal balance, such as annual reports, websites, intranets, conferences, teleconferences, videoconferences, newsletters and bulletins, and codes of conducts and ethics.

Juan Carlos Molleda examined the relationships between the public relations function of subsidiaries and their parent companies as well as other subsidiaries and/or sister companies. His research looked at coordination mechanisms (i.e., socialisation, formalisation, and centralisation) used to manage the GPR function. Positive associations were found between integrative communication devices (e.g., website, intranet, and annual reports), communication quality (e.g., relevance/importance, amount, and timeliness), parent company-subsidiary relationship quality, and integration.

Positive associations also are found between corporate socialisation and both global efficiency (i.e., the use of common public relations resources by both headquarters and subsidiaries) and worldwide learning (i.e., sharing successes and failures of public relations practices in various world locations); between integration and communication quality and overall transnational mentality (i.e., the presence of global efficiency, worldwide learning, and multinational flexibility or national responsiveness in managing the global public relations function).

Molleda's study found that more than 60 percent of the MNCs reported a medium-level of centralisation, meaning that 50 percent of the coordination and control in the hands of the headquarters and the other half under the responsibility of the subsidiaries. More than 50 percent of the public relations executives at a subsidiary report having a mentor at the MNC's headquarters. More than 40 percent of public relations managers have worked at the headquarters and more than 30 percent at a sister subsidiary or company; both reported the length of the stay to be less than one year. The public relations personnel also reported to keep in touch with the parent company via trade shows and special events, committees and meetings, annual assembly of shareholders, teamwork and taskforces, and training programs.

International business scholars offer several studies exploring the relationships among units in MNCs. Some scholars explored coordination and control of the public relations or public affairs function, such as M BMeznar and T Blumentritt. Others studied coordination and control function as it pertains to marketing activities and advertising. Meznar explored MNCs' use of coordination and control mechanisms to cope with the complexity of global public affairs management. He explored the relationships between two public affairs strategies, buffering and bridging, using the boundary spanning literature, and the coordination and control systems used to manage the public affairs function in MNCs. Buffering is a defense strategy with which an organisation seeks to alter or influence social contract terms. In contrast, bridging is an adaptive and collaborative posture an organisation holds to assimilate and accommodate itself to the changes in both the political/legal and social environments.

Meznar reported a strong positive association between the control mechanisms-goal internalisation and performance evaluation-and the use of bridging and buffering strategies. He also found a strong positive relationship between the control mechanisms and the centralisation of the public affairs function. Similarly, he found strong positive correlations between coordination mechanisms-impersonal and personal-and the use of buffering, bridging, and public affairs centralisation. Other sets of associations are reported by Meznar, such as public affairs effectiveness and goal internalisation, impersonal coordination, and an increase of both buffering and bridging activities.

Blumentritt studied the organisational characteristics of foreign subsidiaries and their effects on the subsidiaries' government affairs activities, such as lobbying and relationship building with influential local and national officials and their agencies. He found that the more a subsidiary's top management believes in government affairs as a strategic function, the more the subsidiary will formalise these types of public affairs activities. He also reported a positive association between the extent of economic integration with affiliates and the subsidiary's degree of inter-subsidiary coordination of government affairs activities.

Transforming PR

The science and art of PR is about influencing perceptions. As individuals, we build perceptions of the world around us based on the inputs we receive. Those inputs include traditional media, daily experiences, conversations, interactions and more. The term 'public relations' is still more or less valid, as PR is ultimately about shaping people's relationships with organisations. Yet it is also misleading, as today PR entails being involved with every aspect of how people encounter information and make sense of it. It is far more about being engaged in the flow of messages through an intensely networked world than it is about formal communication.

The traditional domain of PR is swiftly changing. Just over 10 years ago, very few people had a personal email account, mobile phone or internet access. The graphical web browser with which we spend so much of our lives interacting didn't even exist until late 1993. Today, the nature of how information and messages flow, and people build perceptions of the world in which they live, is entirely different to how it was just a decade ago. And this is merely the beginning.

Traditional media will soon relinquish its role as the primary source of our input about the world. Mass media is becoming relatively marginalised as our world becomes one of multiple and highly varied inputs. Yet the underlying shifts cover far more than changing communications technologies.

High Client Demands

For the past decade or so, clients have become vastly more demanding in their dealings with their professional services providers. An entire industry has arisen of consultants that help companies to pin down their suppliers, expose costs, cut fees and enforce accountability. In short, clients are seeing their PR agencies and marketing peers as readily replaceable commodities. The majority of PR agencies have, perhaps unwittingly, encouraged this by firmly positioning themselves as 'black-box' providers. Far too often, firms describe their services as 'outsourced PR' or similar, deliberately disengaging the client from the process. This makes it very easy for the client to replace them. The future belongs to those firms that can successfully engage their clients in true knowledge-based relationships that are based on deep mutual knowledge, and a high degree of collaboration in achieving outcomes. For example, since 2000, Ketchum PR has been using online collaboration spaces with its clients, enabling them to participate in the messy work of creating messages and achieving objectives.

Transformed Media

Mass media will never disappear. Societies are bound together by having a common reference point to discuss and engage with. Yet at the same time, media is fragmenting into a multitude of channels and perspectives. The new wave of 'citizen journalism' includes blogging, as well as the active contribution of pictures, video, words and ideas to media by their audiences. Already the audience of the most widely read blogs, such as Boing Boing, Gawker, and Engadget, rival or exceed that of the major newspapers' online presence.Media has become a participatory sport, in which not just journalists, but literally anyone can provide their perspectives on what they are seeing and what is happening. If the content is interesting or they uncover something of note, they can quickly garner a significant audience. From a narrow pool of arbiters of what is newsworthy, is growing a vast array of deeply interlinked news sources and filters.

Transforming Business Conversations

Consumers are people, and they expect to be treated like people. Companies also happen to employ people. It is extraordinary that companies have always chosen to communicate with the formal, stilted, self-promoting language of the press release and corporate brochure. Would you like someone you met who spoke like a press release? Why then is it surprising that people do not like companies that strive to be impersonal on every level? Running cool 'street-cred' advertising campaigns does not create a conversation. Organisations must enable human conversations, between the humans that work for them, and the humans who buy from them.While this is fraught with challenges, there is no question that customers will flow to companies with which they can have human interactions, and move away from companies that persist in presenting unassailable formal corporate faces to the world.

Information Flows

Information flows used to be largely unidirectional. From organisations and their agencies to the media, and on to the masses. Now information flows in all directions. One of the most powerful trends is towards massive and widespread audio and video production and communication. From podcasting to mobile video calling to home video studios, and video screens soon to appear on every surface you can imagine, audio and video will predominate in our world. PR has traditionally been rooted in the world of words. While that will remain important, the new skills required to play in a world driven by other media forms will be critical.

Transparency

Do not expect to be able to hide anything. The old catch-cry of 'information wants to be free' remains true, and now it has the means to escape. When news is interesting, word spreads like wildfire through the blogosphere. In this world, PR is not about hiding or manipulating the truth; it is about providing access, being open. Know and expect that the truth will come out. PR's traditional role is almost turned on its head. Even more than before, the role of PR must be trusted. Broken trust is not soon forgotten. The only way to gain trust, to be credible, is to be transparent. It is an immensely challenging shift to make, yet those who do not truly believe this will soon find a day when their credibility and livelihood disappears.

Influence Networks

As mainstream media becomes an ever-smaller part of our information input, organisations need to understand and get involved with the influence networks that really form decisions. People form opinions and make decisions primarily from the input of the people around them that they know well and trust, not from advertising and media. A number of major PR firms have launched services to identify and access key influencers in any specific domain. PR will become largely about how to identify, access and influence the key influencers, either individually, or by understanding how influence networks are structured.

There is no question that the above facets of the future of PR pose pointed challenges to the profession. PR as it has traditionally been purveyed will not stand up to any one of these key drivers, let alone all of them simultaneously. Yet at the same time, these drivers offer some fabulous opportunities for the profession. First and foremost, companies will need massive assistance to be able to engage effectively in a world built on dialogue and transparency. Shifting from a default policy of being closed and communicating by press release, to building genuine human interactions and conversations, is far from easy. Guidelines and parameters need to be established and communicated, senior executives need to be coached and technologies need to be implemented.

PR has the core experience and understanding to be able to do this effectively. Yet practitioners also need to extend their capabilities into new domains such as technology and new media in order to be able to deliver on this. As the role of perception becomes ever more central, senior executives must pay attention to these issues directly. Previously, PR executives rarely had access beyond the chief marketing officer, and often were managed by considerably more junior client staff. Those PR executives that demonstrate they can understand their clients' strategic issues, and engage at that level of the organisation, will have the opportunity to do so. Moving beyond the ever-more trenchant issues of reputation management and related spheres, agencies can extend themselves to work with clients on other critical and highly relevant issues such as customer-driven innovation. One of the strongest trends today is increasing specialisation.

References

Coombs, W. T. "Interpersonal communication and public relations" . In R. L. Heath & G. Vasquez (Eds.), *Handbook of Public Relations* (pp. 105–114). Thousand Oaks, CA: Sage. 2001.

Cutlip, S. M., Center, A. H., & Broom, G. H. *Effective public relations* (8th ed.) Upper Saddle River, NJ: Prentice Hall. 2000.

Ewen, Stuart. *PR! A Social History of Spin*. New York: BasicBooks. 1996.

Friedman, Marsha. *Celebritize Yourself: The Three Step Method to Increase Your Visibility and Explode Your Business*. North Carolina: Warren Publishing, Inc. 2009.

Galloway, C. Cyber-PR and "dynamic touch." *Public Relations Review, 31,* 572–577. 2005.

Hall, Phil. *The New PR*. Mount Kisco, N.Y.: Larstan Publishing. 2007.

Robert J. Key. "How the PR Profession Can Fluorish in this New Digital Age: Why You Must Challenge Old PR Models," *Public Relations Tactics*, November, pp. 18-19. 2005.

Seib, Patrick and Fitzpatrick, Kathy. *Public Relations Ethics*. Fort Worth: Harcourt Brace and Company. 1995.

8

Public Relations and New Media Technologies

Technological innovations in the last 25 years have changed many aspects of public relations practice. Public relations practitioners began using computers for word processing, budgeting, and media database management, but soon were using them for public relations program evaluation and communication with colleagues. Telecommunications innovations brought not only telephone hotlines, but teleconferencing and satellite video feeds. Now public relations has entered the "fourth wave" of technological change in the field, and there are many questions about the impact of information highway technologies.

In the past few years, professional trade communication journals have devoted considerable space to describing how to change public relations practice by employing new communication technologies. Advice on changing tactics often centers on technology's capabilities rather than on the needs of the audiences with whom an organization is communicating—or normative roles practitioners should fill.

Public Relations and Technology

Rigorous public relations research about use of new technologies has been limited. Professional trade journals have done a better job of covering the range of technologies used in public relations, but they have done it in an anecdotal, unsystematic way. In addition, the terms *new technologies, emerging technologies, computer-mediated technologies,* and so forth have been used in organizational communication studies, public relations research, and mass media-new technologies research, sometimes without clear definition. One challenge for researchers in the area is that the definition of new technologies continues to shift.

Along with an ever-changing concept definition, new communication technologies do not fit neatly into once separate constructs of interpersonal, mass media (uncontrolled), and controlled media used in public relations. "New media create a continuum between formerly discrete categories of interpersonal and mass-mediated communication". This adds complexity to choosing a public relations tactic. For instance, an executive addressing employees via teleconference is~aiTth-person form of communication, mediated by satellite technology. It is not a preproduced video, nor do audiences perceive the communication in the same way they view an in-person speech by the top executive. New technologies have made former ways of organizing what practitioners do outdated. One gap in the public relations research and professional literature is that there is no organizing framework that merges new technologies with existing communication tools used in public relations. A possible structure that emerges from the literature is that of public relations roles.

Four role concepts developed by Broom and Smith have been widely used in public relations research to look at differences in gender roles, differences in salaries, environmental scanning and external environmental changeability, and strategic planning and research. Although practitioners play many roles within their practice, they enact one role more frequently than others. This dominant role could be one of four conceptual roles derived by Broom in his original work on public relations roles.

One is a *communication technician.* While functioning as a technician, the public relations person is mainly concerned with producing communication materials—such as brochures, videotapes, newsletters, news releases, and so forth. He implements communication programs but does not participate in the decision-making process that planned the programs.

Another role is the *expert prescribes* Unlike the technician, the expert prescriber is the authority on public relations challenges and solutions. However, she is pigeon-holed as "the expert," without integrating the public relations function into the management of the organization. Because there is no executive management vested interest, according to Broom and Dozier , this is a high-risk role for public relations professionals.

The third role that public relations managers enact is the *communications facilitator.* This person spans the organization's boundaries to act as a mediator between the organization and its publics.

The fourth conceptual role is *problem-solving process facilitator.* When a practitioner plays this dominant role, he or she participates on the management team to define organizational problems and collaborate on the strategic planning and programming to meet the challenges. Collapsing the manager roles into one role and separating the technician role as a second dimension has been useful in a number of studies. In his reanalysis of roles data from three studies, Dozier concluded that the manager and technician roles were stable and robust and a useful way of reducing the four roles into a simplified typology.

Broom's research on roles has focused on public relations practitioners, whereas Grunig's concept of roles looks at the way the function is practiced in organizations, what J. E. Grunig and L. A. Grunig described as "the public relations behavior" of organizations.

J. E Grunig and L. A. Grunig used the terms *asymmetrical* and *symmetrical* to describe public relations that aims for balanced rather than unbalanced communication effects. Like the two-way asymmetrical model of public relations, the two-way symmetric model relies on use of research by the public relations practitioner. However, the research's intent is todevelop relationships between an organization and its publics, not merely to further an organization's goals. Two-way symmetric public relations relies on negotiating and conflict resolution strategies to further relationships. In short, the "models describe the mind-set and overall purpose of communication programs, roles describe daily behavior patterns of individual communication practitioners".

Fundamental to the public relations manager role is two-way symmetric communication especially because of the environmental scanning and research that is necessary to fulfill a manager role or practice two-way communications. Both of these models flow from a foundation in systems theory. Two-way symmetrtc_cornmunication contributes to organizations functioning as open systems, and the public relations manager role ensures that the environmental surveillance necessary for adaptation and change can take place. Dozier and Broom "accept Grunig's two-way models of public relations as integral to the function". This study positions the concepts as compatible ones, especially for the exploratory objectives of this research. In conclusion, then, it is useful when investigating how public relations practitioners are using, or not using, new technologies, to consider not only the concepts of public relations technician or manager, but the concept of two-way symmetric communication, as well.

Technology and Public Relations Roles

Studies have shown that technology can enhance technician and manager roles. In addition, research has explicated technology's enhancement of elements of public relations management roles (i.e., research and environmental scanning). The following discusses technology research related to key aspects of the public relations manager role.

Computer databases and online services allow professionals to spot trends, monitor issues, and note sensitive changes among targeted publics while still in latent stages of public opinion. Managers can hear about research affecting their organizations before other publics. A key advantage to the diversity of information available online, and the speed of access and delivery, is that it allows for early identification of emerging issues. Through issues management, a public relations professional can help prevent crises. But, an organization in crisis in the 1990s no longer needs to rely on media to get out the first message because it is possible to alert employees, large stockholders, government officials, and other key publics immediately via a World Wide Web page announcement, E-mail, or teleconference.

A crisis has the potential to adversely affect the bottom line of a company (i.e., lost product sales, reduction in stock price, or lawsuits). In an Exxon case study, Calloway reviewed the critical role technology can play in crisis communication. "What surfaces from the Exxon Valdez press coverage is that media had just-in-time technology and used it, and that the management of Exxon did not".

Technology's aid in research and decision making—other dimensions of the management role—is described in research and professional journals. Research and evaluation can be quicker and more productive with the use of computer-mediated technologies. E-mail surveys to target publics can be distributed, and focus groups can be conducted online. Its role in enhancing strategic counsel to management and clients is another reason cited for the importance of technology. Thomsen pointed to the autonomy of practitioners in establishing their own search agendas as an important distinction is use of databases as a management function rather than technician function. The other way that new technologies affect the role of public relations in the organization is in management decision making. Thomsen found that public relations professionals using technology had "a greater sense of inclusion in their organization's decision-making coalitions" .

Media Relations

Probably more has been written about use of computer-mediated technologies improving traditional mass media relations activities than any other area, because so many practitioners are engaged in it and most journalists are accustomed to computers. Recent studies show that reaching reporters and editors via computer is appropriate for some media practitioners, but not all of them. Two surveys found 33% to 37% of journalists preferred to receive information via E-mail. Descriptive information in the literature suggests that computer- or telecommunications-mediated technologies are improving media communication and evaluation of media coverage. Activities include identifying media contacts more readily via criteria, customizing messages to media contacts, learning about reporters and other stories they have written before returning their calls, pitching stories electronically, keeping electronic records regarding media contacts, tracking online to determine immediately whether releases issued were used, and tracking news for information about competitors.

Employee Communication

Organizational communication studies have analyzed various aspects of employee communication, although the studies have not been limited to public relations tactics. Professional public relations journals also have documented use of new technologies in employee relations. Some uses of computer- and telecommunications-mediated technologies include electronic publishing of employee newsletters, employee teleconferences, employee E-mail, World Wide Web pages, and employee electronic bulletin boards. Floppy diskettes, CD-ROM, and other multimedia delivery systems are being used to inform employees, communicate employee benefits programs, recruit new employees, and train existing employees.

Customer and Consumer Relations

A number of interactive media have been employed to expand brand awareness, build knowledge of products and services, and sell products.

Although the ability to expand relationships between consumers and organizations through new technologies is enormous, articles in practitioner journals have tended to focus on the sales message potential. Key technologies include interactive kiosks devoted to informational or sales messages, CD-ROM, floppy diskettes. World Wide Web pages, and extensive use of consumer database information used for asymmetric communication with audiences. For instance, faced with decreased sales of distilled spirits, Cutty Sark devised a virtual reality game and sent it on tour. This adventure-oriented game, featuring Cutty Sark logos, was aimed at increasing brand awareness and involvement. The ethical implication of such a tactic is an area ripe for review.

Lobbying and Government Relations

Constituents are E-mailing the U.S. President, their senators, and even community representatives. Politicians have World Wide Web pages. Organizations can delineate the potential impact of a bond issue or ballot proposition on their World Wide Web pages, and issues are discussed in electronic newsgroups.

Investor Relations

Practitioners have a few techniques for using new technologies in communication with shareholders, security analysts, and registered representatives. Companies are including current press releases, executive biographies, executive speech "reprints," product info, company fact sheets, and so forth on World Wide Web pages, substituting for the traditional investor mailings. When investor relations practitioners call on security analysts or portfolio managers, they can tote a laptop computer featuring multimedia presentations. Investor relations managers also can monitor the financial markets, analyze target publics, or gather investor information using computer-mediated technologies.

Technology and Productivity

In addition to technician and manager role enhancement, technology has affected practitioner productivity. The downsizing trend has paralleled die explosion of global knowledge, which requires public relations practitioners to investigate ways of being more productive and do more with less time and less staff. Productivity enhancements include electronic calendars; improved list management; automated media relations with databases like

MediaMap; broadcast faxes for news releases; and E-mailing clients, media, employees, and other target publics

Public relations office computer networks offer more effective file management, shared project files, improved accounting and automated time sheets for public relations firms or cost-accounting-based public relations departments. The ability to store and retrieve massive amounts of data, photos, audio clips, video clips, and so forth on CD-ROM has also improved productivity. Audio and video conferences have reduced travel time and costs. When traveling, public relations professionals are using cellular phones and laptops to decrease waiting times for information and increase productivity. Capital investment in technology should continue to reduce ongoing general and administrative expenses like travel, postage, and secretarial assistance.

Effective Public relations with Digital Technology

The digital age has profoundly changed the demands placed on public relations professionals and the ways they do their work. In fact, it is not an exaggeration to say that the digital age has profoundly altered the nature of the public relations profession itself. With the media now fragmented into thousands of communication channels, high-level public relations advice and planning are more critical than ever before, as companies, product marketers, and organisations all compete to develop, enhance, and project positive public images.

Effective public relations writing forms the core of nimble, innovative marketing made possible by digital technology. Today, businesses and nonprofit organisations use digital communications, as well as traditional PR tools, to reach target audiences, communicate with customers, and expand audiences. E-mail, websites, digital newsletters, blogs, viral marketing, search engines, live conference calls, RSS, and podcasting are just some of the tools now available to PR professionals.

Companies are experimenting and diversifying their approaches to reach niche audiences, and they are using public relations to achieve their communications goals. Computers, the internet, e-mail, broadband, and wireless all increase the ease and decrease the cost of researching, writing, publishing, printing, and, especially, distributing written materials, as well as producing graphics, short videos, audio downloads from the internet, and multimedia presentations.

Public relations professionals have found themselves on a sharp learning curve as they discover more uses for digital tools. The first challenge of the digital age was learning to save money and eliminate time-intensive, repetitive tasks such as stuffing envelopes with press releases or faxing them to a hundred media outlets one by one by one.

The next challenge of the digital PR revolution is discovering how to go beyond saving time and money to create new methods of communicating effectively with customers, employees, investors, media, and the general public. Creativity and public relations training, combined with people skills and computer savvy, have enabled new ways of communicating a company's image, or a product's benefits, or an organisation's community goals. The demands of this stage are to harness the potential of e-mail, interactive communications, handheld devices, the convergence of computers with telephones, television, and digital music players to communicate ''personally'' with hundreds, thousands, or potentially millions at a time. You may be writing for a company website, a blog, a social website, a live chat, or the PR war room of a large company facing a public relations crisis. In every case, clear, persuasive written communication, the stock in trade of the public relations writer, is the core skill that can be leveraged by each new technology and technique.

Whether you are writing for newspapers, broadcast outlets, books, or public relations purposes, the basics of good expository writing remain the same and never go out of date:

— Clarity.

— Accuracy.

— Vividness.

— Aptness of details, examples, and quotations.

— Correct grammar.

— A clear, varied style.

The digital age, however, has put new pressure on the media, and therefore on public relations, for speedy responses and on companies for accessibility and forthrightness. Today, news stories can be posted on the internet around the clock. The mass media used to have specific deadlines: once a month (monthly magazines), once a week (weekly magazines), once a day (daily newspapers and network evening news), twice a day (local television news), or more frequently for radio and wire services such as the Associated Press that fed updates throughout the day. Having a deadline meant that media outlets and their sources knew the time by which details needed confirmation, so that the story was as complete as possible when printed or aired.

Public relations writers and other PR professionals were well aware of the deadlines for the media outlets they covered. They knew how much time they had to write a thoughtful response approved by upper management or to find a ten-minute gap in a top executive's schedule for an interview to present the company's point of view or set the record straight.

Now, many editors are pressuring journalists not just to complete the story for the next deadline, but also to post it immediately on the media company's website to beat the competition. More media websites now opt for a scoop on a partial story, with updates—and corrections—as new details are gathered, rather than waiting to file a complete, correct story after an in-depth investigation.

Traditionally, there has been a give-and-take between journalists and the public relations or information officers they deal with. PR people interact with journalists as sources, sounding boards, and restraints on the impulse to go to press too soon with too few facts.

Thousands of rants and rumours are being written and posted on the World Wide Web (WWW or web) by anonymous bloggers who have no particular interest in earning a reputation for accuracy or fairness. Not contacted by the blogger, the company learns about a rumour only as it gains traction and readers, and rises to become a page-one result on the major search engines.

Both public relations and traditional journalism are challenged by the digital age. In addition to new deadline pressures, the way stories are structured is changing. To tantalise and tease readers, headlines used to employ sophisticated rhetorical techniques such as puns, word play, alliteration, and literary allusion. Now headlines must meet the demands for literal meaning of digital search engines, which are computer programs that crawl the web aggregating keywords. Headlines for both web stories and print stories that are simultaneously posted on the web are now more literal and direct or have two headlines: a clever headline on the first page to attract a human reader and a literal, descriptive headline on the second page to attract web crawlers.

People responsible for web pages that sell advertising, products, or subscriptions are all concerned about 'keyword optimisation, search engine optimisation, search engine marketing, or page one results. All of these terms equate to finding a way for your company's website URL to appear on the first page of search results for popular search terms, either by your company's buying a pay-per-click ad or by appearing among the first five to ten listings after becoming one of the most popular choices of recent searchers.

Internet search engines such as Google find and post stories worldwide. The global exposure that stories, press releases, and websites can receive through search engines can result in new readers for publications and bloggers and new customers for products and companies.

In addition to competing with other media companies' websites, professional journalists now battle for scoops and readers with uncounted numbers of ''citizen journalists'' and bloggers who are posting stories, rumours, reviews, and their sometimes fevered speculations about what ''should, would, could, might'' happened. Therefore, public relations professionals need to monitor what is said in the blogosphere and make quick decisions about which misstatements or allegations or rumours require a correction or response to head off a viral rumour that can permanently damage the reputation of a brand, a client including a celebrity, or an entire hundred-year-old company. The 24/7 deadlines, intense competition, and trigger-finger readiness to post an unconfirmed story—a rumour—all put pressure on public relations writing, companies, and the client approval process.

Both the media and the public have heightened expectations for accessibility and speedy response. Management and the media expect the public relations representative or official company spokesperson or public relations writer to be reachable at any time by PDA, cell phone, e-mail, or even instant messaging. At the same time, hastily written press announcements, official statements, web publications, and video remain retrievable indefinitely by using search engines and electronic archives.

Media fragmentation means, for example, that there are hundreds of niche cable channels instead of three or four main broadcast networks; thousands of online forums and blogs in the computer industry versus three or four main trade publications; and millions of websites and blogs versus a few thousand local newspapers and local television stations. This fragmentation has decreased companies' reliance on advertising and increased the importance of public relations.

The value of PR as a resource to corporations, government and institutions has increased, based on the need to address complicated issues and fragmented targets. At the same time public relations initiatives need to be more nimble and creative because a decade ago, only one or two different media channels would be used to reach targeted groups.

Internet Public Relations

The internet has given us e-mail for use in contacting and keeping in touch with editors. It has given us newsgroups, where there can be a liberal exchange of ideas with others who have similar interests. The internet has given us gads of information and the ability to choose what information is on a website. It has given us search engines, which are capable of cataloguing every word on websites and directories, which list websites and their pages. The internet is shrinking the world. It has made it possible for every person to research any subject as thoroughly as desired from his home or office. Thus, it has become an avenue for reaching potential consumers of products worldwide and is an important part of the marketing mix available to every company.

Effective internet public relations approaches use a different focal point for public relations communication than you typically have using traditional PR. Of course you need a catchy headline and a newsworthy story angle. However, when using internet public relations, the words you use to convey your ideas are nearly as important as the ideas they are conveying. It is very important to use words and phrases that are identical to those that potential customers might enter in a search engine when looking for your product or service. Where these words need to fall in your news releases and online blogs are also important.

Using internet public relations as a public relations communication strategy is a win for service providers as well as consumers. Service providers recognise tremendous cost savings related to marketing. Good public relations efforts can get a marketing message delivered to consumers at little or no expense to the provider. When media outlets and the internet deliver messages to a market, for free, the service provider can save lots of money. Internet public relations experts realise the importance of the consumer trends becoming less dependent on information from traditional media outlets. They realise the power of taking their message directly to consumers as part of their public relations communication strategy. Just like there are time-tested approaches for attracting the attention of reporters and journalists who can write about your organisation and share it with the general public, there are specific ways to get your message in front of customers looking for what you have to offer while they're on the internet too.

Blogs

A growing body of research documents the impact of blogs in public relations. Some research also confirms that regardless of the medium, including blogs, writing quality is still a deciding factor in effective communication. One of the more recent developments in blogging is twitter. Twitter is a technology developed in 2006 that enables persons to use their cell phones to send text messages to blogs. Although limited to about 140-150 characters, twitter can nevertheless provide extremely up-to-the-minute updates to blogs.

Content and Messages

Technology has many significant implications for the content or messages developed and utilised in public relations. Blogs, podcasts and websites in general all present vehicles for distributing messages to a variety of publics. Expanded use of audio and video files—podcasts, vodcasts—is a major trend. Moreover, these media can shape the character of the messages themselves.

Text messaging via cell phones has emerged as a viable means to reach mobile publics, especially youthful targets. Because of the nature of the medium, the messages must conform to certain strict parameters. Among these parameters are text-only, short messages, and often messages encoded in short-hand, such as "LOL" for Lots of laughs or "c2it" for see to it. The Lingo 2 Word website provides a comprehensive alphabetic listing of text messaging terminology and characters. It also provides a conventional text to texting translator for the texting neophyte. News releases must also be adapted to cell phone and mobile media formats.

Web 2.0

There is an important difference between technologies that modify existing channels of communication and technology that is changing the environment for all communication, observes Peter Debreceny, chair of the Institute for Public Relations Board of Trustees, retired VP-Corporate Relations for Allstate Insurance and authority on new technology and public relations. The new media, especially Web. 2.0, is of the latter type of influence. Video news releases are an example of the former. They are not really any different than a press release, but in electronic, visual and sound form. They are important, but are essentially just tailored to the particular medium.

Public relations professionals who wish to provide value to their employers and clients in the future will have to adjust their strategic perspective accordingly, from planning and research to counselling, media relations and crisis communications. The media environment has undergone several major transformations—primarily, the establishment of the internet as both national and global communications media, the proliferation of vertical media nationally, and a general shift from objectivity to advocacy in news reporting.

The internet has successfully introduced three revolutionary elements into the communications equation. First is the publication of electronic versions of print and broadcast news products. Second are online databases of credible sources of information, such as scientific literature and public records. Third are inexpensive weblogs published by private individuals, many of whom use news coverage as a base upon which to provide commentary and analysis by themselves and their readers, who sometimes are experts in the field, but participate anonymously, for the most part.

Stakeholders can now communicate with each other about an organisation in a very public way. The public relations function will in most cases be the department dealing with these unplanned messages. As stakeholder strength increases, PR practitioners will have to develop strategies that deal with the rising power of different stakeholders on the web.

There is also an important difference between Web 1.0 and Web 2.0. From a strategic communication perspective, Web 1.0 was basically adding a technological capability to existing techniques ideally suited to public relations or marketing. Web 1.0 meant better pathways to sending information to publics, editorially based, and right up our alley. Those in PR did a very good job in 1994-2004 in taking advantage of the opportunities the web offered. Web 2.0 is different because it's not just a technological enabler of existing methodologies.

Web 2.0 is breaking down barriers. Much of the change is about control. Although conceptually the 2-way symmetric model of public relations is the ideal, it's not usually the practice. PR people like to be in control and get messages out and see the messages resonate and the audience respond accordingly. Web 2.0 is empowering citizens to communicate directly online and the organisation can be left out of the conversation entirely. "The field of public relations needs to come to terms with that.

Among the most important Web 2.0 technologies is RSS, or Really Simple Syndication. RSS is a family of Web feed formats used to publish frequently updated digital content, such as blogs, news feeds or podcasts. A growing number of online publishers utilise RSS feeds to distribute their content on a timely basis. Users of RSS content use software programs called 'feed readers' or 'feed aggregators. The user subscribes to a feed by entering a link of the feed into the reader program. The reader can then check the user's subscribed feeds to see if any of those feeds have new content since the last time it was checked, and, if so, retrieve that content and present it to the user.

Video News Releases

Another example of how technology has influenced public relations messages is the video news release (VNR). With the rise of video tape technology, VNRs emerged in the 1980s as a video version of the traditional news or press release. Having started as often times amateurish promotional video on analog tape, mailed or sent by overnight delivery to selected television stations for possible inclusion in the evening newscast, the VNR has evolved into a sophisticated digital public relations tool and a frequent part of television news, particularly at the local level. Further, new technologies have made it increasingly effective to distribute VNRs in digital format via satellite or other broadband technologies.

On CBS Newspath, VNRs are transmitted digitally in a separate area and are clearly identified as a video news release feed, explained John Frazee, senior vice president, CBS News Services, in a telephone interview January 10, 2006. CNN Newsource has a similar process of formally vetting VNRs before they are accepted for transmission. VNRs must adhere to a variety of formatting requirements including ensuring the script approved corresponds with the video.

The advent of electronic, digital tracking of VNRs has greatly improved the accuracy of determining how widespread the use of VNRs has become. One leading electronic system is SIGMA by Nielsen Media Research. It covers VNR use in all 210 U.S. television markets.

VNRs are rapidly being transformed in the age of digital convergence. They will morph into a form of marketing communication that will be available for viewing on portable devices, such as mobile phones, and other technologies. Perhaps more importantly, there will be no need to deliver these videos through news channels. They are already available online and are becoming increasingly so. Viewership is easier to measure online and consumers are able to easily find them through search engines such as Google and Yahoo. In fact, the rise of digital video production and online distribution through sites such as YouTube is propelling organisational uses of video to communicate directly with publics such as consumers, without traditional media filters or gatekeepers.

Mash-up Media

An emerging form of content or message technique is called "mash-up" media. Mash-up media are those formed by merging two or more sets of data. An example comes in the form of Chicagocrime.org, which merges together crime data reported by the Chicago Police Department, the Citizen ICAM and mapping and satellite data provided by Google. Citizen ICAM stands for Information Collection for Automated Mapping, a system developed by the Chicago Police Department for use by its police officers. Chicagocrime.org provides users a detailed, interactive and useful look at where crimes have been reported in Chicago. Data can be sorted by type, such as arson, homicide, assault and gambling; by street or block, and map nearby crimes; by date and much more. Users can view the crime sites on a map; or plan a route based on where crimes have or have not occurred.

Conducting research is also significantly being reshaped by technologies, especially those of the internet. Studies show that Google Scholar and CrossRef can greatly enhance the effectiveness of research investigations conducted by public relations practitioners, helping them find relevant scholarly research in a timely, cost-effective fashion. Another system is a subsidiary of MediaLink and is called TeleTrax. It utilises an electronically embedded "watermark" securely measuring VNR use even when digitally altered. The watermark is almost impossible to strip off in editing, so monitoring is highly reliable.

Implications for Performance of Organisations

Technological change presents many significant implications for the structure, culture and management of organisations, particularly from the point of view of public relations. Perhaps among the most significant is the opportunity to flatten the hierarchical nature of many organisations, at least from the point of view of communication.

Digital communications makes it possible for more efficient management of organisational communications, including both internally and externally. This also means organisations can be more open and transparent to facilitate better understanding between and among various groups. It is also possible to better transcend time and distance constraints via digital communications. We are witnessing the rise of decentralisation, with increasing use of collaboration group decision-making software. Organisational openness and transparency are increasing as online technologies have become ubiquitous and powerful.

Openness and transparency includes things such as extranets used as part of expanded, special-purpose organisational structures and relationships with suppliers and distributors who have access to at least a portion of an organisation's systems. Materials online might be read by the organisation's expanded community. Internal communications has been transformed with the abandonment of printed materials—including written memos, employee publications, employee benefits communications.

As audiences have increased their use of the internet and have grown more savvy with digital media of all types, public relations has needed to evolve with them. Audience members, or members of often key publics, maintain their own websites, blogs or podcasts, often circumventing traditional media outlets. Practitioners monitor such online sources alongside traditional media outlets. These citizen-produced online media can be influential and widely seen and accounting for them may be essential to a public relations campaign. Gauging public opinion can also involve the use of online media. Conducting public opinion surveys online is now a common practice in public relations.

Facilitating two-way, or interactive dialogues with various publics can depend upon the use of e-mail, discussion boards or other online media. In this context, digital, networked communications such as those possible on the internet and web make possible the cost-effective advent of two-way symmetrical communications. This is a profound opportunity for public relations professionals to implement more effective, balanced communications with various publics.

As communication technology has evolved, society has come to expect ever more rapid communications. This can be both a boon and a bane to human existence. For public relations, it often means great expectations for fast and efficient communications between and among organisations and their publics.

It is increasingly feasible to monitor news media coverage via computer-based systems that employ natural language processing, a branch of artificial intelligence (AI), to monitor and synthesise press coverage and automatically track coverage of topics, organisations and individuals. One interesting example of an AI-based system monitors, sorts and summarises news coverage is the Columbia Newsblaster.

Related are various tools on Google Labs, including google.com/trends. Google Trends allows the automatic tracking of user search queries and tied to current events. For instance, on February 19, 2007 a sort using Google Trends for searches for the Super Bowl, NCAA, Oscars, and election revealed not only the absolute and relative search volume of each term, but provided the data by cities, regions and languages, as well as year-long trends since 2004 and by news events. Such data may be useful in tracking the consequences of news coverage.

Online technology is especially valuable when people are seeking information about organisations—so anticipate needs, concerns and interests of publics. Involve people when they are interested. Optimise search engine searches, make content useable. Be accessible 24/7, maximise the interactive nature of web and mobile media. Such access is especially important in times of crisis or risk. Technology plays a critical role in facilitating two-way communication. Among the useful tools are sponsored chats and newsgroups, game sites, cookie technology that allows recognising users and customising content, and providing options for users to personalisation content on websites, portals and mobile phones to suit their preferences. Also useful are fill-informs, query and ordering mechanisms—provided that the organisation can fulfil requests promptly, pop-up and other web surveys.

The computer-based technologies can potentially provide highly cost-effective methods for not only tracking news media coverage and correlated public opinion indicators, but help in assessing media agenda setting and news media framing. Emerging digital technologies enable the automatic tracking of video based on the content features of the video. For example, computer systems can scan a video clip and identify patterns of action, scenes, or edits.

Social Networking

Social networking sites such as MySpace and video file sharing sites such as YouTube also have enormous implications for public relations. As millions of users populate such websites and spend increasing amounts of time immersed in them, these online environments become increasingly relevant to the communication strategies for organisations. Yet, how to appropriately participate or communicate in these online environments where sometimes the social and cultural rules are stricter than the legal requirements can present a slippery slope. At the same time, consumers are empowered by digital technologies to voice their opinions more easily and more powerfully via social networking sites, including creating and posting their own videos, sometimes griping against corporate practices they find objectionable. How to respond effectively is an increasing challenge for many organisations. Transparency, immediacy and clarity are among the key elements in the process.

One of the challenges raised by social networking sites and other new technologies is the notion of privacy and security in the digital age, with all of the attendant public relations issues. Many organisations of various types will likely be confronted by privacy and security concerns as online technologies bring together both increasing ability to track individuals and data about them and facilitate convenience at the potential sacrifice of personal privacy and data security.

A variety of technologies present similar communication opportunities juxtaposed against privacy concerns. Jonathan Donner, of Microsoft Research India, points out the dramatic growth of mobile technologies internationally. In China, for example, more than 600 million persons use mobile phones, and 100 million more persons begin using mobile phones there each year. While mobile communications is a powerful communication tool, there are also significant privacy implications. A growing number of online services are providing free or low-cost cell phone location-tracking capabilities. Plazes is one online service that provides free cell phone location tracking. Users enter a cell phone number, and their cell phone is then placed on the tracking service, and can be tracked by other users.

Another powerful online technology is Google Earth. Users can quickly and easily travel visually to any location on the Earth and see in high resolution any precise location. Users can populate specific locations by geographic coordinates with high-resolution three-dimensional imagery, and embed textual communications associated with those locations. Yet, privacy concerns may arise as well as citizens become increasingly aware of the ease with which any one from anywhere in the world can observe their home or other locations.

Interactive Public Relations

Public relations is the management function that identifies, establishes, and maintains mutually beneficial relationships between an organisation and the various publics on whom its success or failure depends. Online public relations is about much more than people in large, powerful organisations using the most expensive new technologies to communicate at relatively powerless publics. Relationship building is still about people, and the technologies are merely tools that people can use—ideally—to get along better. Nonetheless, these technologies do different things than the media that came before them.

One of the most often-discussed but least-understood characteristics of online media is interactivity. Although all good public relations is interactive at some level, online media offer practitioners the opportunity to enrich the interactive exchanges between organisations and publics in the absence of face-to-face communication.

Converging mobile technologies that combine the functions of messaging with calendaring, computing, phoning, browsing, purchasing, photography, and entertainment offer a more fluid environment for the practice of public relations. Keeping in touch with the online but wireless publics of "cyber public relations" as part of a relationship-building process means thinking of public relations as a communicative activity that entails "stimulating feelings such as connectedness, involvement, appreciation, and meaningfulness". Such goals pose new challenges in commu-nicating with more physically dispersed publics.

Tools for mobile-based interactivity must increasingly be considered along with static reception equipment. When communicating via mobile devices, researchers have found that with websites, there is an emotional advantage to making online communication more interactive—reminiscent of pressing-the-flesh. The best of the new, then, is still driven by concepts as old as conversations and handshakes.

Interactivity is not new to new technology. There is two general ways to look at it: functional interactivity and contingency interactivity.The concept of functional interactivity focuses on the features of media such as response forms, e-mail links, discussion forums, RSS, and so forth. Some have assumed that more features mean more interactivity. However, the degree to which these functions are used and the extent to which they actually serve the dialogue or discourse is often left out when people think about online media without also thinking about how people actually use the media.

Media effects researchers describe contingency interactivity as a process involving users, media and messages in which communication roles need to be interchangeable for full interactivity to occur. Contingency in this line of research and theory means that messages in an interactive process of communication are contingent on previous messages. The sender now is a receiver later, and vice versa. Broad views of public relations reflect similar thinking.

In organisation-public relationships, the organisation in one case is a public in the next. Of course, if you work in public relations for an organisation, as opposed to studying one from outside, you will almost always think of your employer as the "organisation" and those you communicate with as publics. But interactive public relations will still mean basing your actions and communication on the actions and communication of those with whom you communicate.

Consider how trends in employee relations, for instance, have been articulated in light of emerging media. New media have empowered employees to the point where they now can—and do—play a much more dominant role in the communication process. And how organisations build and maintain relationships with activists might well be the area in which the idea of balanced conversations has come the furthest. Consider the contingency theory of public relations. Public relations strategies and tactics range from aggressive advocacy to total accommodation in contingency theory. It is no accident of semantics that the contingency view of interactivity and the contingency view of public relations dovetail so well.

Good public relations, like good online communication, depends on the situation and the people involved. Emerging communication technologies may de-massify public communication, but public relations people should work to ensure technologies don't dehumanise communication.

Web and Integrated Public Relations Strategy

On-line communications is strongly nicheoriented, the equivalent of going door-to-door and neighbor-to-neighbor in a grass-roots effort. Electronic commerce via the Internet continues to intensify, providing a strategic blend of marketing, public relations, and technology. Projections on the expansion of electronic commerce have been consistently understated.

The Internet has become a communication vehicle that can enable business-toconsumer and business-to-business electronic commerce. Its ease of use has resulted in rapid worldwide expansion. However, while some businesses thrive on the Internet, many have collapsed or are currently on life support. Over the past five years, electronic commerce has exploded, with a significant technological impact on business strategy. Estimates of current use and expectations for the future vary, but in each case, the actual use continues to exceed expectations.

Most major companies have developed a web site presence that aims to boost bottom-line results, raising their awareness level or enhancing customer loyalty. For companies doing business on the Internet, effective web design, an e-commerce strategy, and relationship-building will affect their ability to compete.

It is vital for a company to have an integrated marketing, public relations, and information technology strategy to develop a lasting, value-added presence on-line. Public relations practitioners have found that technology can supplement tasks such as maintaining media lists, analysing media clips, and obtaining immediate feedback on the impact of press releases. Specialisation and targeting continue to be significant trends in public relations, and vast web-based databases support these trends.

Yet, it is not uncommon today for business executives to tout success on the Web, based solely on gross revenues and increased traffic to their web sites. While these two metrics are important indicators of success, the authors contend it is equally important to ascertain that customers are satisfied with their experience on the site, and that future sales are linked to customer trust, loyalty, and community-building.

Relationship – building or humanising the digital experience involves becoming interactive and having an intelligent dialogue with customers – in short, becoming connected to customers in multiple forums: on-line, by phone and direct mail, and with toll-free numbers. Interactivity is a building block that leads to lasting customer relationships.

A relationship on the Web today competes with the handshake and the warm reception that customers are used to receiving in a showroom or retail store. E-commerce marketers can learn from the marketing philosophy of the popular home-shopping TV channels, with their consistently boosted sales over recent years.

Customer relationships in that medium are built entirely on interactivity-toll-free numbers flash on the screen; customers talk with the host; the blinking countdown clock warns viewers of a few minutes left to buy before the item is replaced on the screen; and money-back guarantees are stressed. Information satisfaction contributes to consumer satisfaction, which occurs when the product or service which a firm offers consistently matches consumer expectations.

Of course, many on-line customers fail to hit the buy button before they leave a web site because it does not meet their expectations. Customer satisfaction also depends on relationship-building, finding the customers' shared values and helping them become loyal lifetime customers. Therefore, an effective electronic commerce strategy should match the desired consumer response with the web site design.

The consumer response web site design model was developed to provide a framework for describing the relationship between web site design and a consumer's intention to return to a web site. Here included a public relations dimension, to explain how to build long-term customer relationships. The theoretical basis for the model is explained along with its relationship to information satisfaction.

The model purports that the public relations dimension provides a mechanism to build loyalty and trust and that will result in an increase in information satisfaction. How information technology (IT) and public relations (PR) executives working together on e-commerce strategy can build meaningful long-term relationships with Web customers. IT web site design is enhanced by an integrated public relations strategy, thereby achieving a state in which customers not only return to the web site more often, but also have a more favorable image of the organisation.

Web Site Design

Web site design is beginning to mature as a component of an organisations overall information technology strategy. No longer are organisations racing to develop a web site pressence, but instead must establish lasting relationships with their customers. To accomplish this it is important to establish a relationship between the information satisfaction that a customer perceives from a web site.

Information Satisfaction

Consumer satisfaction occurs when the performance of a product or service matches the consumers' expectations. The concept of information satisfaction, which influences the overall feeling of satisfaction that a consumer experiences when given information about a product or service. The importance of information satisfaction increases when the buyer-seller exchange occurs in an on-line environment through electronic commerce.

The marketing interaction that transpires between business and consumer as the creation of real virtuality. Real virtuality states that users' interactions with electronic environments are enhanced by their cognitive experience, which is created not only by what is seen on the screen but also by the communication of the experience. Therefore, real virtuality is enhanced by the amount of information that is made available on a product or service.

Electronic commerce via the Internet is an enabling technology through which firms can provide customercentric marketing. Sheth, Sisodia, and Sharma (2000) define customer-centric marketing as a strategy that seeks to satisfy the needs of individual customers rather than a mass market. Three reasons underscore the growth in customer-centric marketing. First is concern over the effectiveness of marketing activities by senior management. Second, market diversity increases the consumers' wants and needs.

Third, new technologies have enabled marketers to better meet the needs of individual consumers. The degree to which people place their trust in the Internet as a means to motivate commerce will affect consumers' intentions to return to a web site. Competence trust has a significant influence on consumers' pre- and postpurchase decisions. Further, competence trust affects consumer satisfaction. Consumers, however, are concerned about doing business on-line.

Some 65% of on-line customers bail out of a transaction before the final step. Information satisfaction then becomes a critical component to consider in the design of a web site, there must be a strategy that supports repeat customers.

Significance of Electronic Commerce

Electronic commerce has led to dramatic changes in the definition of a firm. From electronic commerce over the Internet has emerged virtual companies that are capable of delivering products and services largely because they are able to create and maintain a network of business relationships. The three significant benefits of using electronic commerce are:

- reducing cost for routine business transactions;
- collapsing cycle time to complete business transactions, regardless of geographic dispersion; and
- eliminating paper and inefficiencies in handling paper.

Four business benefit criteria to evaluate the potential for electronic markets, including:

- Extending the firm's reach
- Bypassing traditional channels
- Augmenting traditional markets
- Boosting service and advertising

Extending the firm's reach refers to the firm's ability to reach any potential customer, regardless of geographic location. Bypassing traditional channels refers to the ability to reduce dependence upon intermediaries. Augmenting traditional markets refers to the emergence of new means for marketing products and services. Boosting service refers to the ability to utilize electronic commerce 24 hours per day.

Advertising assumes special significance in an electronic commerce market. Firms are not constrained by boundaries of length, time, and place. A model of electronic commerce consisting of three elements: content, context, and infrastructure. In the electronic marketplace, content is information-based, with a focus on electronic transactions. The context of marketing via electronic commerce changes from a real to a virtual environment that is available any time, any place.

The infrastructure, where transactions occur, is completely different as well. Electronic commerce changes the context of product and place in its definitional context. The use of the Internet as a channel of distribution enables interactive commerce to occur. The term interactive as consisting of two features of communication: the ability to address an individual and the ability to gather and remember that individual's response.

When a consumer visits a web site, many exchange cycles can occur within a brief time period. Moreover, when a consumer returns to a web site, exchanges can resume where the previous exchange left off. In addition to time independence, one benefit to consumers is that they need not repeat previously-entered information to resume interrupted transactions. Marketing on the web dilutes the difference between large and small companies, enabling them to perform one-on-one marketing.

One-on-one marketing as the ability to use information about an individual to market specific products or services that are assumed to be of interest to that individual. While this is not a new concept, the use of the Internet has opened a new channel of distribution, based on the premise that if a company can develop a personal relationship with a consumer, the consumer will continue to buy more products or services from that company.

Two categories of data as essential for enabling one-on-one marketing. The first is the variety of needs an individual consumer is looking to satisfy through the firm's products or services. The second is the value skew of the distribution of profits that current customers generate for the firm. Dividing the variety and value presents a customer differentiation matrix. This matrix of low to high value and skewness can help define the electronic commerce strategy for the firm.

One useful outcome of this approach is that a company can learn from the data it collects. If a company begins with the wrong electronic commerce strategy but effectively monitors and controls its web site, it can more easily make interim adjustments until it achieves the right mix of differentiation.

It was necessary to examine the user's overlapping roles and technical perspectives to create an effective e-commerce strategy. Several areas must be evaluated to understand the effect of consumer response from ecommerce. The first is web site design. Various factors affect web site design, the most important factor being page-loading speed. Consumers who do business electronically do not want to wait while web pages are downloaded.

The use of graphics, animated gifs, and files that require plug – in device drivers to maximise page – loading speed. Additionally, the use of plugins should be avoided because the average person does not want to download and install software in order to return and access a web site successfully. Nor should graphics be overlooked as an important way to distinguish between web sites. To effectively compete in an electronic commerce environment, a company's e-commerce strategy should address, among other issues, how it will handle graphics.

One way is through the use of thumbnails, which can be expanded into larger pictures. With myriad options available to consumers who are doing business electronically, an effective web site strategy will consider the transmission speed that a consumer is likely to utilize and design appropriately. The business content of the web site should contain clear concise language that readily describes the business. It should also include contact information via telephone and/or email for user follow-up. The web site content should be changed regularly to remain attractive for repeat customers.

Navigation efficiency refers to the easy use of the entire set of web pages. A well-defined web site should have no broken or non-existing links. The use of frames garnered mixed responses. On the plus side, they break up the web page, provide more flexible functionality, and display the company logo across each page. Among the disadvantages are that frames are not supported by older browsers and make bookmarking more difficult. Frames can also add horizontal and vertical scrolling to a page.

Whether or not frames are used, however, navigation should be consistent throughout a well-defined web site. An e-commerce strategy should also define other factors that affect web site design. These factors include the business content of the web site, navigation, efficiency, security, and customer focus. It is important to consider the existing telecommunications infrastructure when defining an e-commerce strategy. Because it is consumed at a rapid rate, telecommunications bandwidth should be considered when designing resource intensive web sites.

Marketing to businesses that utilize T1 lines to access a company's web site may present different design options than marketing to consumers who access the web site via a 28.8 or 56.6 modem. More than 75% of Internet traffic is HTTP-related. Network planning is critical to obtaining acceptable user response time. It is important to consider what type of web server an organisation needs to compete in an electronic commerce market.

There is no one single type of web server. Web servers can be used as proxy servers, electronic commerce servers, or search engines that are image-intensive and highly dynamic or primarily static. E-commerce consists of two domains: business-to-business inter-organisation systems, usually implemented via electronic data interchange (EDI), and electronic markets that exist on the World Wide Web.

The World Wide Web has been described as having two primary roles. First, it serves as a distribution channel that allows the quick delivery of products and services via the Internet. A consumer can not only order goods, but also obtain an on-line view of exactly how they will look prior to delivery.

Service models are used in an e-commerce environment to support customers or provide additional products or services. The types of services identified were: product/service updates, inquiry processes, frequently asked questions (FAQs), and transaction tracking. A good example of transaction tracking can be found on the United States Postal Service website. For an additional charge, a customer can receive a number with which to track the status of a mailed item. Exchange models are used to offer products or services for sale.

The types of exchanges identified were on-line catalogs, targeted marketing, integrated sales, and integrated sales fulfillment. Targeted marketing seeks to influence customer behaviour through customer profiles, customised information, and narrow cast messages. Integrated sales link front-end and back-end sales activities through the web site. For example, Dell Corporation has effectively integrated its entire sales operation through the Web and dramatically reduced its cost structure by integrating its operation with its supporting vendors.

Dell automatically triggers UPS at three different times to pick up a PC, monitor, and software to synchronise their arrival at a customer's location. This integrated marketing strategy distinguishes effective e-commerce marketing and will become more widely used as companies expand into the e-commerce marketplace. Web site performance management needs to be integrated into an e-commerce strategy.

Firms with clearly-defined web objectives have firmer performance measures to evaluate the actual performance of their web site than firms without defined web site objectives. Further research to measure the linkage between web site performance and achieving the firm's business objectives. Specific metrics can determine if the web site is achieving these objectives. Special performance considerations, such as web pre-fetching, may be needed.

Web pre-fetching is a strategy of loading documents into a client's web site before the user has selected them for browsing, thus reducing the user's access time. Pre-fetching can be characterised as client-side or server-side, depending upon which device initiated the prefetch operation. The longer the estimated time to retrieve web pages, the more likely they will be pre-fetched. Web pages that are quick to fetch, dynamically generated or beyond certain limits will not be pre-fetched.

Effective Web Site Design

Effective web site design can be more rapidly developed utilizing prototyping, which is useful for developing a proof of concept to quickly determine the web site's cost effectiveness. Four steps in web site prototyping.

The first step, define needs, involves identifying and articulating the client's description of what the users want. The second step, define ideas, extracts concepts from all of the participants and turns them into a meaningful entity. Step three, design, builds an entity that is the culmination of all ideas. The final step, deliver, is bringing specifications to the client to construct the application. This is based upon the assumption that once the prototype is developed (as part of the design step), the client will be responsible to transform it into a production-ready application.

This can be useful in determining the cost benefits of web site development and support. The rapid surge of electronic commerce has allowed existing industries, such as telecommunications providers, to expand their support services. As well, new industries, such as infomediaries, are better able to help consumers find businesses on-line for their own growth.

New markets and increased electronic commerce have resulted in businesses transforming themselves to remain competitive. Full cybermarketing organisations that operate exclusively through the Internet have emerged rapidly. A well-designed web site should result in developing a customer base that will more likely purchase goods and services on-line. Customers are expected to purchase more because of the complete, timely, and effective presentation of web site information.

Two significant marketing factors that affect electronic commerce. Time-specific assets have value if they reach users within a specified time period. The complexity of the product description determines the amount of detail information that a consumer needs to make a purchase decision. Together, these lead to the electronic integration effect, which occurs when information technology is used not only to speed communication but to change the processes that create and use information. The use of the Internet as a channel for electronic commerce capitalises on these factors.

Loyalty and Trust

Loyalty programmes are being introduced to e-commerce marketing as a way to build relationships with customers. Affective and conative loyalty can influence customers' perceptions of products. Affective loyalty, for example, may influence how well customers speak about a product. Conative loyalty, on the other hand, may determine whether customers continue to buy products into the future.

European banks on what determines loyalty when bank services move from the traditional marketplace to on-line commerce. They found that customer satisfaction, followed by brand reputation, had the greatest impact on both affective and conative customer loyalty. Two other determinants in the study, switching costs and search costs, had less influence on loyalty.

Readers of The Wall Street Journal typically have a strong loyalty to the printed version of the newspaper. Yet when customers buy an electronic version of it, they expect that the reading experience will match that of the printed version in delivering high-quality business news. The electronic version, of course, has a potential for greater success if customers remain satisfied and loyal. Organisations that choose to build a web relationship with their customers find it an effective way of developing brand loyalty.

Manufacturers and retailers are also learning that treating their customers as faceless individuals jeopardises their loyalty and future business. Four loyalty drivers that influence customer buying decisions, which also apply to web sites and web entities:

— product offering,

— quality,
— price, and
— image.

Most organisations understand the power of the first three-product, quality, and price. The image driver or relationship-building driver, however, determines whether an organisation retains its loyal customers for the future. Companies need to work at creating e-loyalty. "What the web does for e-loyalty is make building relationships easier, faster, and cheaper". People who are loyal to each other can also be loyal to web sites.

Another strategy for building e-loyalty for a web site is intelligent dialogue, implying that Web interactions must sound, feel, and appear human to create successful relationships. Extending beyond merely providing web information such as flights on line, for example, the site must offer customers real – time valuable information about flight cancellations, ways to rebook, and a toll – free number for advice. In addition, this information must be delivered in a timely format attractive to the customers. The nature of intelligent dialogue is influenced by the type of product offered, the customer's sex, education, and age, and the culture of the organisation. It will also be based on research of customer values that influence buying decisions.

The rationale for making e-loyalty work as a strategy on the web is based upon sound business principles:

— retaining customers is more costeffective than acquiring new ones;
— loyal customers are typically more profitable as a segment based on lifetime purchasing value than non-loyal customers;
— loyal customers defect less often; and
— loyal customers are more likely to boost one's brand and image.

In sum, on-line customer loyalty can only be achieved with a close bond between seller and buyer. As active participants in the transaction, customers will often recommend the organisation to friends, family, and co-workers.

Community Building On-line

Just as the Industrial Revolution prompted people from their communities to find work and share interests with others, virtual communities are becoming the social organising mechanism to unite consumers in the 21st century. Because customers apparently want to meet and share information in cyberspace, this development has triggered the need to expand on-line communities among members with common interests. This power of community-building is not lost on information technology and public relations executives who are challenged by trying to satisfy customers on-line.

The Web is slowly becoming America's collective "town square," a place to buy products, find medical advice, join a club or self-help group, play games, trade items, and share information and news through e-mail and chat rooms. As part of an on-line community, customers are no longer limited to joining local neighborhood groups or buying locally; their reach has become national and global, while also choosing to remain anonymous or declare their identity on-line.

Community-building on the web is a relatively new public relations strategy which gained momentum once the Internet was launched and became a community of dialogue. For example, a company's communication on the Web can elicit immediate response from customers, creating a wave of positive or negative publicity that directly impacts the organisation's image. Four categories of on-line communities: geography, demographics, topic, and shared activities.

These categories provide a typology for sharing information and ascertaining and meeting customers' common needs. It is important to note that on-line communities are not static and should evolve over time; Village, for example, renamed itself the Women's Network after it discovered that its members were interested in parenting, health, relationships, and money issues.

Communities on the Web have humanised the on-line experience by letting individuals use message boards that provide a live link or a feeling of personal involvement with the organisation. Real-time chatting is another form of customer interaction. New software for real-time chatting allows for synchronous communication among residents in different parts of the world. Companies can also schedule special on-line events for their customers, thus attracting a crowd of compatible consumers to their web site.

Furthermore, to build strong relationships with customers on the Web, companies should offer real-time support and guidance. A live support option is a good complement to FAQs (frequently asked questions) because it can increase the probability that customers will return to the site to purchase more products or services. One of the best ways to ensure success on the Web is to understand the qualities that a community values the most.

In the auto sector, for example, price, design, and service are important, while in the fashion industry, style, brand, and freedom of choice are drivers that influence buying habits. Effective public relations strategies allow the organisation to express these qualities through web design, image, language, and feedback. To stand out from the competition, organisations must communicate a distinctive persona. In the final analysis, e-marketers need to understand that content alone may lure visitors to a site initially, but their decision to stay is tied in with discovering a community that shares their values.

For example, the community aspects of the Women's Network define its shared values. Its "better health" section resembles a visit to a local spa with experts offering healthrelated advice. Whether an auto company promotes a fan club for its most famous car brands or movie stars contact their on-line fan clubs around the world, the power of community shapes both image and brand, and humanises the Web's digital experience.

E-commerce Web Site Design Model

The E-commerce web site design model provides a framework to explain the type of marketing and public relations integration needed to support consumer satisfaction. The model assumes that consumers in a B2C (business-to-consumer) environment access web sites either because

- they seek information about a specific product or service;
- they require specific choices about products or services, including complimentary or substitute products; or
- they seek to make on-line purchases.

Electronic commerce web sites attempt to satisfy consumers' needs through one of four classifications of integrated marketing-technological strategy. These four classifications-introductory, informative, interactive, intelligence-explain how an organisation chooses to organise and present its web site as well as what consumers desire and how they will respond.

Organisations seek to optimize responses to the desired goal of the web site when they have an effective integrated marketing plan. Each classification represents a specific set of design characteristics for web sites. Each web site classification should have a public relations dimension to build customer loyalty and enhance the probability that the customer will frequently return to the site to buy products.

Every customer interaction is an opportunity to make a sale or make a friend. The public relations dimension can build support for a site in three important ways: credibility, cachet, and community. Credibility is a value-added process because it generates an audience's willingness to believe that the business will be sucessful. A special feeling from the site that intrigues consumers enough to return to it. Key influencers can drive traffic to a site with a mere mention in a major magazine, national newspaper or network.

Finally, community consists of online customers who dialogue with the organisation through e-mail or other feedback mechanisms and share their interests and concerns about the organisation's products or services. For example, Sony and Yahoo have strong public relations dimensions on their sites that help build customer trust and loyalty.

Public Relations Strategy Dimension

The introductory site might have a distinctive logo, a tailored message from the CEO, an annual report or press releases to help build good will and customer loyalty. The informative site may choose to use testimonials from satisfied customers or celebrities who have used the products or services.

The interactive site may include a video message from the CEO or a video that shows how the transaction is completed and the product will be delivered. A pledge or endorsement similar to the Good Housekeeping Seal of Approval may be used to build credibility or trust. It also includes ways to humanise the digital experience and build strong communities that share common experiences.

Dependence on E-Commerce

The intelligence site has options for personal customer feedback and opinions, including a money-back guarantee with the option to talk with a representative on an 800 number if necessary to close the sale. Community dialogue options and cachet are for important to lure customers back to this site. Organisations competing in the world of e-commerce must develop e-commerce strategies to guide and maintain their web site development.

These strategies should define which type of e-commerce web site classification the organisations employ and they should be updated as organisational needs change. Organisations that rely heavily on e-commerce will more likely utilize interactive and intelligence-based web site designs. The ecommerce web site design model postulates the following:

— *P1:* Consumer response is affected by web site design.

— *P2:* An organisation's web site design is affected by its dependence upon e-commerce as a channel of distribution.

— *P3:* Consumer satisfaction increases when the web site design classification matches the desired response.

Consumer satisfaction is an important determinant in evaluating electronic commerce as a long-term strategic technology that benefits and enhances the firm. As part of that strategy, a well-designed public relations dimension would enrich customer satisfaction and loyalty. By integrating public relations into web site design, organisations can strengthen their relationships on the web; build brand awareness that promotes loyalty in their customers' hearts and minds; and create on-line communities that share values with the company.

Today, a strong Web presence is becoming more imperative than traditional marketing communications tools such as fancy brochures, direct mail, and select advertising. The e-commerce web site design model provides a framework for analysing how a web site design with a public relations dimension impacts consumer satisfaction.

Further empirical testing is planned to validate the relationship between web site design classification and consumer satisfaction. Additionally, a sampling of web sites will be conducted to support the web site classifications. In particular, one method will sample web sites by industry type to assess the significance of industry type. Data mining on the Web is an emerging technology.

Companies highly dependent on electronic commerce and utilizing intelligence-based web sites are interested in evaluating consumers' purchasing and browsing patterns. Future work will focus on evaluating consumer satisfaction through data-mining as a means of creating intelligence-based web sites as well as on public relation strategies that support data mining-based web sites. Imagery impacts consumer intention to return to a web site, this future work will consider image mining in addition to text mining.

The most important attributes of measuring good relationships are trust, understanding, credibility, behaviour, mutuality of control or conflict avoidance, and maintenance of that existing relationship between an organisation and its key constituencies. If organisations are serious about understanding the type of experience their customers are having on their web site, they should employ qualitative and quantitative gathering techniques such as exploratory customer focus groups, representative mail and telephone surveys of current and lapsed customers, and in-depth interviews on customer buying habits.

Qualitative focus groups can also be utilized with on-line user groups to learn which values and buying habits customers consider important. Quantitative mail and telephone surveys should follow to confirm statistically the findings of the focus groups. An easy method for keeping track of customers' opinions and behaviours on the Web is through feedback loops, both conversational and behavioural.

Conversational feedback includes e-mail, message boards, chat sessions, and interviews, while behavioural feedback includes page hits, time spent on site, message boards and chat sessions, and responses to direct marketing. Feedback loops provide excellent clues to how effectively a web site offering matches the needs and values of its key constituencies. Additional ways that organisations can learn about their e-commerce relationships with customers. First, customer advisory panels for B2B customers are useful, particularly if organisations are trying to build long-term relationships.

Second, employee surveys measure how well organisations are delivering quality service on the Web. Finally, mystery shoppers can be used to test the Web site experience by buying a product and reporting their experiences. Finally, Microsoft's Usability Guidelines (MUG) can be a valuable metric to assess the quality of a firm's Web presence. These guidelines are organised into five major categories:

— content,
— ease of use,
— promotion,
— made for the medium (personalisation), and
— emotion (affective).

A heuristic evaluation procedure using multiple web sites from four sectors engaged in electronic commerce: airlines, on-line bookstores, automobile manufacturers, and car rental agencies. They noted that the evaluation procedure as well as the usability metric exhibited good properties. Three of the categories-promotion, made for the medium, and emotion-have public relations aspects directly related to building relationships that support customer satisfaction.

Future Concerns

Today public relations is everywhere you look. When you watch the news, the footage you see while the newscaster speaks is sent from the public relations department of the company. It is called "B-roll." When you get an employee newsletter you can bet public relations wrote it. Public relations magazines like the ones distributed to AAA members have become popular tools. Public service announcements are usually written by public relations practitioners to raise awareness for a particular issue. The latest development in the practice is writing for company web sites.

The internet has rapidly become the most-used resource for information. Now companies can save money in printing costs and distribution by getting messages out via the internet. A company can display employment, products, services, its mission, and values. Many computer experts have the knowledge and knack for design, but they can not write to reach the company's publics like a public relations writer can.

As public relations course offerings are evolving to include web design and HTML writing for students, the practice is evolving to include public relations practitioners that can design and write an entire company web site.

> "An advantage to using the Web as a PR tool is the ability to get closer to your customers and other stakeholders."

Many company sites do not have an email link. When sites have an email link, it is likely that the response is from an automated response or a generic pre-written response. A company site should be used to maximize lines of communication. It should not be another place to stonewall the public.

Technology means more to public relations than websites and email.

> "Public relations has shifted from a traditional, print-oriented emphasis to that of a multi-faceted marketing discipline. P.R. used to mean writing, media

> relations and special events.Now there are no limits; it may be direct mail or a presentation to Congress. There isn't anything under the marketing umbrella we aren't capable of doing. We never say 'that's not our job'. If it's part of the marketing mix, it's our job."

The future of public relations is limitless. This is the very reason most people do not understand exactly what it is now. The hardest thing about public relations sometimes, is getting a company's executive board to recognize exactly what it is and why it is needed. The new president of Public Relations Society of America commented on the biggest issues facing public relations practitioners today.

> "First is the need to continue to precisely define the role of PR in terms of providing counsel, building relationships with constituents, and helping to shape strategy, rather than being seen only as communicators or publicists. Yes, media relations and shaping/delivering information are part of what we do — but they're only one part, they're the tactical part, and they're the last stage of a PR program."

Many public relations students do not find a career easily. Most companies have public relations in some form, but have labeled it marketing, human resources, or customer service. Yes, each of those functions may have a part in internal or external communications. People with human resources or marketing degrees are not disciplined in writing for mass media or writing for specific publics. Any large company that does not have an internal public relations department might have to hire a firm that knows little about the issue in a time of crisis. Although these external firms are seasoned in handling crisis, an internal public relations practitioner would be more cost-efficient.

It is interesting to juxtapose traditional definitions of the public relations manager role with the clear orientation toward publics that these informants had. When one looks at the measures that have been used in most of the role studies described in the beginning of this article, one sees that the focus for a key manager role is on the organization and the organization's management A manager in that role is organization-oriented and is, or attempting to be, a member of the dominant coalition. This, of course, is central to the success of the public relations mission within the organization, along with practitioner salary and job satisfaction.

There is a possibility that tactic-oriented practitioners are more audience-oriented than those who more frequently enact the management roles. Technicians may be more immersed in media relations programs, community relations activities, and so forth. But more importantly, new technologies will allow feedback from audiences to be embedded in the tactic itself. One could argue that before online communications, environmental scanning and evaluation tasks were segregated from technician-oriented "creative" tasks. In future quantitative studies, it will be important to ensure that measures of the technician role account for that. As currently measured, the technician role appears to be more audience-centered, and the management role appears to be more organization-centered or public relations profession-centered.

Practitioners perform activities of both managers and technicians, but are categorized depending on how frequently they enact each. If used strategically, practitioner use of technology can further several dimensions of the management model, thereby furthering two-way symmetric communication models in organizations. Even empowering technicians with more interactive media improves two-way symmetric communication, coaxing them toward management role enactment. Although the greatest impact of technology is on management role enactment, new media have the capability of shifting more public relations practitioners from technician roles to manager roles.

Public relations will continue to evolve as technology evolves. The secret to being successful in public relations is to rely on two-way communication, be proactive - do your research and issue tracking, and have a clear consistent message.

References

Anderson. R., & Reagan. J. Practitioner roles and uses of new technologies. *Journalism Quarterly. 69(1),* 156-165. 1992.

Dozier, D. M. The organizational roles of communications and public relations practitioners. In J. E Grunig (Ed.), *Excellence in public relations and comunlcation management.* 1992.

Botan & V. Hazleton, Jr. (Eds.), *Public relations theory* . Hillsdale. NJ: Lawrence

Hauss. D. Technology forecast. *Public Relations Journal, 51(4).* 16-19. 1995.

Lindlof, T. R. *Qualitative communication research methods.* Thousand Oaks, CA: Sage. 1995.

Bibliography

Anderson. R., & Reagan. J. Practitioner roles and uses of new technologies. *Journalism Quarterly. 69(1),* 156-165. 1992.

Aronson, M., Spenter, D., & Ames, C. *The Public Relations Writer's Handbook: The Digital Age*. San Francisco: Jossey-Bass. 2007.

Bernays, Edward *Public Relations*. Boston, MA: Bellman Publishing Company. 1945.

Bivins, T. H. "Ethical implications of the relationship of purpose to role and function in public relations" . *Journal of Business Ethics*, January, 65-73. 1980.

Blood, R. "Activism and the Internet: From e-mail to new political movement" . *Journal of Communication Management*, 5(2), 160-169. 2000.

Botan, C., & Hazleton, V. *Public Relations Theory II.* New Jersey: Lawrence Erlbaum Associates. 2006.

Brock, S., Sandoval, J., & Lewis, S. *Preparing for Crises in the Schools: A Manual for Building School Crisis Response Teams.* New York: John Wiley & Sons. 2001.

Cahn, D. & Abigail, R. *Managing Conflict through Communication*. Boston: Pearson Education. 2007.

Cancel, A. E., Cameron, G. T., Sallot, L. M., & Mitrook, M. A. "It depends: A contingency theory of accommodation in public relations" . *Journal of Public Relations Research, 9,* 31–63. 1997.

Carstarphen, M., & Wells, R. *Writing PR: A Multimedia Approach*. Boston: Pearson Education. 2004.

Center, A., Jackson, P., Smith, S., Stansberry, F. *Public Relations Practices: Managerial Case Studies and Problems.* New Jersey: Pearson Prentice Hall. 2008.

Coombs, W. T. "Interpersonal communication and public relations" . In R. L. Heath & G. Vasquez (Eds.), *Handbook of Public Relations* (pp. 105–114). Thousand Oaks, CA: Sage. 2001.

Cutlip, S. M., Center, A. H., & Broom, G. H. *Effective public relations* (8th ed.) Upper Saddle River, NJ: Prentice Hall. 2000.

Dennis L. Wilcox, Phillip H. Ault and Warren K. Agee. *Public Relations Strategies and Tactics.* New York: Harper & Row.1986.

Dozier, D. M. The organizational roles of communications and public relations practitioners. In J. E Grunig (Ed.), *Excellence in public relations and comunlcation management.* 1992.

Friedman, Marsha. *Celebritize Yourself: The Three Step Method to Increase Your Visibility and Explode Your Business.* North Carolina: Warren Publishing, Inc. 2009.

Grunig, J. "Two-way symmetrical public relations: Past, present and future" . In R. Heath (Ed.), *Handbook of public relations* (pp. 11-30). Thousand Oaks: Sage. 2001.

Hall, Phil. *The New PR.* Mount Kisco, N.Y.: Larstan Publishing. 2007.

Hansen-Horn, T., & Neff, B. *Public Relations: From Theory to Practice.* Boston: Pearson Education. 2008.

Harlow, R. F. "Public relations at the crossroads". *The Public Opinion Quarterly, 8(4),* 551-556. 1945.

Harris, T., & Whalen, P. *The Marketer's Guide to Public Relations in the 21st Century.* Mason, Ohio: Thompson Higher Education. 2006.

Harvard Business Press. *Managing Crises: Expert Solutions to Everyday Challenges.* Boston: Harvard Business Press. 2007.

Hauss. D. Technology forecast. *Public Relations Journal, 51(4).* 16-19. 1995.

Heath, R. (Ed.). *Encyclopaedia of public relations.* Thousand Oaks, CA: Sage Publications.2005.

Hendrix, J., & Hayes, D. *Public Relations Cases.* Belmont, CA: Thomson Arts and Sciences. 2007.

Hon, L. C. & Brunner, B. "Diversity issues and public relations". *Journal of Public Relations Research, 12,* 309-340. 2000.

Kelleher, T. *Public Relations Online: Lasting Concepts for Changing Media.* Thousand Oaks, CA: Sage. 2007.

Kerr, M. *School Crisis Prevention and Intervention.* New Jersey: Pearson Education. 2009.

Kruckeberg, D. & Stark, K. *Public relations and community: A reconstructed theory.* New York: Paeger.1988.

Ledingham J. & Bruning S. (Eds.), *Public relations as relationship management: A relational approach to the study and practice of public relations* (pp. 3-22). New Jersey: Lawrence Erlbaum. 2000.

Lindlof, T. R. *Qualitative communication research methods.* Thousand Oaks, CA: Sage. 1995.

Littlejohn, S. *Theories of human communication.* Belmont, CA: Wadsworth.1989.

Lockhart, J. *How to Market Your School: A Guide to Marketing, Public Relations, and Communication for School Administrators.* Lincoln, NE: iUniverse, Inc. 2005.

Lowery, S. A., & DeFleur, M. L. *Milestones in mass communication research: Media effects* (3rd ed.) White Plains, NY: Longman. 1995.

Mayhew, L. *The New Public*. Cambridge: Cambridge University Press.1989.

McElreath, M. P. *Managing systematic and ethical public relations campaigns* (2nd ed.). New York: Brown & Benchmark. 1996.

Moore, R. L., Farrar, R. T., & Collins, E. L. (1997). *Advertising and public relations law*. Mahwah, NJ: Lawrence Erlbaum Associates.

Moss, D., & DeSanto, B. *Public Relations Cases: International Perspectives*. New York: Routledge. 2002.

Oliver, S. *Public Relations Strategy*. London/Philadelphia: Kogan Page. 2001.

Ries, A., & Ries, L. *The Fall of Advertising & The Rise of PR*. New York: Harper Business. 2002.

Schonfeld, D., Lichtenstein, R., Pruett, M., Speese-Linehan, D. *How to Prepare for and Respond to a Crisis*. Alexandria, VA: Association for Supervision and Curriculum Development. 2002.

Schramm, W. *Men, messages and media: A look at human communication*. New York: Harper & Row. 1995.

Scott: D. *The New Rules of Marketing & PR: How to Use News Releases, Blogs, Podcasting, Viral Marketing, & Online Media to Reach Buyers Directly*. New Jersey: John Wiley & Sons. 2007.

Seib, Patrick and Fitzpatrick, Kathy. *Public Relations Ethics*. Fort Worth: Harcourt Brace and Company. 1995.

Sriramesh, K., & Vercic, D. The *Global Public Relations Handbook: Theory, Research, and Practice*. New Jersey: Lawrence Erlbaum Associates. 2003.

Stacks, D. *Primer of Public Relations Research*. New York: Guilford Press. 2003.

Wilcox, D. & Cameron, G. *Public Relations: Strategies and Tactics*. Boston: Pearson. 2003.